Capitalism
and
Progress

CAPITALISM AND PROGRESS

A Diagnosis of Western Society

by
BOB GOUDZWAARD
Professor of Economics
at the Free University of Amsterdam

Translated and edited by
Josina Van Nuis Zylstra

Wedge Publishing Foundation, Toronto, Canada,
and *William B. Eerdmans Publishing Company,*
Grand Rapids, Michigan

This book originally appeared in the Netherlands in 1978 under the title *Kapitalisme en vooruitgang* (second, revised edition), published by Van Gorcum in Assen. ISBN 90-232-1583-4

31429

Printed in the United States of America
This edition published 1979 through special arrangement with Wedge Publishing Foundation, Toronto, by Wm. B. Eerdmans Publishing Co., Grand Rapids, Michigan 49503.

Library of Congress Cataloging in Publication Data

Goudzwaard, B
    Capitalism and progress.

Translation of Kapitalisme en vooruitgang (2d. rev. ed., 1978)
    Bibliography: p. 251
    Includes index.
    1. Capitalism. 2. Progress. 3. Civilization, Occidental. I. Zylstra, Josina Van Nuis. II. Title.
HB501.G62713   330.12'2   79-20818
ISBN 0-8028-1809-9 (Eerdmans)
ISBN 0-88906-106-8 (Wedge)

Contents

Translator's Acknowledgments

In January 1976, when I first began translating this book, I could not have imagined that I would be writing these acknowledgments on Labour Day 1978. The translation, editing, and organization of the text was all but finished when a second, substantially revised Dutch edition was being prepared. As a result, a major section of Part Four of the English version had to be translated anew if the book were to do justice to the author's insights and the readers' expectations. Since I had meanwhile undertaken a new task, Albert Wolters of the Institute for Christian Studies in Toronto deserves considerable credit for translating the revisions in the second edition. Without his assistance it would have been impossible for me to complete this work. Having finished the final editorial correction and re-organization, I can now look back with gratitude on this challenging opportunity. I would like to thank not only Al Wolters but also those who in other ways contributed to the completion of this book.

I wish to express my appreciation to the Association for the Advancement of Christian Scholarship in Toronto for having entrusted me with this task. The personal confidence of its executive director, Robert VanderVennen, was both stimulating and encouraging. I am equally grateful to Bob Goudzwaard, the author, for the same measure of confidence and for the fine and speedy cooperation which bridged the inconvenience of the Atlantic Ocean. His openness toward editorial improvements and organizational changes greatly facilitated my endeavors.

Since I am not a social scientist, I am also much indebted to my husband, Bernard Zylstra, for his readiness to discuss and elucidate sections of a problematic nature, especially those with a complex philosophical content. He read the entire first draft and made numerous valuable comments which enhanced the clarity of the English text. The first completed English version was read critically by Glenn Andreas, a close friend from Pella, Iowa. I would like to thank him for the time and energy made available and for the incisive, constructive criticism offered from the point of view of the North American reader.

Finally, I am indebted to the University of Toronto, whose extensive holdings in the Robarts Library and affiliated college libraries were indispensable for a major editorial facet, namely, the preparation of a new bibliography. Access to these libraries enabled me to check every quotation used by the author; to substitute, where possible, proper English equivalents for quotations in foreign languages in the Dutch edition; and to include English titles and publication information in both footnotes and bibliography.

Since I feel personally enriched by the experience, knowledge and insight gained, I sincerely hope that my contribution to the English edition will be of equal benefit to many English readers.

Toronto, Canada   *Josina Van Nuis Zylstra*

Preface

Approximately half a century ago Oswald Spengler's famous book *Decline of the West* appeared in Germany. In two extensive volumes Spengler expounded the well-known thesis that the law of birth, maturity, and death applies not only to plants and animals but holds equally for civilizations. He was convinced that within the foreseeable future the culture of the West would disappear in the twilight of world history as had the Roman Empire. As evidence for this assertion he pointed to the disintegration of authority, the exaggerated attention paid to youth, and the craving for power and luxury as ends in themselves. He interpreted these phenomena as signs of cultural deterioration, comparable to that which accompanied the fall of the Roman Empire.

Meanwhile more than fifty years have passed. Admittedly, with reference to the life of civilizations, one must think in terms of centuries rather than decades. Nevertheless, enough time has passed to judge whether the course of events has confirmed Spengler's prediction. It has not. Western society still exists and often strikes us more by its zest for life than by its death wish. Civilizations simply are not plants which emerge, flower, and die according to a set rhythm of life. We feel more at home with Arnold Toynbee who claims that the destiny of civilizations is primarily shaped by man himself, particularly by the manner in which he responds to challenges in his cultural development.

Whatever the case may be, the present condition of western culture definitely gives cause for deep concern. This is due not only to the fact that distinct signs of deterioration can be detected; it is perhaps of far greater significance that the West is gradually being faced with several interdependent problems of such an incisive character that together they could become a decisive challenge to the whole of western culture.

CUMULATION AND FRUSTRATION

This rather forceful language does not seem inappropriate in light of the following considerations. To begin with, it is important to note that the many issues which face the West are particularly stiking, not because of their novelty, but because of the unusual manner of their accumulation. Environmental problems, for instance, are not new, nor is chronic unemployment. The former were encountered in the English industrial cities during the middle of the eighteenth century while the latter marked the economic crisis of the 1930s. Moreover, periods of increasing uncertainty and even of impending doom have also existed previously. The chronicles record that on New Year's Eve of the year 999 the pope and the emperor knelt together on one of the towers of the City of Rome to prayerfully await the end of the world. Similar feelings of gloom were common at the end of the Middle Ages. Again, shortages of raw materials are not new: around 1870 the English economist Stanley Jevons was highly concerned about the near depletion of the coal mines in England.

Indeed, none of these problems is new in the history of the West. We have experienced them before—one at a time. But today the situation is strikingly different. Not only are we confronted with all of these problems at the same time, but they are interdependent and mutually reinforce one another. Unemployment and inflation now occur together; a shortage of energy aggravates environmental problems and coincides with predictions of serious food crises. Moreover, while differences abroad increase, especially between rich and poor countries, at home tensions rise, especially between labor and capital, young and old, black and white. Economists raise warning voices. So do scholars of international relations who regard the growth and proliferation of nuclear arms—now at the stage of "overkill capacity"—with fear and trembling. And so do biologists, because of their deep concern for the world's ecosystem. Psychologists, who see their waiting rooms crowded with people no longer able to cope with the pace of modern society and ready to bury their loneliness with pills and drugs, similarly express their concern. The combination of all these problems, which mutually reinforce one another, must certainly be considered unusual.

But there is still more which strikes us as unusual: solutions to these problems are hard to come by. With regard to the economic issues it is noteworthy that the "familiar" methods of combating inflation and unemployment are no longer successful. Prominent economists tell us that up to a certain point we will simply have to learn to live with inflation. Unemployment increasingly displays "hard" cores which can no longer be fought with "classic" measures, such as tax reductions or public works policies. And we are already being told that the food crises predicted for the 1980s cannot be prevented and can hardly be combated.

Similarly, no effective solutions seem available for problems of a noneconomic nature. What are the real answers to the emotional tensions so common today, such as the loneliness of many persons in our large cities? What can actually be undertaken against the brutal force of armed terrorists who can attack nearly every facet of our complex society?

Finally, we also experience the shortcomings of many political solutions. Effective control over the manufacture and distribution of nuclear weapons has become practically hopeless. The rich western countries are growing politically impotent because of an increasing dependence on the indispensable import of energy and raw materials. As a result of this dependence, these countries are hardly in a position to support truly impartial solutions to problems in Africa, South America, and the Middle East. A sense of powerlessness is present in the West; and this, of course, adds to the temptation to employ recklessly the remaining means of power.

Western culture is indeed challenged today. It is challenged in the accumulation of problems, but also in the ineffectiveness of the classical solutions. Will we be able to find the correct answers in time? That is the unavoidable question confronting us. Because the continued existence of western society is at stake, the search for solutions has become a matter of life and death, especially since impotence can readily nourish despair.

NEED FOR REFLECTION

Fortunately, the public gradually realizes that the situation in which the West finds itself is cause for deep concern. This, however, increases the risk of a wrong reaction. The danger exists in particular that in a panic we will try to find a *separate* answer to each of the problems confronting us, in the manner to which we are accustomed. This reaction is especially dangerous because it can prevent the necessary in-depth reflection on the *causes* of the present predicament—and such reflection is indispensable for finding truly effective solutions. An analogy will make this clear. When someone breaks an arm, the solution is simple—the arm has to be set. However, when a patient displays several negative symptoms simultaneously, ranging from listlessness to physical pain, an effective treatment is often possible only after a search for a single cause of those symptoms. At any rate, one shouldn't exclude the possibility that these symptoms indicate a single, deeper cause. Thus it is with the predicament of western society—by treating merely the symptoms we might well overlook the true cause. As a matter of fact, the typically western manner of solving problems might aggravate the underlying causes. For example, a patient's condition worsens when he or she is given stimulants to counteract the lethargy resulting from pain relievers. In the West we run a similar risk of being satisfied with superficial remedies which only aggravate the disease. Perhaps we are afraid of a genuine reflection into the causes because that would inevitably lead to a confrontation with ourselves. Does western culture dare to behold itself in a mirror? Nevertheless, an in-depth reflection and diagnosis must take place, if only for the sake of that which is still dear to us in western civilization.

This book is a personal contribution to such reflection on the causes of our ills and our failures. The word *personal* is appropriate in this context, for I would not want to argue that my diagnosis is the only correct one or the only possible one. Moreover, in my analysis I am handicapped since I do not have the qualifications of a philosopher, historian, or a cultural sociologist. Rather, I am an economist by training and profession. This limitation is a drawback in a study which will also have to deal with several sociocultural and philosophical aspects of western society during the past and present. At the same time I think there is merit in having an economist tackle this subject instead of a philosopher or a sociologist, for at the frontier of western culture we are constantly being challenged primarily by *economic* issues.

I would like to make an additional comment here especially for the benefit of American readers. European studies about the problems of our time usually have a stronger tendency to look back to the past than the more practically oriented American studies. In this respect this book is European. In my opinion an in-depth reflection on current issues cannot really take place without due attention to roots. When we encounter problems in our personal lives, we search for their roots in the past. By understanding the past, insight into the present becomes more profound. This deepened insight must concern all of us in the critical situation of today.

In conclusion, a few technical and personal comments are in order. The English edition of this book was initially prepared on the basis of the first Dutch edition published in the fall of 1976. A second Dutch edition was required within a relatively short time. Instead of merely republishing the book, I decided to rewrite those parts that had been subjected to constructive critique in the Dutch press, with the result that Part Four has been almost entirely revised and considerably expanded. Changes of lesser significance were made in the other parts. Nearly all of these alterations have been incorporated into the English text.

I owe a debt to many persons who have helped make this book what it is. I cannot mention them all by name, but I would like to single out two individuals who have made a truly indispensable contribution to this edition: Josina Zylstra, who translated and edited this book with great dedication and accuracy, and Bernard Zylstra, who made numerous valuable suggestions which improved the text. I thank both of them wholeheartedly for what they have accomplished.

Free University
Amsterdam
                                        Bob Goudzwaard

Introduction:
A Statement of the Problem

TWO DEPTH LEVELS

When we try to discover the causes of the accumulation of present-day problems in western society and attempt to establish how these problems are mutually interdependent, we soon notice that in large measure they are related to societal structurations. Often they are entirely intertwined with the structure or architecture of western society as a whole. The problems of inflation and unemployment readily illustrate this. These problems, of course, are also present in nonwestern societies, but their specific character in our context is definitely tied up with the economic *system* in which we live, that is, with the manner in which we have organized our socioeconomic life. Such an interdependence is also present—although less pronounced—between the economic system and the current problems with the supply of mineral resources and with environmental control. Finally, many emotional and sociocultural problems cannot be divorced from the specific way in which we organize relations of production, employment, and consumption. Here we encounter a *depth level* which underlies the problems occupying us so intensely today.

There is nothing new about relating a multiplicity of problems to a common, underlying structure. In fact, this relationship has led to the widely held conception that the real cause of these problems lies in the wrong structure of our society, and that therefore the majority of these ills would quickly be eliminated if we only had the courage to replace the present structure of society with a better one.

We have become so accustomed to this type of argument that generally we do not notice the weakness inherent in its logic. In the first place, it apparently is assumed that the structure of society has not only come into existence outside ourselves, but even continues to exist outside ourselves as an objective entity. Is that really true? Isn't the structure of society, at least in part, an expression of our deepest intents—an expression of a culture which we helped shape? The obvious relationship between our problems and an apparently distorted social system does not warrant the conclusion that this system itself is the deepest cause of the ills. Such an argument only holds in a kind of "scapegoat theory" in which we first separate the economic system from our own lives as an independent factor; next we impute the guilt for the difficulties around us to this factor; and finally we delude ourselves into the belief that we go scot-free by sending this "scapegoat" into the desert!

It is imperative to point out the serious flaws in our economic system, but it is dangerous, and wrong, to conclude that the system itself is at fault while we—the human agents operative in the system—are without blame.

Singling out the structure of western society as the real culprit is a mistake for other reasons as well. It is noteworthy that the accumulation of problems we have discussed is also present in the social structure of countries behind the iron curtain. In connection with the rapid increase in production in the communist economic systems, problems emerge with respect to ecology and the supply of energy and raw materials; we also find similar emotional tensions as a result of loneliness and alienation. In other words, in discovering a parallel set of problems in societies with distinctly different structures, we should be quick to realize that, no matter how intertwined these problems are with social structures, the latter cannot be the only and decisive factor in their emergence.

The conclusion is self-evident: in our reflection we will have to penetrate to a second, more fundamental depth level underlying the structures of societies—a depth level which co-determines and shapes these structures. This *second depth level* can consist only in the central, religious motives which fundamentally direct a culture and its society. These motives can be described as *religious* because they embrace hope for the future, faith in God or man, and love for self or others. From this depth level we have always received, and still receive today, the impulse to think, to live, to work, and thus to contribute to the ongoing construction and reconstruction of that gigantic coral reef which is called western society.

THE ROLE OF FAITH IN PROGRESS

By establishing a relationship between the central, religious motives of western culture on the one hand and the western social order on the other hand, we have touched upon a theme which has caused so many problems in the past that it is nearly impossible to discuss it meaningfully once again. The relationship between religion and the social order is one of the most difficult problems in the sociology of culture, particularly since 1904–1905, when Max Weber published his famous essay about the connection between Calvinism and capitalism.[1] Subsequent discussions have shown how dangerous it is to generalize with respect to the relationship between religion and social structures. This is particularly so since this issue has incessantly been the target of vehement attacks on the part of Marxist and neo-Marxist historians and sociologists who absolutely reject the idea that religious impulses could codetermine the nature and constellation of social structures. In Marxism the socioeconomic substructure determines the cultural and religious superstructure—not vice versa.

Nevertheless, we must not let ourselves be discouraged by this. As a matter of fact, it remains to be seen whether it is truly necessary to reconsider this debate. It may well be that in western countries today we are confronted with problems which in essence result from cultural and religious impulses—assuming that these impulses exist—other than those which can still be ascribed to the "Calvinistic Puritan ethics" of the sixteenth and seventeenth centuries.

With this sketchy background, I acknowledge that in this book a conscious though slightly hazardous choice has been made. Instead of undertaking the impossible search for exact influences which each of the main spiritual currents—humanism, Catholicism, and the Reformation—has in various ways exerted on the structure of western society, in this study one

1. Max Weber, "Die protestantische Ethik und der Geist des Kapitalismus," *Archiv für Sozialwissenschaft und Sozialpolitik,* vols. 20, 21 (1904–5). English translation by Talcott Parsons, *The Protestant Ethic and the Spirit of Capitalism* (London: Allen & Unwin, 1930).

distinct current or motif is brought to the fore. This motif provides perhaps the most plausible basis for explaining the rise and development of modern capitalism to the present, including today's problems to which capitalism gave rise. That motif is the idea of *human progress*. Quite late in the history of western culture—namely, in the eighteenth century—this idea first fully unfolded as a *faith* in progress. Before this, however, it had gone through a long period of incubation or preparation—from the time of a lingering scholasticism and the beginning of the Renaissance until far into the period of the Enlightenment. During this period of preparation every spiritual movement in western culture, but notably humanism, influenced the idea of human progress. Therefore, we must be able to detect in this motif of human progress the rivalry between all of the spiritual impulses which have made an impact on western culture.

The following grounds can be advanced to justify this choice. In the first place, it cannot be denied that the theme of human progress has never been completely absent in western culture, and that it flourished particularly during the Enlightenment, just prior to the time of the industrial revolution. It is not at all unlikely that precisely the impulses from the era of the Enlightenment have had a distinct shaping effect on the pattern of modern western society.

In the second place, it is intriguing to note that this motif of progress has indeed presented itself frequently as a faith, and that as a result it has often been described in terms of the inspiring dynamics of an authentic faith.[2] The word *faith* in this context does not, of course, refer to the formal adherence to a distinct religio-ecclesiastical confession. Rather, it refers to the propelling, all-embracing visions which direct persons in everything they feel, think, and do. Insofar as an opinion or conviction becomes a matter of faith in this sense, its influence will inescapably be noticeable in the architecture of society.

In the third place, it is striking that the mutually intertwined problems of which we spoke earlier are also, in one way or another, related to the technically and economically oriented progress of the West. This is true not only for environmental and resource problems but also for the peculiar character of

2. Cf. the titles of the well-known studies by Christopher Dawson, *Progress and Religion: An Historical Inquiry* (London: Sheed & Ward, 1929); and John Baillie, *The Belief in Progress* (London: Oxford University Press, 1950).

inflation and unemployment. Moreover, alienation and loneliness are also closely connected with technical and economic progress. The same is undoubtedly true of what Alvin Toffler describes as "future shock"[3]—the emotional inability to keep up with rapid change in the modern world. Furthermore, the theme of progress has been a welcome occasion for several interpreters of our culture to entertain notions of fatalism and feelings of profound impotence.[4]

In the fourth place, it is no accident that the word *progress* has served a number of writers in their description of the essence of capitalism. The briefest delineation of capitalism has perhaps been provided by Joseph Schumpeter, who defined it as "a form or method of economic change."[5] The change he had in mind is primarily one of economic and technological progress. According to Schumpeter, capitalism would come to ruin not because it failed but because of its technical and economic success.

In reviewing all of this, we can certainly conclude that it will be rewarding to investigate the following questions: a) whether the western social order has indeed undergone distinct influences from western faith in progress; and b) whether such influences continue to exert themselves in the emergence of contemporary challenges to western society.

In our reflection on these questions, the reader should keep in mind that this book is not intended as a treatment of the entire relationship between culture and the societal structuration of western civilization. This would be far too ambitious an undertaking and would hardly be of any avail. The theme of this book was consciously made more specific. It concerns the possible connection between *one* dominant cultural motif in western society—the pursuit of, and faith in, *progress*—and *one* crucial component of the societal structure of western society— capitalism. This is undoubtedly a considerable limitation. In the first place it should be acknowledged that there are many more determinative factors in our culture, also those affecting the

3. Alvin Toffler, *Future Shock* (New York: Random House, 1970).
4. Cf. for instance Karl Löwith's expression, "the *fate* of progress." Karl Löwith, *Nature, History, and Existentialism and Other Essays in the Philosophy of History* (Evanston, Ill.: Northwestern University Press, 1966), chapter 9: "Fate of Progress," pp. 145–161.
5. Joseph A. Schumpeter, *Capitalism, Socialism, and Democracy* (New York/London: Harper and Brothers, 1942), p. 82.

structure of society, than the will to progress alone. This is certainly true if progress is further specified as the advancement of humanity in comprehending, dominating, and developing the surrounding nature. In the second place, the structure of our society consists in a constellation of components which certainly cannot all be simply brought together under the heading "capitalism." For instance, attempts to explain the western legal order and democracy as products of the profit motive do not only make a forced and artificial impression but are absolutely misleading and dangerous. An investigation, therefore, into the relationship between western culture and societal structure in terms of the two concepts *capitalism* and *progress* is one with very clear limitations. But that does not make it meaningless; if anything, the opposite is true. This is clearly evident, for example, from the fact that the pursuit of progress has been the constant "cultural companion" of western society ever since the latter was submitted to a program of radical reconstruction from the time of the industrial revolution. And is not capitalism itself by nature progress-oriented? Capitalism is a form of societal organization that is specifically directed toward growth and change. In this specific orientation toward progress, capitalism appears to this day to be a recognizable and essential element of our societal structuration.

THE INTENT OF THIS BOOK

If it is true that the progress motif has played a decisive role in the unfolding of modern capitalist society, then we must be able to trace that in the history of the West. This is what I intend to do in Part One. I will begin by posing the question as to which successive barriers had to be broken before modern capitalism could indeed establish itself within western culture. If my assumptions are correct, then we will discover that in this breakdown of barriers the motif of progress emerged as a decisive factor.

In Part Two I will deal with the internal development of modern capitalism from the time of the industrial revolution until the present. Here again we shall try to establish a relationship between this development and the progress motif.

In Part Three I will attempt to show that the analyses in the first two parts can clarify our understanding of the origin of the problems which are accumulating in our own time. This should place the present challenge of western culture in a proper light. Here I will also discuss the question of to what extent the idea of progress itself is involved in the present crisis of our culture and, further, whether this very involvement is perhaps a cause of the current accumulation of problems.

Finally, in Part Four our attention will first be focused on various diverging solutions to the emerging crisis in our society. After that I will sketch the skeleton of my own alternative. This will be introduced under the theme of *the disclosure of society.*

A NOTE TO SPECIALISTS

This book is not addressed specifically to economists or experts in related fields. Nevertheless, at the end of this Introduction I would like to address them briefly, in particular concerning an important matter in economic theory. In the discussion up to this point I have implicitly taken a position with respect to the subdiscipline in economics called *theory of economic systems.* Moreover, my position diverges in certain respects from commonly accepted approaches.

Roughly speaking one can distinguish two main directions in the theory of economic systems. The first direction, influenced especially by Marxism, is *deterministic* in outlook. It views the economic system as an object of determined evolution in time, whose main contours are therefore subject to prediction. In this evolution the development of the technique of production puts a decisive stamp on the economic systems as the patterns of society; and at a given moment this development causes the transition from an earlier system—for example, the capitalistic—by way of a qualitative leap to a new economic system—for example, the socialistic.

Partly in reaction to this deterministic conception, a more *voluntaristic* theory was developed which emphasizes the free choice, in principle, of an economic system as the organizational and administrative system of society. The contrast, for instance, between a planned economy and a market economy derives from this voluntaristic theory. For example, if the behavior patterns of economic subjects in a national economy have to be coordinated, then the system of coordination has to be either the market, or the plan, or a mixture of both. In this conception the economic system is viewed first of all as a voluntarily chosen system in which a national economy is administered or organized. Most textbooks in the area of economic systems represent slightly different positions within the voluntaristic framework.[6]

Both of these conceptions of economic systems display distinct shortcomings. The deterministic approach asserts too much since it interprets an economic system as a blind, impersonal force which goes its own, absolutely sovereign way through history. The voluntaristic interpretation, on the other hand, asserts too little since it tends toward a too static and timeless approach to the entire problem by reducing an economic system to a mere technical system of organization.

In response to these two interpretations I am attracted to a third alternative, where economic systems and their development are approached especially from the entire societal *culture* within which they originate and of which they are at least partially an expression. An example can illustrate what I have in mind. The deterministic approach interprets the Japanese economy as capitalistic, while the voluntaristic approach interprets it as a market economy. But does either interpretation touch the essence of the Japanese economic system? Not really! The Japanese economy displays many traits, varying from lifetime employment to the practice of dumping, which can only be explained in terms of the unique Japanese culture which puts its stamp on nearly all economic relationships and institutions in that country.

Another example illustrates the same point. In theory both the Chinese economy and the Soviet economy belong to socialistic or planned economies, but in reality they differ radically. In these differences one can clearly detect varying cultural influences. So the question can properly be asked whether the commune economy of China is not at least in part a direct reflection of Chinese culture itself. For this reason it simply does not fit the category that describes the Russian system.

In this light it is meaningful to approach the origin and development of the western economic system against the background of western *culture* and its *central driving forces.* I readily

6. Cf. for instance Gregory Grossman, *Economic Systems* (Englewood Cliffs, N.J.: Prentice-Hall, 1967); George N. Halm, *Economic Systems: A Comparative Analysis* (New York: Holt, Rinehart and Winston, 1960); William N. Loucks, *Comparative Economic Systems* (New York: Harper & Row, 1965); and Jan S. Prybyla, *Comparative Economic Systems* (New York: Appleton-Century-Crofts, 1969). Perhaps these titles reflect a lack of originality.

acknowledge that my dissatisfaction with the present a-cultural approaches within the theory of economic systems has motivated me to write this book.

One final comment, intended again primarily for specialists, is still in order. It concerns my use of the word *capitalism.* I employ it to describe the main features of the structure of western society. I could have chosen another word to describe that structure, but since every key descriptive term is loaded with unintended meanings, a measure of arbitrariness in choice can hardly be avoided. The reader should keep in mind, however, that I do not employ the term *capitalism* in its classical Marxist sense with its concomitant concepts of proletariat, exploitation, classes, class struggle, and so forth. Moreover, by using this term I do not want to give the impression that the *entire* structure of western society can be fully described by a single word, as if that structure is a holistic system which no longer permits personal freedom or institutional redirection in any sense. This also implies that my interpretation of capitalism and communism as dialectical counterparts in the progression of humanism should not be viewed as a leveling of important qualitative differences in communist and noncommunist societies. But these qualifications should in no way detract us from a thorough diagnosis of the crisis within our *western* world. This book is intended as a small contribution to that end.

PART ONE: THE RAZING OF THE BARRIERS TO PROGRESS

1. The Social Order as an Expression of Culture

We know from the Gospels that every faith, no matter how small, contains within it the power to move mountains. There is no reason to think that the western faith in progress would not have this power. If the notion of progress indeed developed into a genuine faith, we can confidently assume that it possessed the power to change the world, even to move the massive mountain of the western social order.

Did this faith really develop such power? That is the question we must answer. In a comparison between the structure of society during the industrial revolution and during the Middle Ages one quickly detects several contrasts. But how are we to determine whether this change in social structures is to be attributed largely to faith in progress? Why couldn't it be simply the result of a development of historical necessities, such as an internal change in human production techniques? Isn't the advance of science and technology the real motor behind nearly all social changes in the West?

NO AUTONOMOUS TECHNOLOGY

Several arguments can be presented against this too simplistic interpretation. To begin with, a change in production techniques definitely does not fall out of a clear blue sky. A certain spiritual nurturing soil is necessary for such a change. In the Middle Ages the climate for a drastic breakthrough in technology definitely did not exist. Of course even here there are exceptions. We can illustrate that with the "scientific" advice of the Franciscan monk Roger Bacon to the ecclesiastical authorities for their missionary endeavors, namely, to equip the crusaders with reflectors to enable them from a distance to burn alive the Mohammedans occupying the Holy Land.[1] Another illustration of technological change is the entertaining and amazing tale of the Benedictine monk Eilmer who in 1010 built a glider with which he jumped from the tower of Malmesbury Abbey in England. After a flight of 600 feet he crashed and broke both legs. As explanation for this mishap he pointed to the fact that he had forgotten to put a tail on the rear of his machine—"caudam in posteriore parte."[2] Further, it is a matter of common knowledge that during the Middle Ages significant changes occurred in agricultural production methods.[3]

However, these incidents are exceptions rather than the rule. Indeed, in the Middle Ages we encounter a certain apprehension toward technological change, especially if it could substantially affect the social order and its inherent power relationships. Even as late as 1623, according to Heilbroner,[4] a revolutionary patent for a stocking frame was refused in England, and the authoritative Privy Council demanded the abolishment of this dangerous machine. A similar machine was, however, greeted enthusiastically two centuries later, during the first stage of the industrial revolution. The chronicles also relate that in a French city on a single occasion early in the seventeenth century 77 people were sentenced to death by hanging, 58 were to be broken upon the wheel, and 631 were condemned to serve in the galleys because of their vicious crime of having traded printed cotton.[5] But in France, too, that attitude toward the advance of technology changed drastically in a few centuries. For instance, in 1783 half the population of Paris turned out to watch Montgolfier's first balloon ascend from the earth, and the

1. Karl Löwith, *Nature, History, and Existentialism and Other Essays in the Philosophy of History* (Evanston, Ill.: Northwestern University Press, 1966), chapter 9: "Fate of Progress," p. 155.

2. Lynn White, Jr., "The Expansion of Technology 500–1500," in Carlo M. Cipolla, ed., *The Fontana Economic History of Europe*, vol. 1: *The Middle Ages* (London: Collins, 1972), p. 168.

3. Cf. White, "The Expansion of Technology 500–1500," vol. 1, chapter 4.

4. Robert L. Heilbroner, *The Worldly Philosophers* (New York: Simon & Schuster, 1953), p. 28.

5. *Ibid.*

people enthusiastically embraced each other while weeping for joy because of this new dawn for humanity.[6]

These contrasts indicate that technological changes need their own climate and nurturing soil in order to break through. One can readily point to parallel examples. We regard Columbus as the discoverer of the American continent, yet prior to him several others, such as the Vikings, had already undertaken voyages to America. Columbus, however, gained the reputation of being the actual discoverer because his generation regarded his journeys from an entirely new perspective, that is, the Renaissance aspiration to conquer the world.

Naturally this should not seduce us into adopting the opposite point of view, to the effect that *only* cultural factors were determinative in the rise of capitalistic society. It must be recognized honestly that the advent of modern capitalism was also the result of a series of practical developments and circumstances, such as the rise of nation-states, the extension of geographical range (voyages of discovery, planting of colonies), the gradual growth of cities and of crafts, the increasing replacement of payment in kind by monetary transactions, and not least also the advancements in the natural sciences whereby new products and techniques were made possible. We certainly should not deny a direct influence of the development of production technology upon the formation of our society. Clearly the structure of society differs in proportion to the complexity and sophistication of production technology. For instance, the structuration of society which accompanies a production system based on manual labor will be different from a system based on atomic energy. Once a development in production technology has gained a certain momentum, it may well, in course of time, begin to show independent features. Technological development can thereby react back upon the values and views existing in a culture. (This assertion will be illustrated further in the remainder of this book, especially in Parts Three and Four.) But however true all of this may be, no societal order can be established or maintained unless there is a cultural matrix in which it can thrive.

This also seems to be true of the rise of modern capitalism. The societal order which preceded capitalism (medieval society) was not just one among many. It was a societal structure with

6. P. J. Bouman, *Van tijd naar tijd* [From Time to Time] (Assen, the Netherlands: Van Gorcum, 1972), p. 12.

a unique spiritual foundation and with a specific cultural matrix. It cannot be denied that capitalism as a new social order could take lasting shape only by means of a demolition of this complex whole of religion, culture, and structure. Therefore the rise of modern capitalism in western society is indeed much more than the application of a somewhat different method or organization in socioeconomic life, or than the transition to a new system of societal management. It is at the same time an irrevocable relinquishment of the spiritual and cultural foundations underlying medieval society. The choice in favor of a capitalistic order of society was, in an important sense, a *cultural* choice, and one of worldwide significance.

But what in the matrix, in the nurturing soil of medieval society, both spiritually and culturally, presented obstacles to the rise of the later capitalistic structure of society? This is a question to which we must now first address ourselves.

THE NURTURING SOIL OF MEDIEVAL SOCIETY

There is a second reason why the transition from medieval society to a modern capitalistic society cannot be regarded merely as a process of technological historical necessity. This concerns the spiritual basis upon which medieval society was founded and which, as long as it prevailed, formed an essential barrier to a breakthrough of new social structures.

One of many expressions of medieval society can be found in the Gothic cathedrals which were built all over western Europe. These cathedrals can be regarded as a mirror image of the society which gave birth to them. Like the Gothic cathedral, medieval society itself was structured vertically. Everything in it was ordered and related in such a manner as to ascend from the realm of nature to that which alone can ultimately provide meaning to earthly existence—the realm of grace.

The high altar in a medieval cathedral is located either at the head or at the intersection of the cruciform plan. Here the sacraments are served for the blessing and sanctification of the entire congregation. Whoever enters through the portal of judgment at the foot of the cruciform plan can immediately behold the sign of his own deliverance and redemption in the distance, illuminated by heavenly light filtering through stained-glass windows. Along the aisles flanking the nave of the cathedral we often see windows and prayer chapels representing the various medieval guilds. These also, with a social hierarchy of their own, belong to the fullness of the congregation which is built on "the foundation of the apostles and prophets,"[7] who for that reason together are represented by the lowest row of sculptures in the Gothic cathedral.[8] The medieval cathedral, in its very architecture, proclaims that man's natural life is not holy and perfect in itself but is constantly in need of sacramental mediation offered by the holy mother church which can raise natural man before the throne of the living God in heaven. Transubstantiation, the belief in the transformation of blood and wine into the real body and blood of Christ during mass, fits this picture perfectly. Our flesh and our blood cannot inherit the kingdom of God; matter, our natural life, must be transformed and willing to be transformed in order to share in God's grace.

Medieval society outside the cathedral is characterized by a similar mystery. We encounter ranks and classes which cohere like the stones of a cathedral, displaying the stepped pattern of a gradually ascending hierarchy. Agrarians, artisans, and merchants constitute the lowest rung of the ladder of society, followed by the military. Above both are those who direct and govern society: the nobility and clergy. This image, notwithstanding certain Platonic characteristics, reminds us of the image Paul uses in his letter to the Corinthians when speaking of the Body of Christ:

> But as it is, God arranged the organs in the body, each one of them, as he chose. If all were a single organ, where would the body be? As it is, there are many parts, yet one body. The eye cannot say to the hand, "I have no need of you," nor again the head to the feet, "I have no need of you." On the contrary, the parts of the body which seem to be weaker are indispensable. ... Now you are the body of Christ and individually members of it.[9]

Like Paul, the medieval scholastics drew the same conclusion for their society: "Everyone remains in the class to which he has been called." "So brethren, in whatever state each was called, there let him remain. ..."[10] Only those who attend to their own

7. Cf. Ephesians 2:20.
8. Cf. among others Hans Jantzen, *High Gothic* (London: Constable, 1962), part 2: *Ecclesia Spiritualis,* pp. 169–181.
9. I Cor. 12:18–22, 27 (R.S.V.).
10. I Cor. 7:24 (R.S.V.).

limited task in the entire body can be included in the process of sanctification of society through the official ecclesiastical means of grace.

In this light we will have to come to a better understanding of the complex medieval rules and regulations concerning prices imposed on the merchant class. Both the doctrine of the *justum pretium,* the just price, as well as the prohibition of interest served to keep the merchants and artisans in their proper social place. These regulations prevented classes from superseding each other on the social scale by increasing their wealth or power. If that were to happen, the sanctification of society as a whole would be threatened, and the societal cathedral itself might partially or entirely collapse.

Medieval society is shrouded in a mystery all its own. For this reason it escapes banal and vulgar criticism. At the same time, we should not idealize its social structure by holding it up in every respect as a model for our own time. We should not overlook the fact that medieval society was permeated with an often unbearable hierarchy in which slaves and serfs had to suffer a generally miserable existence alongside of knights and noblemen. Moreover, viewing the whole of human life in the context of a nature-grace perspective frequently led to a deformation of natural life because it was forced into the straightjacket of a goal-oriented, vertical social structure and thus denied the opportunities for normal development. During the Middle Ages the manner in which the development of commerce was at times dealt with reminds us of a too strict, authoritarian approach to the rearing of children which in part becomes the cause of their rebellion. It also reminds us of those medieval cathedrals in which the sculpture on the columns has been unnaturally elongated and twisted to make it fit into the structure of the cathedral as a whole, or of the cathedrals which were built so high that during their construction they collapsed, like the one at Beauvais. Not until the Reformation did the consciousness break through that nothing in natural life in and of itself is sinful, and that in every area, including the economic, man lives and works directly before the face of the living God— *coram Deo*—without requiring the mediation of the means of grace of the church to make life holy.

Without a doubt, the origin, background, and nourishing climate of medieval social structure are of a spiritual nature, deeply influenced by Christianity. We find evidence of this influence also within the various ranks and classes and within the individual households making up the building blocks of this hierarchy. However limited, medieval guilds and manors revealed an authentic element of human community. For instance, on a medieval farm even the labor of the serfs was regarded as part of a whole body of social rights and duties, which included the right to care in times of sickness, the right to food in times of famine, and the right to protection in times of attack.

THE NURTURING SOIL OF CAPITALISTIC SOCIETY

The structure of medieval society was deeply rooted in religiously shaped cultural impulses or motives. But what impulses or motives are at the root of capitalism as a type of society? This is a legitimate question at this stage of our argument. Both the demolition of an existing social order and the establishment of a new one are in an important sense a matter of style, of "doing" culture. Every style of culture is in turn related to the religious question of how people view the ultimate meaning of their life and society.

However, the question concerning the religiocultural impulses behind the rise of capitalism is easier to pose than to answer. A famous thesis in this connection, proposed by Max Weber, states that the spirit of capitalism was shaped especially by Calvinism. In his famous essay *The Protestant Ethic and the Spirit of Capitalism,*[11] Weber argued that capitalism can be characterized, in terms of ideal types, as a societal system in which the accumulation of capital is central, and in which, therefore, it is constantly imperative to save. This system thus presupposes a *Wirtschaftsgeist,* a spirit of industry, which considers labor, production, and accumulation of capital to be meaningful even when they do not lead directly to a commensurate increase in consumption possibilities. The rise of this spirit, Weber asserted, was due to Calvinism, which not only stressed the idea of vocation in socioeconomic life, but also combined this vocation idea with a doctrine of election which asserts that a person can confirm his own election through labor in his vocation. Thus, on the one hand rational labor acquires an ethical significance apart from the consumption possibilities which it creates, while on the other hand saving and investing become independent

11. See Introduction, footnote 1.

virtues, in the knowledge that every human being will later have to give an account of his possessions before God.

This is not the place to review the discussion provoked by Weber's thesis. The interested reader is referred to the excellent studies by Richard H. Tawney,[12] Kurt Samuelsson[13] and André Biéler.[14] Three very general conclusions can be drawn from this discussion, though. First, historically speaking there is definitely a connection between capitalism and Calvinism through the intermediary of later Puritanism. Secondly, it has proven far more difficult to establish a direct historical connection between capitalism and Calvinism. Finally, doubts have been raised by some writers as to whether the material derived from Calvinism and Puritanism is sufficient to explain the characteristic spirit of capitalism.

Evidence for the first point—the relation of Calvinism and capitalism via Puritanism—is found especially in the emphasis in Calvinism on personal dedication and effort in labor, the "work ethic" which it is claimed was fostered by the identification of all useful labor with the fulfillment of a divine vocation. With respect to the second point the following comments are relevant. The fact that Puritanism must serve as an intermediate link depends upon the circumstance that in original Calvinism the positive appreciation of human labor was accompanied by explicit warnings against the dangers of wealth, great possessions, and excessive interest. Tawney observes that Calvin handled interest the way a pharmacist handles poison. Calvinism, he argues, "did its best to make life unbearable for the rich. Before the Paradise of earthly comfort it hung a flaming brand, waved by the implacable shades of Moses and Aaron."[15] It is indeed difficult to make original Calvinism responsible for the rise of the capitalist spirit. With respect to the third point, Brentano has pointed out that the rationalism which is so characteristic of the spirit of capitalism clearly can be proven to stem from the Renaissance rather than the Reformation. The "ideal-typical" characterizations of Max Weber, therefore, seem to be disput-

12. Richard H. Tawney, *Religion and the Rise of Capitalism* (Harmondsworth: Penguin Books, 1938).

13. Kurt Samuelsson, *Religion and Economic Action* (Stockholm: Svenska Bokförlaget; London: Heinemann, 1961).

14. André Biéler, *La pensée économique et sociale de Calvin* (Geneva: Librairie de l'Université, 1959), chapter 6.

15. Tawney, *Religion and the Rise of Capitalism*, p. 139.

able both in the case of Calvinism and in that of capitalism. They give the impression of having been written with a view to combining common traits with the result that evident differences are neglected. Thus, Weber's description of capitalism fails to mention the pursuit of income and greater consumption as an independent original element, whereas his description of authentic Calvinism omits the emphasis (characteristic of the Reformers) on *sola gratia*—living and being saved by grace alone, rather than by man's activities.

But if the impulse of Calvinism cannot serve as a sufficient explanation of the rise of capitalism in western culture, in what other directions must we look? Would it be meaningful, instead of starting with Calvinism, to take our point of departure in the Reformation and the Renaissance together? It would certainly not be meaningless. But again the same objection holds that more than two centuries separate the Renaissance from modern capitalism. Therefore, it seems advisable to follow a different path. We might ask ourselves instead *what breakdown of the spiritual background of medieval society was minimally required so as to prepare the soil in which the seed of capitalist society as we know it could take root?* Or, to put it differently, which spiritual barriers related to the main characteristics of medieval society had to be removed successively before modern capitalism, via the industrial revolution of the eighteenth and nineteenth centuries, could become the vanguard of western culture?

Only by finding an answer to this question can we hope to expose more clearly the deepest spiritual impulses underlying the rise of modern capitalist society. It seems very likely that the forces which ultimately made the razing of these barriers possible are the same as those which, in a positive sense, in part evoked the spirit and reality of modern capitalism.

2. The Barrier of Church and Heaven

In the preceding sketch of the contours of medieval society the most notable feature was its vertical orientation. Earthly, natural life had no meaning in itself. It was doomed to eternal sinfulness unless it was lifted, ordered, and directed to heaven and the realm of grace. From that realm it derived its deepest meaning. Only in its vertical orientation would it be sanctified and redeemed through the mediation of the church as the institution of grace.

This is not, of course, a complete picture. Features of a horizontal orientation can also be found in the medieval view of natural life. It is striking, for instance, to observe to what extent the medieval theologians, the so-called schoolmen or scholastics, ascribed an independent role to human reason (*ratio*). Man's acquisition of knowledge, in their view, obeys natural laws which cannot be derived directly from divine revelation. Nature and grace indeed refer to two distinct areas of life, with a certain measure of independence attributed to natural life. An anticipation of modern times becomes visible in this; in the midst of medieval culture the foundation is being laid for a later sense of autonomy and for the advent of a self-sufficient type of man. Yet in all this we should not forget that societal orders rarely change abruptly. Contradictory currents can exist side by side within the same culture. An early capitalistic commercial expansionism was emerging in the Italian (and later also the Flemish) merchant towns when scholasticism reached its culmination in the work of Thomas Aquinas and his followers. Even the medieval ideal of chivalry can be considered in some respects as the harbinger of the enterprising burgher of later times; this has been shown by Johan Huizinga in his magisterial book *The Waning of the Middle Ages*.[16] Nonetheless, it remains true that the cultural and social climate of the Middle Ages was marked by a clear allegiance to ecclesiastic rules and an orientation to the hereafter. As long as these dominated, they of course constituted a real barrier to the free unfolding of the forces of the economy and technology.

It is important to note this, because it is precisely economic expansion and technological innovation which constitute an essential mark of the later capitalist society. We might describe *modern capitalism* as that societal structure (1) in which the legal order, the prevailing public morality, as well as the organization of socioeconomic life grant unobstructed admission to the forces of economic growth and technological development; and (2) in which those forces subsequently manifest themselves by way of a process of "natural selection" as that is given shape by a continual competition in the market between independent production units organized on the basis of returns on capital. In such a social structure an orientation toward a set vertical direction of life does not make any sense. Instead, a horizontal orientation dominates; the purpose of development and expansion is directed to earthly possibilities. For instance, in an unadulterated capitalist society regulations regarding just prices are naturally considered as unlawful interventions in the market mechanism. The same can be said about the prohibition of interest. For that reason, the first barrier which necessarily had to be removed was the one of church and heaven. The vertical orientation of life had to be transformed into a predominantly horizontal one.

This transformation was the accomplishment of both Renaissance and Reformation. But first of all we must mention the Renaissance, for even though the reformers acknowledged that natural life, including economic life, was sanctified by God and therefore did not require the constant mediation of the church for this purpose, they nonetheless stressed the abiding significance of the law of God for economic life. They were distinctly apprehensive of the dangers of addiction to money and wealth which would accompany the expansion and autonomy of commerce and industry. In view of this the contribution of the re-

16. Johan Huizinga, *The Waning of the Middle Ages* (New York: Doubleday and Co., 1924; Anchor Books ed., 1954), chapters 4 and 5.

formers, presupposing the rehabilitation of natural life itself, can better be described as a battle against the unnatural, "elongated" manner of *verticalizing* economic life under the influence of medieval scholasticism than as a licensing of an unlimited and autonomous *horizontal* development. The first primary spiritual impulse for that development must instead be located in the Renaissance.

THE GROUND MOTIVE OF THE RENAISSANCE

Every attempt to describe the ground motive of the Renaissance within a few words is almost bound to fail. What a remarkable time it must have been when—in 1486—Giovanni Pico della Mirandola dared to present his oration about the "dignity of man," appealing throughout to Plato as well as Paul, to Averroës as well as Thomas Aquinas; when Leonardo da Vinci declared that experimental research alone could be the proper interpreter between man and nature, and linked this to the Renaissance prayer: "Thou, O God, dost sell us all things at the price of labour";[17] when the arts, newly oriented to classical principles and mathematical forms, began to flourish, and the plan of buildings was changed from a cruciform to a square, rectangle, or circle (the God of the Renaissance becomes the great mathematician!); when voyages of discovery opened up the world to unknown expansion of trade and human industriousness; and when, finally, even morality became characterized by the unbridled will to human self-expression, impelling the Renaissance author Bandello to write the following lamentation:

> Would that we were not daily forced to hear that one man has murdered his wife because he suspected her of infidelity; that another has killed his daughter on account of a secret marriage; that a third has caused his sister to be murdered because she would not marry as he wished! It is great cruelty that we claim the right to do whatever we list and will not suffer women to do the same.[18]

Rather than provide a summary of my own as to what

17. Cf. among others, Christopher Dawson, *Progress and Religion: An Historical Inquiry* (London: Sheed & Ward, 1929), p. 183.

18. Jacob Burckhardt, *The Civilization of the Renaissance in Italy*, 2 vols. (New York: Harper & Row, 1929; Harper Torchbook edition, 1958), vol. 2, p. 435.

moved men in those times, I shall rely heavily on what author-itative historians such as Jacob Burckhardt, Dagobert Frey, Alfred von Martin, and Peter Gay have written about this period. Their interpretations differ, of course, which is to be expected from good historians.[19] Thus, von Martin[20] sketches the Renaissance primarily as a movement of emancipation of the new bourgeoi-sie, in search of a new manner and style of life to replace the traditional but essentially disintegrated ethic prescribed by the medieval catholic church. Frey,[21] on the other hand, stresses the new perspective on the whole of reality, which now takes its starting point from the view of the individual person; the laws of perspective become the vogue. Burckhardt, in turn, stresses not only the development of the individual and the rebirth of classical antiquity, but also the discovery of the world and man's place in it. It is noteworthy that in his famous book on the Renaissance he opens the chapter on the discovery of man with the following quotation from Michelet's *Histoire de France:* "To the discovery of the outward world the Renaissance added a still greater achievement by first discerning and bringing to light the full, whole nature of man."[22]

In spite of the different emphases in interpretation, these authors share a common underlying theme, namely, the birth of a new image of man and the world, in which, to quote Peter Gay, "man is free, the master of his fortune, not chained to his place in a universal hierarchy but capable of all things."[23] In other words, the earth becomes man's domain as the platform and instrument with which he can realize himself in the arts as well as in science, in trade as well as in his contact with the other sex. Man directs his attention to this world to come to a better understanding of it and consequently of himself.

The contemporary Dutch philosopher and legal theorist Herman Dooyeweerd speaks in this context of the dialectical

19. For a more contemporary interpretation, see Wallace K. Ferguson, *Facets of the Renaissance* (New York: Harper & Row, 1963), especially chapter 2: "The Reinterpretation of the Renaissance."

20. Alfred W. O. von Martin, *Sociology of the Renaissance* (New York: Harper & Row, 1963; originally published 1932).

21. Dagobert Frey, *Gotik und Renaissance als Grundlagen der modernen Weltanschauung* (Augsburg: Filser, 1929).

22. Burckhardt, *Civilization of the Renaissance,* vol. 2, p. 303.

23. Peter Gay, *The Enlightenment: An Interpretation,* 2 vols. (New York: Alfred A. Knopf, 1967–69), vol. 1: *The Rise of Modern Paganism* (1967), p. 266.

character of the ground motive of every form of humanism since the Renaissance. It is dialectical because it tries to unite into one conception the pole of completely autonomous personal *freedom* and the contrary pole of absolute and rational *control* over nature. In essence these poles contradict each other. However, Renaissance man regarded them as extensions of each other.[24] It is precisely in the control over nature, in the disclosure of new fields of research, and in the new direction of the arts and morality that the freedom and grandeur of Renaissance man find their inimitable expression. Even Pico della Mirandola testifies to this in his above-mentioned oration, in the dialogue between the Creator and Adam:

> I have set thee in the midst of the world, that thou mayst the more easily behold and see all that is therein. I created thee a being neither heavenly nor earthly . . . that thou mightest be free to shape and to overcome thyself. Thou mayst sink into a beast, and be born anew to the divine likeness. . . . To thee alone is given a growth and a development depending on thine own free will. Thou bearest in thee the germs of a universal life.[25]

The Renaissance stands at the borderline between the Middle Ages and a new period. It also stands at the borderline between Christianity and humanism, as is apparent from Pico's words. During the Renaissance, Christianity and humanism were still close together, quite intermingled. The putti resemble the angels; the scholars of antiquity, though present, have not replaced the teachers of the church. But then, in the next stage, one can detect the divorce of humanism from Christianity. Burckhardt thus describes the complexity of motives: "It is curious, for instance, to notice how far Gioviano Pontano carried this confusion. He speaks of a saint not only as *divus,* but as *deus;* the angels he holds to be identical with the genii of antiquity; and his notion of immortality reminds us of the old kingdom of the Shades."[26] Such a synthesis, such an effort to fuse two different worlds, cannot survive. And before long we find Christianity and humanism offering different spiritual foundations for the culture of the modern age.

24. Herman Dooyeweerd, *Roots of Western Culture: Pagan, Secular, and Christian Options* (Toronto: Wedge Publishing Foundation, 1979), especially chapter 6: "Classical Humanism."

25. Burckhardt, *Civilization of the Renaissance,* vol. 2, p. 352.

26. *Ibid.,* p. 483.

We can easily perceive parallels between the emergence of the new Renaissance view of man's world and the rapid flourishing of so-called early capitalism. For instance, when Werner Sombart asks which new element is introduced in the organization of economic behavior by capitalism, his immediate response is: "The answer cannot be difficult to find: the enterprise is now autonomous."[27] The Renaissance in particular laid the foundation for this concept of autonomy, this notion of the self-determination of the laws governing one's own behavior. The disclosure of new markets and their control, according to Sombart, constitute the new mentality. Hobbes pointedly described the modern attitude of autonomy in these few words: "No moral rule beyond the letter of the law."

During this same period the cohesion of the medieval manor was broken up by the increased influence of a money-oriented economy. Labor, land, and capital became separate elements of production, each of which could be bought or hired by means of money.[28] Man chose this world solely as his own, also with respect to its economic dimension, and in his conquest of this world he would tolerate no other standards than those of his own making.

27. Cf. Werner Sombart, "Medieval and Modern Commercial Enterprise," in Frederic C. Lane and Jelle C. Riemersma, eds., *Enterprise and Secular Change: Readings in Economic History* (Homewood, Ill.: Richard D. Irwin, Inc., 1953), p. 36.

28. A fascinating survey of this process of *monetization* is provided by Robert L. Heilbroner in *The Making of Economic Society* (Englewood Cliffs, N.J.: Prentice-Hall, 1968).

3. *The Barrier of Fate and Providence*

We have just alluded to the blend of Christian and humanist motives present in the Renaissance world view. The doctrine of God's providence and judgment was still upheld formally. However, in due time an inevitable choice had to be made between two divergent convictions: between the belief that in the final analysis God directs the destiny of human life and the belief that man himself determines that destiny.

This choice introduces us to another barrier that had to be overcome in the transition from the Middle Ages to the breakthrough of modern capitalistic society. This is the barrier of the doctrine of divine providence as it was taught and confessed in the Middle Ages. Much more was involved in this belief than a general realization that God rules the world. It clearly implied a condemnation of the pursuit of happiness and prosperity on the basis of man's own strength and potentials. Since the medieval view of divine providence goes back particularly to Augustine, it will be profitable to turn our attention briefly to this church father.

AUGUSTINE

The term *divine providence* does not appear in the Bible. Rather, it has been derived from the literature of the Stoics. These philosophers, who wrote before and around the beginning of the Christian era, viewed the world as a roughly hewn material entity which received its shape from the deity. This deity pervades the world and is at the same time its soul; it drives world history with absolute necessity. Nothing in world history happens accidentally, according to the Stoics Zeno, Diogenes, and later Cato. Everything that occurs is contained in Providentia, the world's providential order. Everything that happens is foreseen, "pro-vided," by the deity.

The Stoic idea of providence is borrowed by Augustine (354–430); however, he grafts it on a Christian root. The living, personal God not only made the world but also rules it providentially from day to day. His rule pertains to both the city of God and the city of this world. Here the image of the two cities appears, which Augustine worked out so carefully in *The City of God,* and which has had such an immense influence on all later western thought.

For our purpose, what Augustine said about the city of this world is particularly important. It is the city of Babylon, to which the children of darkness belong, and is distinguished from the city of God, Jerusalem, to which the children of light belong. Both cities, according to Augustine, exist next to and intermingle with each other throughout the entire world history, until at Christ's second coming they will finally be separated. These two cities can readily be distinguished, however, by their totally different principles of life. The principle of the city of God is love for God, even to the extent of contempt for one's self; in the city of this world it is love for one's self, even to the extent of contempt for God. Both cities also have their own institutions. The city of this world knows private property, slavery, and the state. The institutions of the state and of property are necessary to curb the sins of man and to prevent the disintegration of the world into a complete chaos. In other words, they exist "because of sin."

It is surprising to see how, in the city of this world, Augustine placed life, including economic life, in the light of his view of divine providence. "God," he says, "can never be believed to have left the kingdoms of men, their dominations and servitudes, outside of the laws of His providence."[29] God does not allow these kingdoms to end in chaos before their appointed time. His divine hand is capable of establishing a relative har-

29. St. Augustine, *The City of God* (New York: Random House, 1950), book 5, p. 158.

mony in the midst of all antagonistic human interests and forms of egoism which come into prominence in the city of this world.[30]

Does this mean that the final end of the city of this world will still be relatively good? Certainly not; for even though God's providence can bring about temporary and relative harmony between antagonistic human interests, the direction of the city of this world is, according to Augustine, its ruin, like the destruction of Babylon as described in the last book of the Bible. And the basis for its destruction is man's reliance on his own ability, prosperity, and expertise. Augustine expressed this nowhere as succinctly and lively as in his commentary on Psalm 137 which describes the destiny of the Israelites who, far away from their beloved city of Jerusalem, wept by the rivers of Babylon:

> The rivers of Babylon are all things which are here loved, and pass away. For example, one man loves to practise husbandry, to grow rich by it, to employ his mind on it, to get his pleasure from it. Let him observe the issue and see that what he has loved is not a foundation of Jerusalem, but a river of Babylon. Another says, it is a grand thing to be a soldier; all farmers fear those who are soldiers, are subservient to them, tremble at them. If I am a farmer, I shall fear soldiers; if a soldier, farmers will fear me. Madman! thou hast cast thyself headlong into another river of Babylon, and that still more turbulent and sweeping. Thou wishest to be feared by thy inferior; fear Him who is greater than thou. He who fears thee may on a sudden become greater than thou, but He whom thou oughtest to fear will never become less. To be an advocate, says another, is a grand thing; eloquence is most powerful; always to have clients hanging on the lips of their eloquent advocate, and from his words looking for loss or gain, death or life, ruin or security. Thou knowest not whither thou hast cast thyself. This too is another river of Babylon, and its roaring sound is the din of the waters dashing against the rocks. Mark that it flows, that it glides on; beware, for it carries things away with it. To sail the seas, says another, and to trade is a grand thing—to know many lands, to make gains from every quarter, never to be answerable to any powerful man in thy country, to be always travelling, and to feed thy mind with the diversity of

30. Cf. Reinhold Niebuhr, *Christian Realism and Political Problems* (London: Faber & Faber, 1954); Werner Stark, *Social Theory and Christian Thought* (London: Routledge & Kegan Paul, 1958); and Theodor E. Mommsen, "St. Augustine and the Christian Idea of Progress," *Journal of the History of Ideas*, vol. 22, no. 1 (Jan., 1951), pp. 346–374.

the nations and the business met with, and to return enriched by the increase of thy gains. This too is a river of Babylon. When will the gains stop? When wilt thou have confidence and be secure in the gains thou makest? The richer thou art, the more fearful wilt thou be. Once shipwrecked, thou wilt come forth stripped of all, and rightly wilt bewail thy fate *in* the rivers of Babylon, because thou wouldest not sit down and weep *upon* the rivers of Babylon.[31]

This eloquent quotation confirms that Augustine's faith in divine providence with respect to this world cannot be explained as a faith in a guaranteed favorable outcome of what happens in the city of this world. The contrary is closer to the truth: God preserves this world, but he does this in part unto its own judgment. The relative harmony which he brings about by his hand serves the flow of the streams of Babylon. In these streams man lets himself be swept along of his own free will to the shipwreck which awaits him at the end.

This is the faith that permeates the medieval sense of providence. Augustine's image of the streams of Babylon finds its parallel at the end of the Middle Ages in the alarming painting by Jerome Bosch entitled the *Hay Wain* (Prado, Madrid). In this painting the hay wain is the symbol of human prosperity and abundance around which everyone, clergy as well as laity, elbows his way to pick and grab. No one seems to notice, however, that the hay wain itself is being pulled by monstrous devils who drag the entire masquerade into the scorching fires of hell and destruction.

Insofar as faith in divine providence entails the preparation of this world for its own destruction, it clearly constitutes an enormous barrier to every pursuit of happiness by economic and technological means. If taking destiny in your own hands is equal to calling forth your own fate, then any development toward an expansive capitalist society is doomed. The building of such a society does not tolerate the image of a God who rules the world, who in his own way sets the destinies of men and women, and at moments of his own choosing interferes directly in their affairs with his judgment. For that reason J. B. Bury correctly observes in his profound study that the idea of progress could establish itself permanently in the West only after

---

31. Cf. Reinhold Niebuhr, *Christian Realism and Political Problems,* pp. 136–137.

orthodox faith in providence had lost its universal impact: "The process [of human development] must be the necessary outcome of the psychical and social nature of man; it must not be at the mercy of any external will; otherwise there would be no guarantee of its continuance and its issue, and the idea of Progress would lapse into the idea of Providence."[32] For that reason also the barrier of the divine shaping of history's destiny, which is part and parcel of the spiritual legacy of medieval society, had to be removed before the structure of the modern capitalist social order could be crowned with success.

This enormous task was accomplished by the spiritual movement known as deism. Almost every western thinker and philosopher of the sixteenth through the eighteenth centuries has been influenced by this spiritual current. Deism indeed maintained the term *providence* but filled it with a totally different meaning.

SELF-ACQUITTAL AND SELF-REVELATION

A short definition of deism in contemporary language might describe it as the conception that God has created the world in such a perfect manner that immediately afterwards he could afford to go into early retirement. The God of deism, in fact, has often been compared with a clockmaker, a superior technician and mathematician, who is capable of making such a perfect timepiece that once it is set in motion, it no longer needs his further attention. In this conception, the history of the world unfolds in accordance with the natural order which the great Mathematician ordained at its beginning once and for all. "According to the Deistic philosophy God's role has already been played in creating the natural order, and . . . he can be safely left out of account as a factor in the present."[33] We can speak of God's providence only insofar as it refers to God's acts before the beginning of world history. It excludes all activity on God's part during the unfolding of world history. Or, to put it in the words of Hugo Grotius, the great Dutch legal thinker, "Natural

32. John B. Bury, *The Idea of Progress: An Inquiry into its Origin and Growth* (London: Macmillan, 1920), p. 5.

33. Eduard Heimann, *History of Economic Doctrines* (London: Oxford University Press, 1945; New York: Oxford University Press, Galaxy Book, 1964), p. 49.

law is so unalterable that God himself cannot change it."[34] It is this natural law, therefore, which replaces God and executes the role of providence in the world.

We hardly need argue that a persistent influence of deism could indeed radically raze the barrier of fate and providence. In fact, it fundamentally changed medieval faith in providence in two ways: first, by forcing the role of a governing and intervening God back to the time before the beginning of human history; secondly, by couching this "indirect" divine control in a cloak of "providence" which guarantees only good results, at least for those who are willing to take the natural order into continuous consideration.

This can also be formulated in more positive terms. As soon as God moves to the background as the shaper of man's present fate, legitimate room is created for man to take this fate into his own hands. The God who withdraws is the complement of man who steps to the fore. And while God in his providence can no longer judge and punish man, the latter can begin to guarantee for himself a good life on this earth. Man can now begin to "provide" for himself! Thus the God who does not *judge* is the complement of the man who *acquits* himself.

This self-providence and self-acquittal, which in effect are self-revelation, will soon take over the leadership in western culture. The western image of God is bent into a deistic direction. Thus Peter Gay correctly describes deism as "a last compromise with religion."[35] God becomes a working hypothesis who can, in fact, easily be eliminated at a later stage. There also is no further room—nor need—for miracles on God's part; "to the deists, the only miracle was the miracle not of irregularity but of regularity."[36]

For our purposes it is important to take note now of the impact of deism on the rise of the science of economics, since this new discipline has exerted an immense influence on the structure of western society from the time of the Enlightenment.

THE DEISM OF ADAM SMITH

Adam Smith (1723–1790) is the father of the science of economics. The fact that he was also a deist is not, as has frequently

34. Gay, *Enlightenment*, vol. 1, p. 299.
35. *Ibid.*, p. 149.
36. *Ibid.*

been noted, purely a coincidence. It was precisely in the spiritual climate provided by deism, which looked upon the social and economic life of man as a cosmos controlled by natural laws and completely accessible to human analysis, that the science of economics could gradually emerge. The character of this science of course presupposed a primarily mechanistic view of the world. The timepiece manufactured by the clockmaker could, so to speak, now be opened up by man, and the wheelwork inside could be analyzed as carefully as possible.

As is well known, Adam Smith connected the functioning of all economic processes with the idea of an "invisible hand." An invisible hand guides man to serve the general good even when he thinks he is engaged only in the pursuit of private interests. Thus, the invisible hand is the deistic version of the role of God's providence. This is clearly evident from what Smith writes in *The Theory of Moral Sentiments* (1759). He states that *"by acting according to the dictates of our moral faculties,* we necessarily pursue the most effectual means of promoting the happiness of mankind, and may therefore be said in some sense to co-operate with the Deity and to advance, as far as in our power, the Plan of Providence."[37] The rich, he writes elsewhere, "consume little more than the poor." Even though they have only their own interests in mind—to increase their wealth by employing thousands who are in their service—nevertheless the poor share in "the produce of all their improvements." Thus the rich are led "by an invisible hand to make nearly the same distribution of the necessaries of life, which would have been made, had the earth been divided into equal portions among all its inhabitants; and thus, without intending it, without knowing it [they] advance the interest of the society."[38]

It should surprise no one that in the context of this world view Smith senses no problems at all in attaching the hope for a better future for humankind to its economic activities. For him the barrier of church and heaven no longer exists, neither does that of a God who provides and judges the world. For that reason, in his view, nothing stands in man's way, within the given order of nature, to pursue "that great purpose of human

37. Quoted by Andrew Skinner in his Introduction to Adam Smith, *The Wealth of Nations* (Harmondsworth, England: Penguin Books Ltd., 1970), p. 27.
38. Cited by Henry W. Spiegel, *The Growth of Economic Thought* (Englewood Cliffs, N.J.: Prentice-Hall, 1971), pp. 230f.

life which we call bettering our condition."[39] In accordance with that great master plan of nature which aims at human happiness, man himself can work out his providential destiny.

The manner in which Smith elaborates this in his own system of thought has been discussed so extensively and competently elsewhere that we need not treat it in depth here.[40] To summarize, he attributes a great significance to the division of labor as the motor of all economic development. This division of labor is nourished by accumulation of capital, and its benefits for humankind become particularly apparent when new competitive markets can be opened up. Only the size of the market, in his view, can limit the possibility for continued division of labor. Therefore, the wider the market, the more the technique of division of labor can advance and the more the "wealth of nations" can increase. Smith's thought pattern is not static; rather, it is thoroughly dynamic. He perceives a gradual progess in the economic life of man. After a period of hunting, gathering, and farming, trade between peoples and nations now has become the key factor in economic progress. It would be senseless and above all in conflict with natural law to subject this free trade, which opens up the world, to any limitations imposed by government. That would be stark defiance of the plan of providence.

BASIC ELEMENTS OF THE CLASSICAL ECONOMIC WORLD VIEW

The world view of Adam Smith and his successors comprises certain elements which at first do not seem to be outstanding, but which are of great importance because of their impact on the later formation of the capitalist spirit. I want to call special attention to four of these elements.

1. Man versus nature

When Adam Smith and later classical economists ask how men and nations can attain prosperity, they pose the problem in the

39. Quoted by Spiegel, *ibid.,* p. 230.

40. For a discussion of Smith's thought and the classical school of economics in general see: Eduard Heimann, *History of Economic Doctrines;* Hla Myint, *Theories of Welfare Economics* (London: London School of Economics and Political Science, 1948; New York: Augustus M. Kelley, 1965); Gunnar Myrdal, *The Political Element in the Development of Economic Theory* (New York: Simon and Schuster, 1954); Joseph A. Schumpeter, *History of Economic Analysis* (New York: Oxford University Press, 1954); and Henry W. Spiegel, *The Growth of Economic Thought.*

specific context of the struggle of man against nature. Hla Myint and Gunnar Myrdal in particular have pointed to this.[41] For classical economists like Smith economic life is characterized by man's attempt to attain the greatest possible prosperity on the basis of an interaction with nature by means of human labor. The most important capacity at his disposal for accomplishing this is rational insight, which enables him to analyze nature and its laws and to use instruments—such as capital—in his labor. In this way he continually advances in the mighty process of division of labor.

In this setting of the economic problem we recognize the persistent influence of the Renaissance world view in which nature is the domain of man's self-realization. This wide ontological scope is given an economistic reduction in the classical school. Specifically, for Adam Smith economic value can only be achieved by way of man's active struggle with nature—in other words, by means of labor. Hence there is no value other than labor value, elicited from nature by man. This economic value is tangible in the goods produced. Thus, production is the result of labor; it is the most important expression of human dignity.

It is quite in place to remind ourselves that this Renaissance world view is not at all a matter of course. Rather, it clearly entails a spiritual choice as to cultural direction, namely, that man's destiny is realized primarily in his relation to the natural things of this world and not in relation to his fellowmen. The centrality of interhuman relations is far more characteristic of oriental civilizations. There a person derives his identity and dignity particularly from the social relationships in which he moves. The centrality of the relationship of man with nature, however, is one of the most characteristic features of western culture since the Renaissance. In the modern age, the value of human personality and the social order depends to a great extent on our individual or collective ability in the areas of productive labor, economy, science, technology, and art. We distinguish ourselves as human beings primarily by the shape we give to this world through thought and creative activity rather than by the meaning of our lives to other persons.

This centrality of the relationship of man to things permeates classical economic thought. A typical western economist

41. For titles see footnote 40 above.

does not view the market primarily as a meetingplace for people, but rather as a meetingplace for each separate individual with a given price. In such a world view the market is ultimately nothing but a mechanism. Similarly, human labor is not regarded first of all as a reciprocal human relation and an expression of communal action, but rather as an individual effort to be performed by means of a particular combination of labor, land, and capital. Labor is an isolated production factor to be put to use at random. In this view a business enterprise is not looked upon as an organization primarily characterized by ties of cooperation between living human beings, but as a workshop where production factors can be combined at will. For that reason the enterprise is referred to as an object of property. The relationship of man to his fellowman is secondary for a western economist; he considers the relation between man and things as primary. Thus the contemporary French economist Perroux correctly speaks of the forgotten aspects of our economic progress: "namely those which tie men to their fellowmen, rather than those which pertain to the contact of man with things."[42]

2. Natural law as suitable servant

We have already observed in our discussion of Adam Smith that he does not expect nations to prosper as a matter of course. Certain conditions have to be met. The primary condition requires that the natural order be respected, that the demands of natural law be taken into account.

Adam Smith was not, of course, the first thinker to employ the term *natural order*. The Stoics popularized this notion, with the result that theories concerning the natural order of justice or the law of nature can be found at every stage in the history of western thought, so that we can speak of the natural law conception of the Roman jurists, the medieval philosophers, the reformers, and the Renaissance thinkers. Schumpeter, therefore, is quite correct in his claim that "natural law" is an analytic concept, that it has served as a *conceptual device* which has been filled with a constantly changing content depending on the diverse spiritual movements in western culture.[43]

42. F. Perroux, "Les mésures des progrès économiques et l'idée d'économie progressive," in *Cahiers de l'ISEA* (Paris, 1956), p. 10. French text: "disons ceux qui relient les hommes aux hommes plutôt que ceux qui se relèvent par le contact des hommes avec les choses."

43. Schumpeter, *History of Economic Analysis*, pp. 110–115.

For instance, the medieval natural law concept was rigid. It was characterized by the same vertical orientation typical of the medieval world view as a whole. Thus Thomas Aquinas derived the medieval prohibition of interest directly from the Bible and natural law: it is *contra naturam,* against the natural order, to assume that money could propagate itself in the manner of animals. Time and again after the Middle Ages, however, natural law is adjusted, mitigated, and newly interpreted. For the medieval scholastic, for example, the "natural price" consisted of a precise remuneration for labor and risk involved in the goods offered by the vendor. But even before 1600 the Italian jurist Luis Molina claimed that the "natural price" consisted of the normal outcome of the process of free market competition.[44] In other words, while medieval scholars considered market exchange only legally justified after the norm of the "just price" had been applied, the Renaissance jurist Molina turned the tables around by making the legal norm depend on the outcome of the market process. Only that which respected the functioning of the free market was considered just.

This reflects a shift of great significance. The form of medieval natural law is maintained, but the new content turns itself against almost everything the angelic teachers, the *doctores angeli* of the Middle Ages, had originally put into it. Schumpeter pointedly describes this shift: "the sword that was forged by angels might easily fall into the hand of devils."[45]

Adam Smith developed his economic system on the basis of this revised natural law concept. In his view also the correct, natural price results from the operation of free competition on the market. Natural law becomes the law of free, unhampered competition. It is precisely this natural order which the government is called upon to guard and conserve. Its task lies first of all in the protection of the civil rights of property, contract, and free enterprise, for these rights constitute the natural order, the indispensable condition for a truly flourishing and prosperous society. If the government would go beyond that by interfering directly in the operation of the free market, it would place itself between man and his potential for self-realization according to the providential plan for this world.

In short, for Adam Smith the concept of natural law has

44. *Ibid.,* p. 99.
45. *Ibid.,* p. 115.

become a suitable servant of the economy. In practice this means that the norm of justice, which applies to all government acts, by definition guarantees for him the outcome of the process of free competition.

3. Equilibrium as harmony

In our discussion of the removal of the barrier of fate and providence we pointed to Augustine who believed that the city of this world is subject to the laws of God's providence. In that context, Augustine suggested, God's own hand fashions a relative harmony in the midst of all conflicting human interests. Credit is due in particular to Werner Stark[46] for having drawn attention to the relationship between Adam Smith and Augustine. Both speak of an "invisible hand" which guides world history, and both make mention of a certain equilibrium in society through the operation of providence, notwithstanding the fact that the human motives involved are in the first place directed to the realization of selfish interests.

A closer look, however, reveals that in at least two respects there are essential differences between these thinkers. In the first place, Augustine speaks only of a relative, temporary harmony. This harmony does not exclude the possibility of the world being driven to its own judgment; rather, it even contributes to that. With Adam Smith this harmony is not relative but absolute. It is the absolute harmony of optimum social happiness, to be attained by the continual balancing of economic interests in the market place, where the interest of the one is matched by that of the other in a free competitive struggle.

There is a second important difference. For Augustine "self-interest" is a negative concept. It sums up the sinful direction of the city of man and drives him to his ruin. For Smith, on the other hand, self-interest is not a negative element in principle. Though it is not one of man's highest motives, it cannot be denied that the pursuit of self-interest is rationally quite defensible because in the end it benefits everyone.

Adam Smith was truly convinced of the positive value of the pursuit of clearly understood self-interest. This is evident from his great aversion to Bernard Mandeville, a student at the Erasmus School in Rotterdam, who in 1714 published a poem

---

46. Werner Stark, *Social Theory and Christian Thought* (London: Routledge & Kegan Paul, 1958).

entitled *The Fable of the Bees,* subtitled *Private Vices, Publick Benefits.* In this poem Mandeville indeed called a spade a spade! He compared economic life of his day with a buzzing beehive bustling with life, prosperity, and industriousness, thanks to the presence of a multitude of bad characteristics in each of the bees, such as selfishness, rapacity, lust for power, avarice, and an enormous measure of vanity. The result of these characteristics is a hive in which

> Millions endeavouring to supply
> Each other's Lust and Vanity;
> Whilst other Millions were employ'd
> To see their Handy-works destroy'd;

so that soon

> . . . there was not a Bee, but would
> Get more, I won't say, than he should.

Nevertheless the rule holds:

> Thus every Part was full of Vice,
> Yet the whole Mass a Paradise;
>
> The Worst of all the Multitude
> Did something for the common Good.

This magnificent parody, which is, as it were, the application of Erasmus' *Praise of Folly* to economic life, at a certain point presents the bees as becoming profoundly conscious of their own wickedness. Thus they decide to change their lives. Soon the disasters in the beehive heap up. The locksmiths walk out because a hive without thieves has no need for locks. They are followed by thousands of others who have lost their livelihood bcause such things as jewelry and fancy clothes are no longer coveted products. In the end life in this rich and bustling beehive turns to dust. For the few remaining bees nothing remains but to fly to a hollow tree in the surroundings, to rest content with their newly gained honesty:

> They flew into a hollow Tree,
> Blest with Content and Honesty.[47]

47. Bernard Mandeville, *The Fable of the Bees: or, Private Vices, Publick Benefits* (First published, London: 1714; Harmondsworth: Penguin Books, 1970), pp. 63–75.

It is easy to imagine why this poem angered Adam Smith and led him to label its author a "profligate."[48] Mandeville makes it clear that one cannot pursue one's own material happiness as fervently as possible and at the same time claim that one supports high standards of morality. At a particular moment it becomes a matter of choice. If one accepts the pursuit of prosperity as an absolute priority, one will also have to accept the morally evil consequences; if, on the other hand, one fully accepts the principles of morality, one ought not lament the prosperity to be sacrificed as a result. This dilemma must have been unbearable for such a proper and well-behaved bachelor as Adam Smith. How could he possibly have been the promotor of a multitude of human vices with his plea for a dynamic economy? That conclusion was in direct conflict with his deistic principles, for providence would most certainly not show us the way to a continual economic improvement in life and at the same time demand that impossible price—acquiescence to the most despicable human qualities!

4. Utility and morality

With this we are confronted almost automatically with a final characteristic of classical economic theory, namely, the direct relationship between prosperity and morality or, more specifically, between utility and morality.

Human happiness, according to Adam Smith and his followers, depends in large measure on the possession and use of material prosperity. Thus Myint correctly observes that "The classical economists . . . believed that quantities of satisfaction are proportional to quantities of physical product."[49] But, as we noted above, such a hypothesis is quite vulnerable from a moral and ethical point of view. Is it indeed *always* ethically responsible to strive for the greatest possible material prosperity? In this context the relationship between economics and ethics demands further elaboration and precision.

This matter has been dealt with in particular by *utilitarianism,* a moral philosophy developed at the end of the eighteenth century. The manner in which it has done so, however, is very peculiar. Instead of testing the economic process of increasing prosperity in the light of certain ethical principles, it

---

48. Spiegel, *The Growth of Economic Thought,* p. 227.
49. Myint, *Theories of Welfare Economics,* p. 9.

did the reverse. It manipulated ethics in such a way that the economic process of material increase could be regarded as ethically proper without prior justification.

The credit for this *tour de force* goes to Jeremy Bentham, the father of utilitarianism and a contemporary of Adam Smith. The word *utilitarianism* already indicates on what footing he based his new moral philosophy, namely, that of the aspiration toward utility. Thus, in the opening words of his Introduction to *The Principles of Morals and Legislation* (1789), he states that

> Nature has placed mankind under the governance of two sovereign masters, *pain* and *pleasure*. It is for them alone to point out what we ought to do, as well as to determine what we shall do. On the one hand the standard of right and wrong, on the other the chain of causes and effects, are fastened to their throne. They govern us in all we do. . . . The *principle of utility* recognises this subjection. . . .[50]

From this we can clearly deduce what Bentham, in essence, is aiming at. For one thing, he asserts that each person in fact only arrives at decisions by weighing right against wrong, utilities against disutilities. Everyone strives toward maximum utility as he sees it, and tunes every activity he engages in to that principle. That even holds, according to Bentham, for people who let themselves be burned at the stake. The disutility of going to hell is apparently so deterrent that in this weighing of utility they are willing to have themselves burned. That, according to Bentham, is a correct observation of what people actually do. At the same time he maintains that this principle of utility indicates what people and governments *ought* to do. If a certain activity is more utilitarian than another, then it is ethically justified. "Pleasure is . . . the only good . . . and pain is . . . the only evil," he grandly states in chapter 10 of his book.[51] His message is: we must not evaluate activities in terms of their *motives*. Good or bad motives in fact do not even exist. The only matter that counts in the evaluation of the ethical quality of an activity is its *effect*—particularly its effect in terms of utility.

It is significant to note that quite soon this train of thought was taken over by the leading economists, especially under the influence of John Stuart Mill, Adam Smith's spiritual heir. They

50. Jeremy Bentham, *The Principles of Morals and Legislation* (New York: Hafner, 1948), pp. 1, 2.
51. *Ibid.*, p. 102.

did this by introducing a slight modification: they regarded the possession of consumption goods as the most important type of "utility" and the performance of labor as a clear instance of "disutility." All classical economists speak of the "pain of labor."

Thus it becomes evident how the relationship between prosperity and morality has come full circle. The only valid moral principle in life is equated with the acquisition of the greatest number of utilities! In addition, goods are positive factors of utility and labor is a negative factor of utility. Therefore, in society the pursuit of the greatest possible possession of goods at the expense of the least possible exertion of labor is declared to be an *a priori* ethically proper matter.

The further adaption of utilitarianism in economic theory of course resulted in a number of problems. One of those concerns the thesis that by maximizing one's own utility, one also maximizes—at least does not diminish—the utility of others. Bentham tried to avoid this problem by establishing "the greatest happiness for the greatest number" as the essential moral purpose of life and also as the norm for the actions of governments. For this reason, in fact, he at times proposed what for his day were rather radical political solutions, such as the nationalization of life insurance companies.

In economic theory this political maxim of "the greatest happiness for the greatest number" did not gain a following until the development of a separate theory of "welfare economics."[52] In general economic theory, utilitarianism has been applied in particular in an individualistic manner. Until today most economists assumed, either implicitly or explicitly, that every individual strove after the acquisition of the greatest possible sum of utilities and attempted to avoid all disutilities.

The ethics of utilitarianism is of course from the outset in complete harmony with the goal of rapid economic growth. Every instance of economic expansion can be seen as a process by which more utilities (goods) are gained than lost. This harmony between economic growth and ethical principle is undoubtedly the most important feature of utilitarianism. Here it exerted its major influence, not only on economic theory but on western society as a whole. Thus, it is not in the least surprising that Alvin Gouldner, a prominent sociologist, has de-

52. This theory was developed around 1920 by Arthur Pigou, with Henry Sidgwick, Alfred Marshall, and Vilfredo Pareto as forerunners.

scribed contemporary western culture as primarily a "utilitarian culture."[53]

---

53. Alvin Ward Gouldner, *The Coming Crisis of Western Sociology* (New York: Basic Books, 1970).

4. Evaluative Intermezzo

At this point there is merit, after everything that has been introduced, in drawing up a kind of balance sheet. We began with a short description of medieval society. This society was characterized primarily by a vertical direction and a strictly hierarchical order in which technology was kept under control. It was a society based on the profound awareness that earthly life is indeed ruled by the will and providence of God, and that, as soon as one pursued this earthly life as an end in itself, it would betray him. In contrast to this outlook we saw that the Renaissance declared the earth and natural life to be the real domain of human existence. Through the domination of nature Renaissance man desired to prove his own dignity and grandeur as a rational being. Finally, we have traced how, under the influence of deism, the barrier of God's providence was razed and the notion of providence was reinterpreted to suit nearly opposite purposes. The order of nature was geared by divine providence to promote the interest of all those who wanted to make sure of their maximum earthly happiness—judged in terms of utility—by means of the free, natural operation of the market mechanism. In this way, so it was argued, we can be certain not only that every man has a chance to determine his own destiny but also that social harmony and equilibrium are achieved. In all this it is clear that the classical tradition of natural law was adjusted to serve the promotion of earthly bliss.

The entire discussion so far has focused on the razing of two barriers. But is this sufficient to explain the rise of capitalism? That is, have we dealt with every cultural obstacle to this development of western culture?

Let us briefly review the *most essential elements of modern capitalism* as described above. Modern capitalism is that societal structure (1) in which the legal order, the prevailing public morality, as well as the organization of socioeconomic life grant unobstructed admission to the forces of economic growth and technological development; and (2) in which those forces subsequently manifest themselves by way of a process of "natural selection" as it is given shape by a continual competition in the market between independent production units organized on the basis of returns on capital. With this in mind, we can answer the above questions affirmatively in several respects, for even before the beginning of the nineteenth century a spiritual climate was established which displayed these characteristics:

1. The urge for economic and technological renewal is considered essential to man's self-realization, which is attained through interaction with nature (Renaissance).
2. The urge for economic and technological renewal is made possible by the notion that free competition belongs to the providential plan as embodied in the natural order in which the equilibrium of the market leads to social harmony (deism).
3. The urge for economic and technological renewal is justified from the outset by the legal norms of the revived natural law conception which regards every price as just if it is a result of free competition, and which further views the task of the government as limited primarily to the protection of the already existing rights of property and contract.
4. And, finally, the urge for economic and technological renewal is also justified from the outset on the basis of the moral norms of a utilitarian ethic—developed in particular after 1750—which evaluates human activities only in terms of utility effects and which considers the increasing acquisition of goods for humankind as the most important source of utility.

These four characteristics constitute the spiritual blueprint of capitalism. Once they have been accepted, the way is cleared for the process of free competition, including the reorganization of socioeconomic relationships if required for the optimum success of free competition. Law and morality function as a justification for competition. Finally, the legal task of the government in the realization of competition consists in keeping out of it.

Nevertheless, with this summary we have not as yet dealt with every condition that must be met if a capitalistic society is to be established. We are looking at a kind of blueprint, but this blueprint has to be given shape; it has to be brought to life. The spiritual spark is still missing.

Could it be that, in effect, the *western faith in progress* is this life-giving element? Could it be that in this faith we recognize the *decisive spark,* at first touching a small élite but gradually also reaching the masses? This is a highly interesting and important question which deserves a careful answer. In our search for an answer we may well discover the third and possibly the most crucial barrier to the rise of capitalism. This is the barrier of paradise lost. In the medieval age, earthly paradise was indeed considered lost. This consciousness limited its temporal aspirations. But can the modern age accept such limits? Isn't the modern age characterized by the effort to overcome these limits in its quest to regain paradise on earth? These questions need our careful attention.

5. *The Barrier of the Lost Paradise*

ENLIGHTENMENT, REASON, AND PROGRESS

The sixty to seventy years preceding the French Revolution are generally known as the period of the Enlightenment. This is the period, according to its contemporaries, in which the light of human reason began to penetrate the darkest corners of Europe. Immanuel Kant, the great Enlightenment philosopher, described it as the era in which man emerged "from his self-imposed tutelage." He suggested as the Enlightenment motto *Sapere aude*—"Dare to know."[54] This was the time when man became conscious of his cultural advance; when he drastically and rationally wanted to break the shackles which chained him in ignorance, superstition, and tradition. In a word, it was the era in which faith in progress became an inherent part of western culture.

This immediately places before us an important question of interpretation. Prior to the Enlightenment we can indeed speak of the presence of a general consciousness of progress. But now this consciousness has become a faith, that is, a profound trust in the constant growth of man's ability, insight, and earthly happiness. How did this notion of progress become a faith in progress? One reason undoubtedly was the fact that in the eighteenth century, especially during its second half, one could look back upon a series of important accomplishments. Achievements in the natural sciences particularly impressed many. Thus in 1706 Lord Shaftesbury wrote: "There is a mighty

54. Gay, *Enlightenment,* vol. 1, p. 3.

light which spreads itself over the world, especially in those two free nations of England and Holland. . . ."[55] The "lightbearers" he mentioned in this context were the natural scientists Newton and Huygens, the philosophers Bacon and Locke, and the physician Boerhaave. In addition, the advance of western man with respect to economic and geographic expansion must be noted. Far-off continents were drawn within his sphere of influence. New markets opened up. There was an amazing revival of new centers of trade and banking in Europe.

One might say that during the period of the Enlightenment the balance sheet of the previous era was made up. The accomplishments were listed and totalled and the credit balance clearly and concisely marked with a single word: *progress.* "For the spokesmen of the enlightenment, progress was an experience before it became a program."[56]

However, the fact that progress was made is not, of course, sufficient reason to explain the rise of a faith in progress. Faith in progress cannot be founded only on the certain knowledge that progress in civilization has occurred in the past. Such faith also requires the conviction that similar progress will definitely be made in the future. "Now faith," we read in the New Testament, "is the assurance of things hoped for, the conviction of things not seen."[57] That also is true for faith in progress. In this context J. B. Bury correctly observes that "Progress of humanity belongs to the same order of ideas as Providence or personal immortality. It is true or it is false, and like them it cannot be proved either true or false. Belief in it is an act of faith."[58]

When we ask ourselves how this faith in future progress could lodge itself in our culture, we notice first of all that western man at that time had acquired a profound confidence in the possibilities of his own rational insight and critical ingenuity. We witness here the triumphal procession of rationalism. As early as 1729 Bernard le Bovier de Fontenelle, a French scientist and Enlightenment man of letters, compared western society with a child who, as he grows older, gains more and more wisdom because, thanks to his rational capacities, he can learn from his

55. *Ibid.,* p. 11.
56. Peter Gay, *The Enlightenment: An Interpretation,* vol. 2: *The Science of Freedom* (1969), p. 56.
57. Hebrews 11:1 (R.S.V.).
58. Bury, *Idea of Progress,* p. 4.

own failures. Thus his knowledge and insight continually increase. In other words, human reason is a guide for the present on which you can also rely for the future. The assurance of future progress is implied to a great extent in the operation of a completely reliable guide in the present which can help humankind avoid every danger and threat with infallible certainty. In this light we can also understand Voltaire, the "Moses" of the Enlightenment era, when he wrote in 1751: "We may believe that reason and industry will always progress more and more; ... that of the evils which have afflicted men, prejudices ... will gradually disappear. ..."[59] Later, Whitehead expressed the same idea as follows: "While the Middle Ages were an age of faith based upon reason, the 18th century was an age of reason based upon faith."[60]

This function of man's critical reason as infallible guide also explains the mystery of why the Enlightenment idea of progress so easily and tacitly involved simultaneous advances in every area of culture. It is a result of the implicit but unproven Enlightenment assumption that two consecutive periods—either the past and the present, or the present and the future—can in every respect be compared with each other, and that the later will emerge as advanced in *every* respect beyond the earlier. If that were not the case, one could at best speak of partial progress. However, only in exceptional instances did Enlightenment philosophers think and write about partial progress. They employed a concept of progress which is indeed integral and all-inclusive. It involves the steady improvement of human customs and mores, progress in education and civilization, flourishing of the arts, growth of prosperity and technology, and improvements in all kinds of social conditions. This integral and all-encompassing faith in progress on the part of the Enlightenment thinkers can be explained only in terms of their acceptance of the infallible guidance provided by man's *critical reason* in which all the threads of human existence come together. Progress in society is governed in every respect from the control center of rationality. In 1752 David Hume wrote in this vein:

> We cannot reasonably expect that a piece of woollen cloth will be brought to perfection in a nation, which is ignorant of astronomy, or where ethics are neglected. The spirit of the age affects

59. Cf. Bury, *Idea of Progress,* pp. 149, 150.
60. Cf. Dawson, *Progress and Religion,* p. 220.

all the arts; and the minds of men . . . carry improvements into every art and science. Thus, *industry, knowledge,* and *humanity,* are linked together by an indissoluble chain.[61]

The same idea was affirmed by Hume's contemporary, Francis Place, who claimed that "The progress made in refinement of manners and morals seems to have gone on simultaneously with the improvement in arts, manufactures and commerce."[62]

However, does all this indeed guarantee the complete, integral progress of society? The answer to that question is negative. Such a guarantee is not automatically obtained, not even in the world view of the Enlightenment in which critical reason is considered an infallible guide toward a better future. The uncertainty lies in the question of whether man will be prepared to continue to follow this guide. The possibility exists that man himself will obstruct progress by allowing considerations other than rational ones to influence his life. Therefore, in order to obtain absolute certainty, faith in progress required a finishing touch; it was, so to speak, in need of a final seal. This was found in the astonishing idea of "le perfectionnement de l'homme," the perfectibility of man himself.

HUMAN PERFECTIBILITY AND THE PARADISE TO COME

Confined to his cell—from which he would be led to the guillotine—the Marquis de Condorcet (1743–1794), past chairman of the French Legislative Assembly, wrote his famous *Sketch for a Historical Picture of the Progress of the Human Mind*[63] in which he lucidly articulated the idea of human perfectibility as the seal on Enlightenment faith. In 1795, a year after his death, and at the expense of the French government, his treatise was published. This book can be regarded as perhaps the most important confession of Enlightenment faith in progress. It received a great deal of attention, both nationally and internationally. At that time international contacts were quite intensive. This is borne out by the fact that Madame de Condorcet translated Adam

61. Cited by Gay, *Enlightenment,* vol. 2, p. 26.
62. *Ibid.,* p. 42.
63. Marquis de Condorcet, *Esquisse d'un tableau historique des progrès de l'esprit humain* (first published posthumously in 1795). English translation by June Barraclough, with an Introduction by Stuart Hampshire (London: Weidenfeld and Nicolson, 1955).

Smith's *The Theory of Moral Sentiments* into French, while Smith himself did the ground work for his *Wealth of Nations* during his three-year stay in France.

It is fascinating to see how Condorcet, in his sketch of human progress, starts from a typical Renaissance setting which we also encounter with the classical economists, namely, man's struggle with nature. Condorcet views this as the cradle of all human progress; for in this battle, fought with the aid of reason, man gains victory after victory over nature which resists this domination with all its powers—but to no avail. Condorcet also regards the fruits of progress as an outcome of this struggle. Man obtains effective technical and scientific control over all natural processes. In addition, because of his critical reason, he is capable of cutting his links with the past, of breaking through all inherited traditions and rigid mores in human civilization. However, such progress is not made apart from or beyond man's own most essential nature. To the contrary—and here we encounter a new, decisively modern element—the essence of man himself changes and develops in this battle with nature. He rises to ever higher phases of humanity. History is the stage of man's humanization, of his *becoming man.* This process of self-realization and self-improvement can ultimately lead to only one point: the perfectibility of man, "le perfectionnement de l'homme." Progress, therefore, is not only made *by* man; it is also made *in* man. Nature, according to Condorcet, "has set no limit to the perfection of human faculties."[64] Thus, he prophesies that a true millennium awaits humankind, a perfect society in which "the human race, freed from all its fetters, withdrawn from the empire of chance as from that of the enemies of Progress, would walk with firm and assured step in the way of truth, of virtue and of happiness."[65] Paradise does not lie in the past; it lies in the future. Western man is now competent to attain that future.

It is not surprising that the paradise motif is so often introduced by Enlightenment thinkers. It is important to note that they do not present it as a utopian dream but as a definitely attainable future certainty. This is true not only in the case of a few grandiloquent French authors; even the more sober English thinkers describe the new Jerusalem, which will be estab-

64. Cf. Gay, *Enlightenment,* vol. 2, p. 119.
65. Cf. Dawson, *Progress and Religion,* p. 13.

lished on earth by man, in almost apocalyptic terminology. Thus, William Godwin prophesies that in that blessed day

> There will be no war, no crimes, no administration of justice, as it is called, and no government. Besides this, there will be neither disease, anguish, melancholy, nor resentment. Every man will seek, with ineffable ardour, the good of all. Mind will be active and eager, and yet never disappointed.[66]

In a similar vein Joseph Priestley (1733–1804), English preacher, economist, and philosopher, declares that "whatever was the beginning of this world, the end will be glorious and paradisaical, beyond what our imaginations can now conceive." He explains this by claiming that "nature . . . will be more at our command; men will make their situation in this world abundantly more easy and comfortable."[67]

We should note carefully what is really taking place here. Certainly more is at stake than some fruitless and idealistic musings of a few ivory-tower scholars. Here the way is being paved for a radically new social *practice!* Let us briefly review the history once more. The removal of the barrier of church and heaven ties western man to this earth as the stage for his self-realization. The overthrow of the barrier of providence and fate eliminates an intervening God, thereby making room for a completely human self-destination. Now the third barrier is razed by the Enlightenment philosophers, who place rational self-destination in the context of an attainable perfect future and of the guarantee that the lost paradise can be regained by man's own activities. The *optimism of being (zijnsoptimisme)* becomes an *optimism of will (wilsoptimisme).*[68] The motif *of* progress becomes a program *for* progress! That is the deeper significance of these new and striking paradise images. Consciousness of progress has matured into a faith which, for the sake of the future of mankind, can summon

66 .William Godwin, *Enquiry concerning Political Justice and its Influence on Morals and Happiness,* 3 vols. (Toronto: The University of Toronto Press, 1946), vol. 2, p. 528.

67. Cited by Carl Lotus Becker, *The Heavenly City of the Eighteenth-Century Philosophers* (New Haven: Yale University Press, 1932), p. 145.

68. These terms are derived from Fred L. Polak, *De toekomst is verleden tijd,* 2 vols. (Zeist, the Netherlands: W. de Haan, 1958). English translation by Elise Boulding, *The Image of the Future,* 2 vols. (Leyden: Sijthoff; New York: Oceana Publications, 1961), vol. 1, p. 47. Boulding's translation of these terms—*essence-optimism* and *influence-optimism* respectively—is misleading. (Translator's note.)

man to *deeds;* and the breathtaking "splendor" of these deeds parallels the moving of mountains, including the massive mountain of the western social order. Faith in progress has become a faith capable of transforming its adherents into revolutionaries of the first order, for who would not follow the direction of an infallible guide which resolutely points the way to paradise regained?

BASIC ASPECTS OF THE ENLIGHTENMENT FAITH IN PROGRESS

These statements do not present a onesided picture of the situation. This will become evident from an investigation of three specific aspects of the Enlightenment faith in progress: the resistance of Enlightenment thinkers to the Christian religion; their interpretation of the future paradise; and their practical attitude toward concrete improvement of society. It is precisely because of these features that the adherents of Enlightenment thought created the spiritual climate for the great revolutions in western society.

1. Antichristian attitude

From the extant correspondence between Denis Diderot (1713–1784) and Voltaire (1694–1778) we know that it was Diderot's habit to address Voltaire with "sublime, honorable, and dear Anti-Christ," while Voltaire closed his letters with the abbreviation "Écr. l'inf." for the French *Écrasez l'infâme,* meaning "Crush the infamous." The infamous for him was in the first place the Roman Catholic Church and its clergy, but in a broader sense it was the Christian religion in general. "Every sensible man, every honorable man, must hold the Christian sect in horror," he once wrote.[69]

Is this hostile stance toward the Christian religion, taken particularly by the French *philosophes,* a mere historical accident or an essential trait of French Enlightenment thought? Peter Gay convincingly shows that the latter is the case. It is significant that he subtitles the first volume of his profound interpretation of the Enlightenment *The Rise of Modern Paganism.*

To a certain extent, French Enlightenment philosophers looked upon deism as a temporary ally; at the same time it was obvious that they did not consider themselves adherents of this

69. Cited by Gay, *Enlightenment,* vol. 1, p. 391.

spiritual movement. Deism was western philosophy's last compromise with Christianity, but it was precisely as a compromise that it could not find favor in the eyes of the *philosophes.* Deism still started from some form of divine revelation, although with important qualifications. It still accepted the notion of good and evil and its effect on human society. It did not reject the recognition of the person of Jesus as the most important historical figure and as a model for a virtuous human life. But right at this point the tension arose with authentic Enlightenment philosophy—for what had the Christian church accomplished with its appeal to divine revelation apart from maintaining the status quo and keeping society in barbarism and traditionalism? Hadn't the doctrine of original sin and total depravity paralyzed man's trust in himself and his capacity to do good? It certainly was no accident that Rousseau tried to shed the trauma of his Calvinistic background in Geneva by proclaiming that man by nature is good instead of evil and that therefore we encounter in a state of nature not depravity but purity and innocence. Against this same background the cross of Christ, erected because of our sins, became for Voltaire a direct source of vexation. Once, after climbing a hill and watching a magnificent sunrise, he knelt down and prayed emotionally: "I believe! I believe in you! Powerful God, I believe!" But when he stood up again, he added nonchalantly: "As for monsieur the Son, and madame His Mother, that's a different story."[70]

During the Enlightenment we encounter for the first time in western history an open and broadly based resistance on the part of leading thinkers to whatever is connected with the Christian religion. Deism no longer suffices; at best it leads to an *optimism of being*—an optimism within the order of nature, achieved without human interference. What we need is an *optimism of will,* which has faith in its own power and therefore is able to change the world.[71]

In the final analysis, this intense emotional resistance to the Christian faith can probably best be explained by the fact that Enlightenment thinkers confessed a faith of their own. This faith collided with the heart of the Christian religion. Carl Becker, more keenly than other historians, has brought to our attention

70. *Ibid.,* p. 122.
71. For origin and use of these terms cf. Polak, *Image of the Future,* vol. 1, p. 47; see also footnote 68 above.

this faith commitment of the *philosophes*—"atheists in effect if not by profession." These thinkers, he says, "demolished the Heavenly City of St. Augustine only to rebuild it with more up-to-date materials."[72] His summary of the articles of faith of the *philosophes* is worthwhile quoting in its entirety:

> The essential articles of the religion of the Enlightenment may be stated thus: (1) man is not natively depraved; (2) the end of life is life itself, the good life on earth instead of the beatific life after death; (3) man is capable, guided solely by the light of reason and experience, of perfecting the good life on earth; and (4) the first and essential condition of the good life on earth is the freeing of men's minds from the bonds of ignorance and superstition, and of their bodies from the arbitrary oppression of the constituted social authorities.[73]

It is no accident that in each of these articles of faith we see as it were a reflection of the Christian confession, more specifically of Roman Catholicism. French Enlightenment religion is not a religion in a positive sense of that word. It is in the first place an antireligion, as it attempts to break radically with the Christian religion and with everything dependent on the latter. Its maximum positive dimension consists of a vague respect for "deity" in general. However, this deity has nothing to do with either revelation or redemption from human evil in this world.

In England and Germany we do not encounter the same bitter and tenacious resistance to the Christian religion as in France. One could claim that in England the deistic tradition remained so strong that these and other radical characteristics of authentic Enlightenment thought to some extent were tempered and restrained. Did this restraint neutralize the antichristian tendency of French thought? Did it maintain the Christian faith in its authenticity? In reply we can say with Peter Gay that "the philosophes paid a price for fraternizing with the Christian enemy. But the Christians paid a far heavier price—it was the defender, not the aggressor, who was paralyzed by his concessions."[74] Salt that has lost its savor serves no purpose but to be

72. Becker, *Heavenly City*, p. 31.
73. *Ibid.*, pp. 102–103.
74. Gay, *Enlightenment*, vol. 1, p. 358.

thrown away. An insipid religion of virtue and immortality was dominant in the English state church at the beginning of the industrial revolution.

2. Paradise image

The Enlightenment conception of a future paradise reveals a number of features which deviate strikingly from the content of the Biblical paradise motif. Parallel traits are also present, of course, such as the disappearance of war and misery, the restoration of harmony with nature, and the return of eternal peace. Kant even devoted an entire publication to the latter theme.

But the differences are marked. We notice first of all that in Enlightenment descriptions of the future the emphasis is on great material prosperity and an abundance of luxury and leisure as a result of advanced technology. Perhaps even more striking is the great stress on the direct beneficial effect of change in social structures and institutions. Such change has a kind of built-in, never-failing healing effect. To what influences can these differences be traced? Or were they an Enlightenment invention? These questions become even more fascinating when we read in the works of several Enlightenment thinkers that the transition to a better society is marked especially by the institution of common property, and when we notice that others hint at the permanent disappearance of the state. In that future era "there will be no government," Godwin prophesied, as we observed earlier.[75] Such ideas could hardly have been voiced arbitrarily. In this respect we note striking parallels between the Enlightenment paradise images of the future on the one hand, and Graeco-Roman, particularly Stoic, paradise images of the past on the other hand. They are separated by many centuries, yet one wonders whether such similarities are merely accidental.

From the writings of the Stoics we indeed receive a fantastic picture of a paradise once inhabited by man.[76] At the beginning of the human era, they speculated, a perfect world existed which lasted at least 36,000 years.[77] They referred to this era as the *golden age,* a term which regularly reappears in western literature in the most unexpected places. This golden

75. See note 66 above.

76. I am following in particular the exposition provided by Ernst Troeltsch, *The Social Teaching of the Christian Churches,* 2 vols. (London: Allen and Unwin, 1931).

77. Bury, *Idea of Progress,* p. 10.

age was characterized primarily by the presence of communal property and by the enjoyment of the fruit of one's own labor. Equality resulted; differences in class or rank were unknown. Even the state was absent, for where equality exists, there is no cause for envy and hence no need for legal protection by the government.

In the Biblical account the sinful desire to become like God causes a breach between God and man and therefore between man and paradise. The Stoics' version is different. They claimed that this period of perfect happiness came to an end because some people violated the institution of communal property so that, for the first time, private property was introduced. But that was not all, for private property caused the emergence of different classes and ranks in society. Further, the individual person lost his right to enjoy the fruits of his own labor. Finally, the state emerged. In the new social structuration—characterized by Ernst Troeltsch with the term *relative natural law* to distinguish it from the *absolute natural law* of the golden age—the state had become a necessity. Its task consisted in the protection of private property rights and the prevention of all-out war in this world of man against man. In other words, the state became the custodian of this new legal order, characterized by divergences in property, social position, and power.

Undoubtedly the Stoics preferred the golden age, with its communal property and equality of all men, above the subsequent era. Nevertheless, they were convinced that a return to this lost paradise was beyond the powers of man. An attempt to regain it would be tantamount to challenging the gods or providence. The only prospect of a better future—marked by the brotherhood of all citizens of the world—lay in virtuously following the providential direction of relative natural law.

This Stoic picture of paradise has left a deep imprint on western thought. We already noticed that fact with reference to Augustine who considered the city of the world characterized by the institutions of ownership, slavery, and the state, each of which corresponds to the relative natural law of the Stoa. With Augustine these have become the distinctive marks of the world after the Fall until the end of times. But this picture of a lost golden age frequently reappears later on. In the seventeenth century, for instance, John Locke devoted a significant part of his *Essay Concerning Human Understanding* (1689) to this theme. Hugo Grotius similarly takes the idea of communal property of all men as his starting point. Perhaps even more explicit are the echoes we hear of this golden age in the utopias or images of the future such as Sir Thomas More's *Utopia* (1516), Francis Bacon's *The New Atlantis* (1627), and Charles Fourier's *Nouveau monde industriel et sociétaire* (1829). These differ considerably from each other, but they have an important element in common. Each of these fantasies of the future give a prime place to the regulation of property, of labor, and of ranks and classes. In other words, they represent modified dream images of the Stoic golden age. We encounter this in almost all western utopias, which manifest a nostalgia for a long-lost paradise projected into the future.

What is the meaning of all this for our understanding of the Enlightenment? To begin with, the old images of paradise gain new life. From the start, however, they are put in a new frame. This is no longer one of nostalgia or dreams of a long-lost past—it does not have to be. Instead, it is one of a future reality to be commanded at will by man's own activity. Two changes are decisive: the golden age image is transformed from *dream* into *blueprint*, and shifts from paradise *lost* to paradise *regained*. A most pointed expression of this is found in the epitaph of the French utopian socialist Saint-Simon (1760–1825) which his pupils engraved on his tombstone as a summation of his entire life: "The golden age does not lie behind us, but ahead of us."[78]

Of course, Enlightenment accounts of paradise reveal divergences and modifications. The socialists remained closest to the original Stoic image of paradise. Karl Marx, for instance, believed in an attainable future society based on communal property, in which everyone enjoys the fruit of his own labor, in which class differences disappear, and—to make the Stoic picture complete—in which the state is abolished. But it shouldn't surprise us that not every Enlightenment thinker was equally charmed by these "radical" ideals. Some entertained reservations about the ideal of total communal property; others maintained an arrogant attitude toward the masses. The *peuple,* Diderot once wrote, is "too idiotic—bête—too miserable and too busy" to be able to enlighten itself, and "the quantity of the canaille

78. For a recent discussion of Saint-Simon's strange career, see Frank E. Manuel, *The New World of Henri Saint-Simon* (Notre Dame: University of Notre Dame Press, 1963).

is just about always the same."[79] But the common link between the whole of Enlightenment thought and the utopian-Stoic paradise motif consists in the shared conviction that in the final analysis the presence or absence of *social institutions and structures,* with their respective *legal* relationships (such as the existence or nonexistence of communal property), determines whether a society will be perfectly happy or unhappy. The Fall of man into sin does not separate him from paradise. Only the wrong social institutions and structures keep him from happiness.[80] For that reason a change in, or the destruction of, such social institutions is sufficient to guarantee the return of happiness in this world.[81]

3. Practical social improvement
In the light of the foregoing we can well understand why the philosophers of the Enlightenment displayed a nearly endless interest in every proposal directed to the practical improvement of the existing social order. "The spirit of the French philosophers in the eighteenth century was distinctly pragmatic. The advantage of man was their principle."[82] Nothing—small or great—escaped their interest if it could promote "utility" in society. Not surprisingly, therefore, they were more attracted to utilitarianism than to deism. Rousseau aptly summarized their common starting point in *Émile:* "It is not a question of knowing what is, but only what is useful."[83]

Placing the meaning of theory—that is, of all scientific reflection—in the promotion of practical social utility was a vital notion long before the era of the Enlightenment. It was already evident in Francis Bacon's *New Atlantis* (1627). His imaginary society is peopled with scientists, gathered in Solomon's House, who are permanently engaged in useful scientific inventions. These vary from artificial sunlight to artificial metals, firework, submarines, and even "Water of Paradise" for the prolongation

79. Cited by Gay, *Enlightenment,* vol. 2, p. 519.

80. Rousseau shares this thought also. "Moral and social inequality," he writes, "were introduced by the man who first enclosed a piece of land and said, This is mine. . . ." Quoted by Bury, *Idea of Progress,* p. 181.

81. Bury correctly describes the orthodox Marxist conception that wrong social structures are the most profound cause of the continued existence of misery and evil in the world as "pure eighteenth century doctrine." Cf. Bury, *Idea of Progress,* p. 234.

82. *Ibid.,* p. 161.

83. Gay, *Enlightenment,* vol. 1, p. 180.

of life.[84] "The principle that the proper aim of knowledge is the amelioration of human life, to increase men's happiness and mitigate their sufferings . . . was the guiding star of Bacon in all his intellectual labour." "For him the end of knowledge is utility."[85]

This line of thought is consistently pursued by the eighteenth-century philosophers of progress. The famous Abbé de Saint-Pierre (1658–1743), for instance, devoted his life to the construction of schemes and plans to increase human happiness. He not only devised a plan for the establishment of perpetual peace, but also a grand system of reform in education, based on free instruction, as well as a project for a thorough revision of the entire government apparatus. He is also known for a number of practical technical projects, such as a plan to make roads passable during winter months. According to his own statements, he had more appreciation for a new canal than for the Notre Dame cathedral in Paris. He viewed the expansion of overseas trade as one of the best avenues to a happier society; for more trade meant more prosperity, and more prosperity provided more leisure time for reading and writing which steadily increases the level of knowledge of the population.[86]

Growth in prosperity and scientifically founded technological progress are the two indispensable allies on the way to a better future. This is part and parcel of the Enlightenment creed. "Where can the perfectibility of man stop, armed with geometry and the mechanical arts and chemistry?" This rhetorical question was asked by Sébastien Mercier, French utopian author, at the end of his book *L'an 2440*.[87] The answer is implicit in the title: Mercier prophesied a perfect society for the year 2440 A.D. Such a society is characterized by perpetual peace, education by the state, and abundance of spare time.

This confidence in future prosperity and technical innovation forms a close link between English and French Enlightenment thinkers. They constitute the visible signs of human progress. "In the century of the Enlightenment . . . the word

84. Francis Bacon, *Essays, Civil and Moral and The New Atlantis* (with essays by John Milton and Thomas Browne), The Harvard Classics, ed. by Charles W. Eliot (New York: Collier & Son, 1909), p. 183.

85. Bury, *Idea of Progress*, pp. 52 and 51 respectively.

86. *Ibid.*, pp. 127ff.

87. *L'an 2440* means "The Year 2440." It was published in 1770. See Bury, *Idea of Progress*, p. 197.

innovation, traditionally an effective term of abuse, became a word of praise."[88] Thus Newton, who was a humble Christian throughout his entire life, was universally admired as a pioneer, an innovator, a discoverer of a new world. "Wer dir will folgen, irret nie," praises Albrecht von Haller, a German poet of the Enlightenment. At the same time Diderot urged that "theoretical and practical thinkers must unite against 'the resistance of nature.' Playful speculation has its place by the side of patient and systematic experimentation; together they make the philosopher of nature into a conqueror."[89]

In general there is agreement among Enlightenment thinkers with respect to their undaunted admiration of scientific, technical, and economic progress as the bearers of the greatest benefit and utility for all of society. They are united in their advocacy of concrete revisions in the existing social and political order. Regarding the question of whether these desired social changes can only be brought about by means of direct, violent force, however, there is a rather important difference of opinion among these thinkers. English and German Enlightenment philosophy is characterized in general by restraint. Here it is thought that the required social and political changes will, in a manner of speaking, automatically come about in the wake of progress. The realization of social utility does not require forceful and violent intervention. The French thinkers, however, consciously went beyond that. For them new social structures and institutions were imperative. They had not only educational reform in mind, but an entirely new political system, based on the sovereignty of the people; a new social order which minimally required the abolition of whatever was left of the guilds; and a new spiritual élite, which entailed the liquidation of the clergy's power over the daily life of the believers. Here again their argument is completely consistent. If it is true that social institutions are capable of determining man's weal or woe, and if the assumption is correct that the "new social machinery could alter human nature and create a heaven upon earth,"[90] then the establishment of *new* social institutions is not a tedious, incidental

88. Gay, *Enlightenment,* vol. 2, p. 3.
89. *Ibid.,* p. 10.
90. Bury, *Idea of Progress,* p. 205.

task, but a dire necessity and a high ethical imperative. In that case the narrow way to the lost paradise can only be the way of *social revolution*.[91]

THE ENLIGHTENMENT AS MOTHER OF REVOLUTIONS

Enlightenment philosophy has played an important preparatory role with respect to all subsequent revolutions in western society. It could do so because faith in progress, inherent in this philosophy, was not a matter of abstract theorizing but was solidly based on the practical proof of a reform mentality and the urge for social renewal. This is the case in particular for the French Revolution of 1789. Its outbreak is indissolubly connected with the specific character of French eighteenth-century philosophy of progress. This philosophy, as we have observed, directly links the arrival of an improved human nature and a better world to a radically renewed political and social order.[92] For this reason the slogan "freedom, equality, and brotherhood" was not a vague hope or pious wish for the French revolution-

91. Guillaume Groen van Prinsterer (1801–1876), Dutch historian and statesman, deserves considerable credit for having shown, at an early date, this close connection between French Enlightenment thought and the French Revolution of 1789. He did this in several of his voluminous writings, but especially in the fifteen lectures which he published in 1847 in his most famous book *Unbelief and Revolution.* "What the eighteenth century has shown," Groen van Prinsterer argued, "is that actual ruin follows hard upon the heels of apparent progress." Cf. *Unbelief and Revolution: Lectures VIII and IX* (Amsterdam: The Groen van Prinsterer Fund, 1975), p. 12. This ruin shatters the paradisiacal hopes: "a golden age was expected, an age of iron arrived." *Ibid.,* p. 8. Groen van Prinsterer locates the cause of that ruin in the self-conscious faith whose implementation necessarily leads to revolutionary violence, as in the case of Diderot who yearned "to strangle the last king with the guts of the last priest." *Ibid.,* p. 72. It is striking how easily and casually the French *philosophes* linked their ideas of enlightenment with the need for revolution and how nonchalantly, almost cheerfully, they anticipated the latter. For instance, exactly twenty-five years before the French Revolution Voltaire wrote: "Enlightenment has gradually spread so widely that it will burst into full light at the first right opportunity, and then there'll be a fine uproar." Cf. Gay, *Enlightenment,* vol. 2, p. 103. The link between Enlightenment ideas and social revolution is profoundly discussed in Eric Voegelin, *From Enlightenment to Revolution* (Durham: Duke University Press, 1975).

92. Cf. also Bury, who states that for French Enlightenment philosophers "the perfectibility of humanity" was based on "the possibility of indefinitely moulding the characters of men by laws and institutions." *Idea of Progress,* p. 167.

aries. It was a program to be carried out directly in actual practice. It was by means of the necessary political and social revolution that freedom and brotherhood would, as it were automatically, become a permanent part of society, in anticipation of the coming perfectibility of man. This proud conviction is openly revealed in the French Declaration of the Rights of Man (1789).

The link which Enlightenment thinkers established between revolutionary social intervention and permanent human progress had vast implications. It gave birth to the *ideology of revolution* which since its inception has accompanied us in the West as a constantly rekindled fire.

How does an ideology of revolution come into being? (1) Such an ideology starts from the general assumption that man by nature is not evil but good, and that consequently the evil that does exist in the world should not be attributed to man himself but to the social order and its structures which force him to do wrong. (2) If this is the case, then the following step is readily taken, namely, that the most dangerous enemies of man and his happiness are those persons who have identified themselves with the existing social order and who make every effort to preserve it. They are the enemy because in doing this they constitute, consciously or unconsciously, the real obstacle to the future happiness of the whole of humankind. (3) The conclusion of the argument is simple: the enemy of the people must be eliminated, no matter how painful the elimination, since salvation can break through in society only if this barrier is removed. Their shed blood can even be looked upon as a kind of guarantee that the world's redemption will indeed be forthcoming. They are the scapegoats whose lives must be sacrificed so that all humankind can have freedom and life in abundance.

The French Revolution indeed fully displayed the style of such an ideology of revolution. Significantly, it was one of the bloodiest revolutions the world has known. The guillotine was in operation daily, simply as a matter of course. That appears to point to more than a short-lived, irrational revenge on former tyrants and exploiters. Liquidation of nobility and clergy, the two pillars of the former social order, also represented the sacrifice demanded by a new religion in order to guarantee the advent of salvation in this world.

Since then such an unadulterated ideology of revolution has appeared countless times. We encounter a similar pattern of thought, for instance, in the Russian Revolution of 1917. There the capitalist class became the scapegoat. Their systematic elimination was regarded as the necessary condition for the advent of society's salvation. In a different, even more lugubrious form this ideology permeated the Nazi dream of a pan-Germanic empire whose realization in world history had been held back by the contemptuous schemes and intrigues of the Jewish race. Hence Hitler's "Endlösung der Judenfrage." This was not merely a systematic and insane attempt to put into practice the "final solution of the Jewish question." Rather, for Hitler and his cohorts the concentration camps and the gas chambers represented the milestones on the way to a better and happier society—*das dritte Reich!*

The road of revolution through Europe runs through the graveyard of "high civilization," where its untold millions are buried, the victims of the demonic forces western culture itself has released. Indeed, the ideology of revolution and the demonic appear to be inseparably bound together. Perhaps this is especially the case because the deepest mystery of the Christian faith—the suffering and death of Christ—is almost nowhere as intensely and consistently parodied, imitated, and dissected as in the ideology of revolution. Moreover, in this ideology that ultimate religious seriousness is present which speaks in terms of fall and redemption, sin and deliverance, and the sacrifice of one's blood as an indispensable condition for the salvation of this world.

THE AMERICAN REVOLUTION

In the light of this critique of the ideology of revolution, it is not altogether out of place to make a few comments about the American Revolution of 1776. The United States of America was founded prior to the French Revolution. If we are to look for possible links between this founding of a new state and western Enlightenment philosophy, we must keep in mind from the very start that the American Revolution of 1776 was essentially different from the French Revolution of 1789 and the Russian Revolution of 1917, both of which were nourished by an *ideology* of revolution. The French Revolution is directly related to the French variant of Enlightenment thought which, with respect to the question of method in attaining a new social order, generally approved the use of violence, while the English

Enlightenment thinkers favored an evolutionary, gradual approach. On this matter there is continuity between England and America. Moreover, the American Revolution should in the first place be viewed as a legitimate attempt at decolonization, an effort to wrestle free from English colonial authority.

Nevertheless, it would be historically incorrect to argue that there are no connections at all between French Enlightenment thought and the American revolutionary experience. The founders of the New World were undoubtedly motivated by their own ideals, but it is not accidental that the later French Enlightenment thinkers regarded the embodiment of these ideals in the American Revolution as their shining example. Moreover, the pioneers of the American Revolution certainly did not reject the honor thus bestowed on them by the French intellectuals. This was not a mere formal matter; there was a similarity in the frame of reference. Benjamin Franklin and Voltaire, Peter Gay informs us, were members of the same masonic lodge in France. And Franklin, as the representative of the American Revolution, bid farewell to Voltaire at his deathbed in Paris. On that occasion Voltaire publicly embraced him and blessed Franklin's grandson in the name of "God and liberty."[93]

Finally, we should note that the American Declaration of Independence, formulated by Thomas Jefferson, also bears clear traces of the continental faith in progress. It is fair to describe this Declaration as an attempted synthesis between Christian Puritanism, deism, and the ideas of progress. Deism is present in the express reference to natural rights which are bestowed on all men by a providential God. The progress motif can be detected in the specific mention of each person's fundamental right to the "pursuit of happiness." In this light it is clear why Peter Gay justifiably entitled the last section of his two-volume study on the Enlightenment, which includes a discussion of the American Revolution, *The Program in Practice*.[94]

93. Gay, *Enlightenment,* vol. 2, p. 557.

94. For a recent treatment of this entire matter see Henry F. May, *The Enlightenment in America* (New York: Oxford University Press, 1976).

PART TWO: THE EVOLUTION OF MODERN CAPITALISM

6. The Industrial Revolution and Its Consequences

From the middle of the eighteenth century a wave of increasing industrialization rolled over western Europe, beginning in the British Isles. Here, between 1760 and 1770, patents were granted for three inventions which would change the face of the English countryside almost beyond recognition: to Arkwright for the water frame in 1769; to James Watt for the steam engine, also in 1769; and to Hargreaves for the spinning jenny in 1770.[1] As a result, the textile industry was the first to expand. "Between 1700 and 1780 British imports of raw cotton increased from one to five million pounds, by 1789 to thirty two and a half million. Between 1750 and 1769 the export of British cotton goods increased ten times."[2]

Soon other industries, especially coal and ironworks, followed suit, taking advantage of the ever-improving models of Watt's steam engine. This entire process was, of course, accompanied by a rapid growth of new industrial cities.

> Until the mid-eighteenth century, Glasgow, Newcastle, and the Rhondda Valley were mostly waste or farm land, and Manchester in 1727 was described by Daniel Defoe as "a mere village." Forty years later there were a hundred integrated mills and a whole cluster of machine plants, forges, leather and chemical works in the area. A modern industrial city had been created.[3]

1. Arnold J. Toynbee, *The Industrial Revolution* (1884; Boston: Beacon Press, 1956), p. 63.
2. Christopher Hill, *Reformation to Industrial Revolution* (London: Weidenfeld & Nicolson, 1967), p. 207.
3. Robert L. Heilbroner, *The Making of Economic Society* (Englewood Cliffs, N.J.: Prentice-Hall, 1962), pp. 82, 83.

This rapid urbanization continued at the beginning of the nineteenth century with increased tempo. "In the first twenty years of the nineteenth century the population of Manchester increased from 94,000 to 160,000; . . . Leeds more than doubled its population between 1801 and 1831; Bradford, which had 23,000 inhabitants in 1831, grew grass in its streets at the end of the eighteenth century."[4]

Historians have asked what caused this enormous change. The Dutch historian and sociologist Pieter Jan Bouman is of the opinion that we can compare it with the rapid crystallization of a supersaturated solution. Not only were the circumstances ripe for it; so was the mentality. "No earlier culture had the materialistic, rationalistic spiritual disposition that characterised particularly the bourgeoisie in the western European cities around the middle of the eighteenth century; in no other culture did the traditional religious and political forces offer so little resistance as in Europe after three centuries of demolition."[5] Bouman defines this bourgeois rationalism as a "vulgarisation of philosophic criticism."[6] In his view it revealed more of an attitude than a profound reflection. It was closely connected with the idea of utility and with "faith in progress which we discover in all currents of the Enlightenment."[7] "The bourgeois citizen lived under the illusion of being the forger of his own happiness."[8]

It is impossible, of course, to present *definitive* proof for the thesis that the industrial revolution not only follows closely in the steps of faith in progress but is related to the latter as a son is related to his father. However, we can furnish sufficient grounds to make this assumption least plausible.

INDUSTRIAL REVOLUTION AND FAITH IN PROGRESS

In approaching this question we should not lose sight of the fact that both individualistic rationalism and economic materialism,

4. John L. Hammond and Barbara Hammond, *The Rise of Modern Industry* (London: Methuen & Co., 1925), pp. 222, 223.
5. Pieter Jan Bouman, *Van Renaissance tot Wereldoorlog* [From Renaissance to World War] (Groningen: P. Noordhoff, n.d.), pp. 120f.
6. *Ibid.,* p. 97.
7. *Ibid.,* p. 104.
8. *Ibid.,* p. 101.

no matter how fundamentally important for this rise of capitalism, far antedate the industrial revolution. In a sense it can be
claimed with R. H. Tawney[9] that these attitudes are as old as
history itself. At any rate, they already made their marked appearance during the Renaissance. The fact that the industrial
revolution did not get off the ground until the middle of the
eighteenth century must therefore be due to factors other than
individualism and materialism. In this context it is hardly a coincidence that eighteenth-century faith in progress enthusiastically considered every individual invention and enterprise as
clear evidence of authentic progress. The adherents of this faith
crowned the new technical and economic pioneers with the
saintly aureoles of a new and better world. They called on society to clear the way in every respect for these heroes. Belief
in progress, much more than Calvinism, attributed a newly sa-
cred significance to the technical and economic pioneering efforts of the industrial revolutionaries. In any case, it is not too
farfetched to assume that this faith in progress was the decisive
spark which ignited the explosion made possible by the available
"ingredients"—the mixture of individualism, materialism, rationalism, and Puritanism.

At least two aspects of this faith seem to confirm this diagnosis. The first is its revolutionary *power to action.* It was not
a faith which got lost in futile self-analysis but one which, so to
speak, pursued its own self-realization, its own self-verification
in and through concrete acts of social change. Voltaire expressed
this concisely at the end of *Candide:* "That is well said, but we
must cultivate our garden."[10] In other words, speculations are
beautiful but forceful intervention demanded by critical reason
is better. Faith in progress, both in England and in France, is a
faith in practicality, in the individual urge to act. And it would
be very odd indeed if this faith, which called forth the French
Revolution and looked favorably upon the American Revolution, should not have exerted a direct influence on the industrial
revolution which emerged at the same time.

The second aspect of this faith, of particular importance

9. " 'The capitalist spirit' is as old as history, and was not, as has sometimes been said, the offspring of Puritanism." Richard H. Tawney, *Religion and
the Rise of Capitalism* (Harmondsworth: Penguin Books, 1938), p. 226.

10. "Cela est bien dit, mais il faut cultiver notre jardin." Voltaire, *Candide,* a bilingual edition, translated and edited by Peter Gay (New York: St.
Martin's Press, 1963), last page.

here, is its emphasis on *technological innovation* as a source of progress. Great admiration existed for the technical inventors of the age. Thus "in 1753, when Watt was a young man, Diderot had, as it were, drawn his portrait in his *De l'interprétation de la nature.*"[11] Faith in progress assumed the role of an essentially infallible guide to a happier future. Happiness in this context is usually described in the first place as an abundance of material wealth. "Humanly speaking," writes the French Enlightenment philosopher Mercier de la Rivière, "the greatest happiness possible for us consists in the greatest possible abundance of objects suitable to our enjoyment and in the greatest liberty to profit by them."[12] Priestley even argued that the very basis of the paradisiacal future is the fact that "men will make their situation in this world abundantly more easy and comfortable."[13] To guarantee this abundance, technological innovation in industry is indispensable. "Steam will govern the world next," prophesied the English poet Robert Southey in 1829.[14] And in 1830, while sitting in the first train from Liverpool to Manchester, the great English poet Alfred Tennyson composed his famous lines: "Let the great world spin for ever down the ringing grooves of change."[15] Condorcet pointed to progress in science, technology, and material welfare as the avenues to improve human nature itself: "The human species can be improved, firstly, by new discoveries in the arts and sciences and, consequently, in the means of well-being and common prosperity. . . ."[16] A similar sentiment is expressed in the inscription on Montgolfier's first balloon which ascended before the eyes of an enthusiastic crowd of Parisians in 1783: "And so the weak mortal can approach God."[17] In this way technology had indeed become a

11. Peter Gay, *The Enlightenment: An Interpretation,* 2 vols. (New York: Alfred A. Knopf, 1967–69), vol. 2: *The Science of Freedom* (1969), p. 10.

12. Quoted by John B. Bury, *The Idea of Progress: An Inquiry into its Origin and Growth* (London: Macmillan, 1920), p. 173.

13. Cf. Carl L. Becker, *The Heavenly City of the Eighteenth-Century Philosophers* (New Haven: Yale University Press, 1932), p. 145.

14. Quoted by Bury, *Idea of Progress,* p. 325.

15. *Ibid.,* p. 326.

16. Quoted by Morris Ginsberg, *Essays in Sociology and Social Philosophy,* 3 vols. (Melbourne/London/Toronto: William Heinemann Ltd., 1956–1961), vol. 3: *Evolution and Progress* (1961), p. 12.

17. "Et le faible mortel peut s'approcher de Dieu." Cited by P. J. Bouman, *Van tijd naar tijd* (Assen, the Netherlands: Van Gorcum, 1972), p. 12.

saving guide, a mediator between man and God. It was the dawn of a new world.

An interesting and important question remains. Why did the industrial revolution begin in England with its sober and moderate disposition rather than in France, a far more passionate culture? This question has occupied many historians and sociologists.[18]

Among the causes for this earlier start in England belong Britain's greater natural resources and colonial possessions and what Jacques Ellul calls the greater "plasticity" of its milieu.[19] This plasticity pertains not only to the early rise of a unified nation-state in Great Britain but also to the enclosure process of the English countryside.[20]

The start of the industrial revolution in England rather than in France is also related, of course, to a difference in cultural and spiritual outlook, notably with reference to the implication of faith in progress. In France, as we observed earlier,

18. Cf. Thomas S. Ashton, *The Industrial Revolution 1760-1830* (London/New York/Toronto: Oxford University Press, 1948); Phyllis Deane, *The First Industrial Revolution* (Cambridge: University Press, 1965); Jacques Ellul, *The Technological Society* (New York: Alfred A. Knopf, 1964), pp. 42ff; D. S. Landes, *The Unbound Prometheus: Technological Change and Industrial Development in Western Europe from 1750 to the Present* (Cambridge: Cambridge University Press, 1969); Heilbroner, *Making of Economic Society,* chapter 4: "The Industrial Revolution"; and Toynbee, *Industrial Revolution.*

19. Ellul, *Technological Society,* pp. 49f.

20. In the eighteenth and early nineteenth centuries the English landed aristocracy increasingly expanded the already common habit of enclosing communal pastures belonging to the manors. It had been customary for the peasants to have access to these pastures for their own bare means of subsistence. (For instance, they were used as grazing fields for their flocks.) As a result of enclosure the peasants lost this privilege and the common land began to be used exclusively by the lords as sheepwalks for the production of wool. Thus countless farmers and their families literally lost the ground from under their feet and were forced to leave the land in search of work. As a result they ended up in the cities, where they became a willing arsenal from which the new industrial enterprises could draw their laborers in return for often extremely low wages. In other words, England's rapid urbanization at the time of the industrial revolution is the counterpart of its equally rapid drainage and uprooting of the countryside. Cf. Heilbroner, *Making of Economic Society,* pp. 60ff; and Karl Polanyi, *The Great Transformation* (Boston: Beacon Press, 1957), part 2. Arnold Toynbee confirms the severity of this drainage of the English countryside in one of his lectures where we read that "between 1710 and 1760 some 300,000 acres were enclosed, between 1760 and 1843 nearly 7,000,000 underwent the same process." *Industrial Revolution,* p. 61. For a detailed discussion of this process, see chapters 8 and 9.

this faith manifested itself first of all in an increasingly radical resistance to existing social and political institutions. For French Enlightenment thinkers the continued existence of these institutions constituted the decisive barrier to total social progress, and hence they had to be eliminated, if necessary by revolutionary methods. Eighteenth-century England, on the other hand, was influenced more fully by deism which—as we saw in Adam Smith—favors the preservation of existing social and political institutions. This difference between radical and moderate conceptions of progress is not indicative of a fundamental "spiritual" divergence but it does—paradoxically—affect the practical results. Because of its moderate stance, England had much more opportunity than France to busy itself with immediate matters of technical and economic progress. In France a good many *philosophes* filled books with elaborate descriptions of the defects of the present social order and the blessings of a paradise to come, while in England the attention was directed to the practical promotion of the concrete well-being of society, the "wealth of nations," within the context of existing social institutions. Christopher Dawson keenly summarizes the differences: "Hence at the same time that the French were attempting to reconstruct society on abstract principles, the English were devoting themselves to a practical utilitarian activity . . . and brought the forces of nature under human control by scientific means."[21]

No doubt a personal sense of calling has often played a role in the work of these technical and economic innovators, which can be seen as a distant, indirect influence of Calvinism. Dawson speaks of a combination of individualism and strict moral discipline which is characteristic of British and American Puritanism. However, this late-Calvinist sense of calling was assimilated in a general faith in progress equivalent to Thomas Jefferson's motto "Faber suae quisque fortunae" ("Every man is the architect of his own fortune"), and consecrated by Voltaire's evaluation: "Great men I call all those who have excelled in the useful or the agreeable."[22]

Perhaps we can best describe the outlook of these first innovators and businessmen as a combination of an individual-

---

21. Christopher Dawson, *Progress and Religion: An Historical Inquiry* (London: Sheed and Ward, 1929), p. 203.
22. Cf. Gay, *Enlightenment*, vol. 2, p. 50.

istic Puritan work ethic, a deistic-utilitarian view of society, and above all uncomplicated humanist faith in progress.

In summary, it can be said—here we return to the discussion of Part One—that the English spiritual climate between 1750 and 1850 provided not only the most suitable context but also the most favorable intention for the emergence of a modern capitalist society. The *context* was most suitable, first of all, because its deistic religion sanctioned "relative natural law" in which the state fares well when it confines itself to the protection of individual rights in the context of an emphatic respect for the free market; and, secondly, because its utilitarian ethics imposed only one moral demand on the new industrialists, that is, to strive for the greatest possible quantity of utilities primarily for themselves. This striving, so it was thought, would automatically result in a maximum of utilities for their fellowmen. The *intention* within this spiritual climate was decisively favorable to capitalism because it found in technical and economic expansion the basis for providing happiness not only for the individual but for society in every one of its domains.

Such a new faith, coupled with a new conception of justice and ethics, could not but lead to a new type of society with its own social forms and structures. The purest social expression of medieval faith, law, and ethics is found in the church, the manors, and the guilds. The clearest expression of eighteenth-century faith, deistic natural justice, and utilitarian ethics, on the other hand, is found in an entirely new and radically different social structure: the industrial enterprise or factory. This, according to Thomas Ashton,[23] is the dominant form of organization under industrial capitalism.

FACTORY VERSUS MANOR

Enormous differences indeed exist between the typical production households of the Middle Ages—the manors and guilds—and those of the new economic structure in the modern age—the industrial enterprise or factory. When we look at them as expressions of a culture, these differences are especially most fascinating, informative, and rich in contrast. Of course, in both we encounter a combination of factors of production: land, tools, and labor. However, while this combination in the manor and

23. Ashton, *Industrial Revolution 1760–1830.*

guild is organic and largely traditional, in the factory common during the industrial revolution it is mechanical and based on the dynamics of technical innovation. The guideline for production in the manor is the internal provision for the sustenance of its inhabitants; the economic motive of profit is of subordinate significance. In the industrial enterprise, on the other hand, the decisive guideline for production is maximum financial yield by means of the most profitable expansion of an external market for its products. In the manor and guild, social, economic, and legal life are permanently and intensively intertwined. Work is done in a totality of social rights and duties. But in a typical factory of the industrial revolution, labor is separated from social and moral obligations to a large extent. It is performed in accordance with an incidental contract that can be terminated at will, which only stipulates the required number of working hours and the hourly wage. In the manor and the guild work is done by means of simple tools. In the factory, tools begin to determine the character and tempo of work and at times reduce labor to a few technical operations. Finally, perhaps the most outstanding difference is the divergence in orientation. In the manor and the guild the meaning of human activity—also of production—in the final analysis is incorporated in the vertical orientation of society. These medieval production units have a fixed and acknowledged place in the social order, which as a hierarchic totality is directed to ultimate sacramental sanctification. However, the dominant orientation of the industrial enterprise is horizontal. It is not rooted in the social stability of a traditionally recognized place in society, but is founded on the flexibility of the will of the individual entrepreneur and his personal initiative with respect to capital. As such the industry's primary concern is to stay ahead of competitors and in this way to serve the highest[24] purpose of society as a whole, namely, the creation of a maximum quantity of goods to increase the common welfare.

Here we indeed encounter two different expressions of culture. Their contrast is so pronounced that the world and life views which lie behind them must also differ with respect to fundamentals. In fact, this contrast can only be satisfactorily

24. I suppose we should not speak of *highest* purpose here, since that would require a vertical orientation, but of the *farthest* purpose, since that fits the horizontal direction of society in the modern age.

explained in terms of the successive and systematic elimination of the spiritual barriers to horizontal materialism imbedded in medieval society. The new social order finds its spiritual and cultural moorings in a vigorous horizontal dynamism which takes for granted the acceptance of profit and technological innovation as near absolute guides toward a better future for humankind.

EVALUATION OF THE INDUSTRIAL REVOLUTION

These observations place directly before us the complex question of how we are to evaluate the industrial revolution as the beginning of the modern capitalistic social order. Medieval society, as we established earlier, should not be idealized. It was too static and too hierarchic, and by and large it failed to appreciate the legitimacy of a technological and economic development of culture. However, that leaves the question of whether the social structure that the industrial revolution gave birth to was the correct response to the medieval one. If not, we must try to discover what went wrong.

These questions were posed even during the industrial revolution itself. The respective answers differ widely, however, because of the divergent attitudes with respect to faith in progress. In 1792 Sir John Byng, while traveling to northern England and looking from the window of his coach, responded to the surrounding landscape in these words: "Why, here now, is a great flaring mill . . . all the Vale is disturb'd." And when he arrived in Manchester he exclaimed: "Oh! What a dog's hole is Manchester."[25] In contrast to that Robert Southey was more appreciative of the industrial revolution. In *Sir Thomas More: or, Colloquies on the Progress and Prospects of Society* (1829), we find the following dialogue between Sir Thomas More's ghost and Southey's imaginary contemporary, Montesinos:

> *Sir Thomas More:* "The spirit which built and endowed monasteries is gone. Are you one of those persons who think it has been superseded for the better by that which erects steam-engines and cotton mills?"
>
> *Montesinos:* ". . . Yet the manufacturing system is a necessary stage in the progress of society. . . . And from the consequences of

25. Robert L. Heilbroner, *The Worldly Philosophers* (New York: Simon & Schuster, 1953), p. 54.

that skill in machinery which the manufacturing system alone could have produced, we may expect ultimately to obtain the greatest advantages of science and civilization at the least expense of human labour."[26]

One's evaluation of the industrial revolution at that time depended on one's personal view of the nature and cultural potentials of human progress. In other words, objective, value-free, or neutral answers to this question were impossible then, as they are now. Therefore, in my own attempt to find an answer, it is no more than fair on my part to reveal clearly my own presuppositions.

As a Christian taking my stance in the line of the Reformation, I would want to relate my views—certainly concerning the problem at hand—first of all to the position of John Calvin, whose outlook is still relevant today. In distinction from the medieval scholastics, Calvin held that in the unfolding of society the development of economic life was entitled to a place of its own. Consequently, he considered it improper that every form of economic expansion and technological innovation should be restricted in advance by regulations imposed by ecclesiastical or political authorities. For even in economic life, said Calvin, man works and lives before the face of the living God—*coram Deo*—who embodied in his very creation the possibilities of technological and economic development. These possibilities for development, however, are subject to God-given norms which guide and define their meaning. As Calvin put it in his commentary on Genesis 2:15: "Everyone must realize that he is God's steward with respect to everything he possesses."[27] The potentialities inherent in creation for increasing the material welfare of humankind are not there to satisfy our selfishness and pride[28] but are intended for our response to God and our

26. Cf. Brian Tierney, Donald Kagan, and L. Pearce Williams, eds., *Great Issues in Western Civilization* (New York: Random House, 1967), vol. 2, pp. 286–287.

27. "Que chacun pense qu'il est dépensier de Dieu en tout ce qu'il possède." Cited by André Biéler, *La pensée économique et sociale de Calvin* (Geneva: Librairie de l'Université, 1959), p. 352.

28. See Calvin's sermon on Matt. 4:8–11, in which he said: "... every day we see it round about us: persons who seek to enrich themselves only give evidence of honoring the devil. . . . God means nothing for them, Satan everything. . . ." Original text: ". . . nous voyons comme tous les jours ceux que se veulent enrichir font hommage au diable. . . . Dieu ne leur est rien, et Satan leur est tout. . . ." Cf. Biéler, *La pensée,* p. 318.

service to our fellowmen. For that reason there is indeed a rightful place for economic life in the whole of human existence. But it occupies that place only when it is an "expression of human solidarity and a sign of spiritual community among men," as André Biéler has summarized the basic pattern of Calvin's social and economic thought.[29] An economic life without consideration for God's nature, without concern for fellow creatures, without solidarity, and without "equity" (a term regularly used by Calvin when he dealt with the "ethics" of trade), is, according to Luther as well as Calvin, no longer an authentic economic life. It deviates from the loving response to God and one another which is expected in economic life also.

One can convey the same idea in different terms. To use a phrase by T. P. van der Kooy, professor-emeritus of economics at the Free University of Amsterdam, economic life can unfold its own meaning and significance only when a *simultaneous realization of norms* takes place.[30] The norms of economic development and those of ethics, the norms of justice and of the unfolding of technique, ought never to be played off against each other. Because God's command is undivided, the norms set by him must be seen and observed in their mutual coherence.

It was precisely at the point of this necessary simultaneous realization of norms in society that the industrial revolution failed. It is imperative to grasp what is meant here. My critique is not directed at the circumstance that at a certain moment in western cultural development increased attention was given to the expansion and innovation of production techniques; nor is it my intention to criticize the conviction that a rise in industrial production contains the potential for improving the extremely low standard of life. In a report entitled *The Results of Machinery*, published in 1831 by the "Society for the Diffusion of Useful Knowledge," it was correctly established that "Two centuries

29. ". . . expression de la solidarité humaine et signe de la communion spirituelle des hommes entre eux." *Ibid.*, p. 414.

30. T. P. van der Kooy has developed this significant theme of the simultaneity of norm realization in several of his works. See, for example, his inaugural lecture concerning the meaning of the economic dimension in his book *Over economie en humaniteit* [On Economy and Humanness] (Wageningen: Zomer en Keuning, 1954), pp. 171–190; and his recent essay "Methodologie der economie en christelijke wijsbegeerte" [The Methodology of Economics and Christian Philosophy] in *Philosophia reformata*, vol. 40 (1975), pp. 1–32 (with an English summary).

ago not one person in a thousand wore stockings; one century ago not one person in five hundred wore them; now not one person in a thousand is without them."[31] The failure of the industrial revolution does not lie here; rather, it lies in the well-nigh *absolute* priority gradually accorded to the advance of technology and industrial production in the development of western culture. The failure does not lie in new institutions. But it does lie in the institutionalizing of new forms of production devoted almost exclusively to technical and economic progress. Simultaneous consideration of socioethical and juridical norms was out of the question because the interpretation of ethics as well as law—via utilitarianism and deism—had placed those norms in the service of the market economy and industrial technology.

This, in my estimation, is the most essential critique which can be voiced against the industrial revolution and resultant capitalism. *Capitalism is subject to critique insofar as, for the sake of progress, it is founded on independent and autonomous forces of economic growth and technology, that is, forces which are considered isolated, sufficient, and good in themselves. These economic and technological forces are indeed related to norms of ethics and social justice, but in such a manner that these norms cannot impede the realization of these forces and the promotion of "progress." These norms are consciously viewed as dependent upon and secondary to the forces of progress: they are placed in the service of the expansion of technology and the growth of the economy.* The combination of independent and primary factors of progress with dependent and secondary socioethical norms prevents simultaneous and harmonious realization of norms—economic as well as ethical and legal. This combination has made it impossible for capitalism to do justice to noneconomic norms for human life. Norms of ethics and justice are allowed to play a role only *after* economic production has already occurred. They are permitted to make limited corrections and modest alterations in the process of industrialization, but only *after* this process has autonomously and sovereignly chosen its path through society.

This can be illustrated clearly from actual practice. When, from the point of view of justice, the process of industrialization gives rise to unacceptable consequences, it appears that in the context of capitalism necessary corrections can at best be of a limited nature, applied as an afterthought. *Limited,* because

31. Cited by Hammond and Hammond, *Rise of Modern Industry,* p. 210.

progress itself should not suffer harm; as an *afterthought,* because priority should be granted to expansion of the economy and technology. We can detect this disharmony in the history of the industrial revolution. The "industrialization" of English society implied that in the acquisition and employment of labor forces, criteria which favor the market economy and technological efficiency play a dominant role. Labor is no longer—as in the manor or guild—a personal relationship between lord and serf, or master and apprentice, which involves social rights and duties on both sides. Labor relations develop into impersonal market relations in which wages are determined on the basis of a quantity of time spent and units produced. Of course, in this new relationship legal norms also exist. But these legal regulations are adjusted to the requirements of technico-economic progress. Initially they contain nothing more than the contractual rights and obligations which both parties must meet. If this meant—as it did in England around 1800—that because of low wages laborers often had to work fourteen or more hours per day, and women and children—even those below seven years of age—were obliged to engage in factory work, then only a *limited* correction was allowed as an *afterthought* to alleviate this excessive exploitation of human beings and their families. What was the substance of the correction? In 1802 in England the work day of pauper apprentices was limited by law to twelve hours! In 1819 children below eight years of age were prohibited from working in cotton mills. But it took until 1842 before children under ten were barred from working in the coal mines, and until 1847 before a general limit of ten hours per day was decreed for women and children.[32]

New Lanark, Robert Owen's Scottish enterprise, shows that production could be organized differently. From its inception in 1815 no child labor was used. Schools were provided for the children of the laborers and two-room homes for each of the working-class families. Most surprising of all is that during the ten years of its existence this enterprise made substantial profits. Owen's early experiment is particularly fascinating because it can be regarded as an effort in an industrial framework to meet *simultaneously* the norms of economy, ethics, and social justice. Owen was not one of those whose naive faith in progress caused them to believe that satisfactory working conditions and

32. Heilbroner, *Making of Economic Society,* pp. 86, 87.

family happiness would gradually, freely, and automatically accompany progress in the market economy and technology. New Lanark reveals traits—such as the effort to make the enterprise into an authentic community of life and work—which on the one hand maintain historical continuity with the medieval manors and guilds, while on the other hand contain an essential message even for today's society.

PROGRESS AND ECONOMIC GROWTH

We can also articulate more theoretically what happens in a society which in its general cultural development gives priority to technologically founded industrial expansion. This can be done by pointing to factors basic to every process of economic growth or expansion. For that purpose we will provisionally define *economic growth* as a process in which human possibilities of choice with respect to scarce goods and other limited elements steadily increase. In this context we think of choice between consumer goods, between labor and leisure, as well as between a more or less intensive exploitation of nature. Thus we must ask which factors condition and contribute to such a process of growth.

According to nearly all textbooks on economics, at least three factors are to be considered here. First of all, the possibility exists of using human labor more efficiently: the application of a division of labor among people and groups can result in a significant surplus. In the second place, the possibility exists of introducing the use of tools: the production of tools does indeed cost labor, but it guarantees greater choice in the future. Thirdly, it is possible to use labor for systematic improvements in tools and working methods. Here again the ultimate yield, measured in terms of increased choice, can outweigh the sacrifice. To summarize, division of labor, use of tools or machines, and technical innovations are the three most important original "producers of growth." They are most effective when they reinforce each other and are applied in mutual coherence.

None of these factors of growth can be considered inherently destructive or bad. Personally, I prefer to regard them as positive potentialities for economic development embedded in creation. However, we must investigate what happens to these factors when, as with the realization of faith in progress, uncurtailed priority is given to rapid economic growth in the entire social fabric. It is obvious that each of these factors of growth will then be employed to the utmost, for attaining universal human happiness in society is considered to be dependent on their intensive usage.

As a matter of fact, this is exactly what took place during the industrial revolution. Division of labor was carried to such an extreme that at times only atomized fragments of impersonal work remained. Every interruption was regarded as a threat to reaching a set, useful goal. The deployment of capital was also conditioned by the same pressure, even if the result was meaningless labor which increasingly assumed the character of machine-like repetition of monotonous operations. Finally, as soon as an opportunity arose to introduce new technical innovations, in accordance with the law of progress, these were applied immediately and as extensively as possible. Hence, during the industrial revolution technical innovations were immediately adopted even if this resulted in the radical elimination of industries still using antiquated tools.

In short, the manner in which these factors of economic growth were used indeed reveals a connection between a cultural element such as the belief in progress and the concrete way in which our society was actually shaped.

It should also be clear from our discussion that certain unavoidable dangers are inherent in every culture which isolates and absolutizes the potentials for economic and technical development. Such a culture seems at first to raise man to the position of sovereign master of his own fate—one who calls forth these economic and technical processes and determines their direction. But in the final analysis such a culture quickly relegates this "master" to the position of utter dependence on the powers of development which he himself has enthroned. He ends by being an object, an extension of his own creations.

AROUND 1850

Toward the middle of the nineteenth century there was as yet no full awareness of the negative aspects implicit in the cultural choice taken with the industrial revolution. To the contrary, we are confronted with a pervasive acceptance of progress and its results in almost every sphere of culture. Faith in progress had permeated society to such an extent that not only were the political and industrial leaders guided by it, but it had reached the masses as well. This is confirmed by the French author M. A.

Javary who in 1850 stated in his book *De l'idée de progrès:* "If there is any idea that belongs properly to one century . . . and that, whether accepted or not, is familiar to all minds, it is the idea of Progress conceived as the general law of history and the future of humanity."[33] Eighty years later Christopher Dawson confirmed this: "In the first half of the 19th century the Idea of Progress had attained its full development. It dominated the three main currents of European thought, Rationalist Liberalism, Revolutionary Socialism and Transcendental Idealism."[34]

The popularization and permeation of faith in progress undoubtedly occurred, at least in part, under the influence of more favorable economic results of the industrial revolution which gradually became noticeable. Wages of industrial laborers were raised somewhat, especially after 1830. In the course of time better quality foods became available for the workers' families. Further, social legislation, no matter how primitive, began to take effect. A striking case in point in this entire development is the opening of the world exhibition in London in 1851, where the most modern products of technology of the time were displayed before the eyes of the public. These included railway products, steamships (in 1832 Sauvage had invented the screw propeller), modern factory machinery (such as Henry's electric motor of 1829 and Nasmyth's power hammer of 1842), as well as the latest consumer products which could be manufactured with these machines. To be sure, the sacrifices required by the industrial revolution had been much heavier than one could originally have imagined. And much of the naiveté of the initial faith in progress had been lost.[35] However, the London Exhibition showed that the harvest was evidently at hand, and all that mattered was to make sure, by means of consistent and mutual exertion, that this harvest would be as rich as possible.

33. Quoted by Bury, *Idea of Progress,* p. 313.
34. Dawson, *Progress and Religion,* p. 201.
35. This is confirmed, among others, by the Dutch historian Johan Huizinga. After observing that "We will have to wait till the eighteenth century—for even the Renaissance does not truly bring the idea of progress—before men resolutely enter the path of social optimism;—only then the perfectibility of man and society is raised to the rank of a central dogma," he continues: "and the next century will only lose the naiveté of this belief, but not the courage and optimism which it inspired." *The Waning of the Middle Ages* (New York: Doubleday and Co., 1924; Anchor Books ed., 1954), p. 38.

It was precisely at this time that a movement emerged which would forcefully disturb this dream of the unhindered advancing progress of capitalism. Marx and Engels, the leaders of this movement, openly revealed their sympathy with the working class and set out to define their aims in the *Communist Manifesto* of 1848. Here we read: "The Communists disdain to conceal their views and aims. They openly declare that their ends can be attained only by the forcible overthrow of all existing social conditions. Let the ruling classes tremble at a Communistic revolution."[36] The time had arrived for the revolutionary socialist countermovement.

36. Karl Marx and Frederick Engels, *Communist Manifesto* (1848), in *Collected Works* (New York: International Publishers, 1975 seq.), vol. 6 (1976), p. 519.

7. *The Socialist Countermovement*

In 1845 Friedrich Engels, faithful friend and fellow worker of Karl Marx, published his famous book about the conditions of the industrial workers in England entitled *Die Lage der Arbeitenden Klasse in Engeland.* With the aid of extensive—though not always entirely reliable—statistical data, he painted a glaring picture of the bitter poverty suffered in the slums of English industrial cities despite widespread labor by women and children and fifteen- to sixteen-hour working days. The book is a violent indictment against the capitalist system which made such conditions possible. It clearly reveals how Engels was moved by a deeply felt sympathy and a seriously wounded sense of justice.

The same is true of Marx. In *Das Kapital* he describes how a seven-year-old boy, William Wood, had to bring ready-molded articles to a drying room, day in and day out, from six o'clock in the morning until nine at night. When Marx then fiercely exclaims, "Fifteen hours of labour for a child 7 years old!"[37] there is not a single doubt that he, too, was deeply moved by this inhuman situation. To this authentic concern we can add Marx's profound analysis of human alienation in the modern capitalist process of production in which the laborer is estranged not only from his work but also from his fellowman. In view of all this, one can seemingly arrive at but one conclusion: in Marxist socialism we are confronted with the most violent protest against not only the assumptions of the industrial revolution but also against the firm belief in progress which is their foundation.

37. Karl Marx, *Capital,* 3 vols., edited by Frederick Engels (New York: International Publishers, 1967), vol. 1, p. 244.

After all, did not Marx himself predict the inexorable downfall of the entire capitalist system in contradiction with the prevailing progressive optimism of his day?

However, this conclusion is arrived at too hastily. The matter of properly interpreting Karl Marx is extremely complex. Enlightenment faith in progress and Marx's "scientific socialism" are much less opposed to one another than it appears from superficial observation. Even in his profound protest against the societal structuration of his day, Marx remained in the grip of a relentless and revolutionary Enlightenment faith in human progress. Marxism is an offspring of Enlightenment philosophy.

DIALECTIC MATERIALISM AND IDEA OF PROGRESS

What did Marx say about the possibility of human progress? Whatever he said about this crucial theme is of course closely connected with his conception of history. Marx views the history of humankind as a dialectical process arising in particular out of the tensions between the technico-economic substructure of society (consisting of the productive forces: *Produktivkräfte*) and the superstructure of society (consisting of the relations of production: *Produktionsverhältnisse*) to which belong in particular the relations of ownership and possession. Marx argued that in every noncommunist society these relations of production in the superstructure have the tendency dialectically to drag behind the changes taking place with respect to the forces of production in the substructure. For instance, in capitalism we encounter the situation that the forces of production have already advanced to the stage of large-scale industries operated by steam power. This stage of industrial production, Marx argued, requires communal property in all the means of production in the social superstructure. But what do we see? We note that in this advanced stage of capitalism the dominant relations of production—private property—still belong to an earlier phase of development of the forces of production. The capitalist class of private property owners in the means of production try their utmost—though in vain—to prevent the leap from private relations of production to communal property. This attempt is fruitless since the capitalists, exploiting and accumulating, only dig their own graves and prepare the destruction of their own social system.

This well-known picture of the development of capitalism

indeed seems at first sight far removed from the stereotyped ideas of progress of the Enlightenment era. However, we will have to take a closer look at the role which the so-called *forces of production* play in this entire process. Marx describes these forces as the methods and means employed in the process of economic production together with the human ability to use them in the proper manner. These forces of production, taken together, consist primarily of the entire complex of technical production possibilities. In Marx's view the whole history of humankind is conditioned and influenced, though dialectically, by changes in production techniques.

But the question now arises: what determines these forces of production? Further, how does Marx explain that this development of technology reveals a definite advance? Marx hardly addresses himself to these questions, even though he clearly regards the development of production technique as the only way toward future happiness. This can be explained only as a typical expression of Enlightenment faith. The technology of labor clears the path, in spite of all opposition, to a better social order.[38]

When Marx speaks in volume one of *Capital* about the enormous potentials of technology, he makes the point that the word *impossible* should never be used, quoting Mirabeau's exclamation: "Impossible? Ne me dites jamais cet imbécile mot!"[39] Marx elucidates his conception of technology as follows: "Technology discloses man's mode of dealing with Nature, the process of production by which he sustains his life, and thereby also lays bare the mode of formation of his social relations, and of the mental conceptions that flow from them."[40] In other words, every essential unfolding of culture is rooted in the guiding function of an inexorably advancing technology.

Other elements of Marx's thought can also be directly re-

38. Marx identified "all the progress of civilization" with "every increase in the *powers of social production* . . . such as results from science, inventions, division and combination of labour, improved means of communication, creation of the world market, machinery, etc." Karl Marx, *Grundrisse,* translated with a Foreword by Martin Nicolaus (Harmondsworth: Penguin Books, 1973), p. 308.

39. "Impossible? Never mention that imbecile word to me!" Taken from the second edition of *Das Kapital*. For a slightly different reading see the final edition, Marx, *Capital,* vol. 1, p. 477: "Impossible! ne me dites jamais ce bête de mot!"

40. Marx, *Capital,* vol. 1, p. 372, note 3.

lated to Enlightenment ideas about progress. This is particularly true of his view of the dialectical relation between man and nature. The *man versus nature* theme is one of the characteristic issues of the Enlightenment era, as we recall from our discussion in Part One. In Marx's thought the dialectical relation between man and nature is not a minor element. He considers it of vital significance for his entire thinking. All of world history is determined precisely by this relationship, he argues in *Economic and Philosophic Manuscripts of 1844.*

In his view, man and nature are so essentially involved with one another that nature cannot reach its destination without man and man cannot do so without nature. Hence for Marx the entire history of humankind is a process in which nature is guided to its human destination by man, and in which man reaches his most essential, his natural destination, only through nature. "History itself is a *real* part of *natural history*—of nature developing into man," he writes.[41] And "communism," the final goal of world history, "as fully developed naturalism, equals humanism, and as fully developed humanism equals naturalism; it is the *genuine* resolution of the conflict between man and nature and between man and man. . . ."[42] But how can nature reach its human destination and man his natural destination? This is possible only by means of human labor. Progress in the world is contained in the possibility of man's interaction with nature through industry. To quote Marx again:

> Labour is, in the first place, a process in which both man and Nature participate, and in which man of his own accord starts, regulates, and controls the material re-actions between himself and Nature. He opposes himself to Nature as one of her own forces, setting in motion arms and legs, head and hands, the natural forces of his body, in order to appropriate Nature's productions in a form adapted to his own wants. By thus acting on the external world and changing it, he at the same time changes his own nature. He develops his slumbering powers and compels them to act in obedience to his sway.[43]

> Thus Nature becomes one of the organs of his activity, one that he annexes to his own bodily organs, adding stature to himself in spite of the Bible. As the earth is his original larder, so too it

41. Karl Marx, *Economic and Philosophic Manuscripts of 1844,* in Marx/Engels, *Collected Works,* vol. 3 (1975), pp. 303–304.
42. Marx/Engels, *Collected Works,* vol. 3 (1975), p. 296.
43. Marx, *Capital,* vol. 1, p. 177.

is his original tool house. . . . The earth itself is an instrument of labour. . . .[44]

It cannot be denied that in this statement we encounter almost every element of the Enlightenment faith in progress in a new garb. In the first place, man's struggle with nature becomes the central theme of human history. Further, there is the firm conviction that in this struggle man himself develops toward self-realization and perfection: "adding stature to himself" ("seine natürliche Gestalt verlängernd"). Finally, we find here Marx's faith in the salvific, redemptive function of human labor, including its technical qualities. *"Industry,"* Marx claims, "is the actual, historical relationship of nature . . . to man."[45] For Marx the beginning of human history is that moment when men and women begin to distinguish themselves from animals because they "begin to *produce* their means of subsistence."[46] "As individuals express their life, so they are. What they are, therefore, coincides with their production, both with *what* they produce and with *how* they produce."[47] All of these elements are present in an incisive passage from the *Economic and Philosophic Manuscripts of 1844:*

> But since for the socialist man the *entire so-called history of the world* is nothing but the creation of man through human labour, nothing but the emergence of nature for man, so he has the visible, irrefutable proof of his *birth* through himself, of his *genesis.* Since the *real existence* of man and nature has become evident in practice, through sense experience, because man has thus become evident for man as the being of nature, and nature for man as the being of man, the question about an *alien* being, about a being above nature and man—a question which implies the admission of the unreality of nature and of man—has become impossible in practice.[48]

MARX AND ALIENATION

If Marx has such a high estimation of human industrial labor as the path toward general improvement of man and his destiny,

44. *Ibid.,* p. 179.

45. Marx, *Economic and Philosophic Manuscripts of 1844,* in Marx/Engels, *Collected Works,* vol. 3 (1975), p. 303.

46. Karl Marx and Frederick Engels, *The German Ideology* (1845), in *Collected Works,* vol. 5 (1976), p. 31.

47. *Ibid.,* p. 31f.

48. Marx, *Economic and Philosophic Manuscripts of 1844,* in Marx/Engels, *Collected Works,* vol. 3 (1975), pp. 305–306.

how can he at the same time present such a profound analysis of the possibility of *alienation* right within an industrial capitalistic society? At first sight, the alienation of *man* from his *fellowman* seems to proceed from a framework of reference different from that of *man* laboring with *nature.* Similarly, Marx's call to solidarity and his hope for the restoration of authentic human community seem to have considerably broader implications than what can be deduced from the man-nature relationship. Are we then perhaps dealing with a *different* Marx?

The answer to that is No! It is the same Marx who speaks here. Alienation for Marx is not a phenomenon to be found in every modern industrialized society. Rather, it is only encountered in a specifically capitalist society, because the different expressions of alienation—man's alienation from his labor, from the products of his labor, from his natural environment, from his fellowmen, and finally from his own self-consciousness (this last expression of alienation Marx calls "religion")—have a common basis in what Marx calls the *Grundübel der Entfremdung:* the basic evil of alienation. This basic evil consists of the circumstance that the worker is estranged from—is alienated from—ownership of the means of production. The entire process of alienation is set in motion because the means of production do not belong to him but to the capitalist. It is not a result of industrialization itself. Rather, it stems exclusively from the existence of private property in the means of production and its consequences.

It is quite obvious why ownership of the means of production is for Marx the basic cause of all forms of alienation in society. This interpretation flows directly from his fundamental assumption that man can reach his destination only through his own active operation upon nature. To take away a person's right to freely dispose of the products of his own hands thus amounts to nothing less than to deprive him of his only possibility of self-realization. The maintenance of private property, with respect to both the laborer's tools as well as his products, simply implies a separation between man and nature. This intervention between the laborer and the means of production prevents the laborer from achieving his human, this is, his natural destination. For that reason Marx believes that "The positive transcendence of *private property,* as the appropriation of *human* life, is therefore the positive transcendence of all estrangement."[49] As soon

49. *Ibid.,* p. 297.

as private property is abolished, all expressions of alienation will disappear.

At that moment the veils will be removed under which capitalism managed to hide the real progress of humankind in all of its industrial activity. Then the fruits of progress, carefully cultivated by capitalism itself, will with one revolutionary act be plucked like ripened grapes from the vineyard of capitalism. At that moment capitalism will have fulfilled its "historical mission"—the development of all productive human forces. Quite paradoxically, when this turning point has been reached, the capitalists themselves will not in the least be conscious of the fact that capitalism has produced these fruits only to make possible an abundant future for the laboring class. This is the socialistic doctrine of election and predestination, Marx's Jewish irony about human history. Capitalism is like Egypt's pharaoh who oppressed the people of Israel but who, because of that oppression and in spite of himself, created the conditions for Israel's liberation and its journey to the promised land, laden with the treasures of Egypt.[50]

What does this mean for our understanding of the mutual relationship between orthodox Marxism and capitalism? Marx's faith in the advance of technology, his limited perspective on the sources of human alienation, and his profound confidence in the perfectibility of man through his laboring struggle with nature are elements of Marx's thought that can only lead to the conclusion that Marxism and capitalism are like sisters who live in hatred and envy toward one another. Both are direct descendents of Enlightenment faith in progress. For both, industrial expansion is the guide to a happier future, the hallmark of the arrival of better times.

Of course this does not mean that there are no radical differences between capitalism and Marxism. The most important difference concerns the question of on what societal basis progress can best be assured and can benefit everyone. Capitalism chooses as its basis the individual will, as this comes to expression in the free interchange of the market, with public protection of all civil rights. Marxism chooses as its ultimate basis the collective will of society, as this comes to expression in a central plan, and is predicated on the assumption that everyone will fulfill his social tasks and civic duties. But even in this

50. Cf. Exodus 12:35f.

undoubtedly sharp opposition Marxism and capitalism betray their original profound kinship. The differences which remain are, so to speak, mirror images of one another; there is similarity precisely in the points of difference. Moreover, the remaining differences share the common denominator of the necessity of progress.

In the light of this background it is not very surprising that soon after Marx died, the main stream of socialism began to feel more or less at home in the development that capitalism was undergoing. The struggle from that point was almost exclusively directed to a different division of the fruits of capitalism. Marx had admonished in *Wages, Price and Profit:* "Instead of the *conservative* motto, '*A fair day's wage for a fair day's work!*' they ought to inscribe on their banner the *revolutionary* watchword, 'Abolition of the wages system!' "[51] However, his adherents increasingly flung this admonition to the winds. If the capitalist vineyard bears such fancy fruits, even for the working class, why should the latter deprive itself of the immediate benefits of progress? This is all the more so when through corrections made as an afterthought, in particular in the area of social legislation, the further cultivation of the vineyard itself often can be stimulated in a more acceptable direction. Thus we observe the curious fact that within a few decades after its inception, socialism, which started as a countermovement to capitalism, is bent into the role of supporter which propels the economic progress of capitalism with even greater speed.

51. Karl Marx, *Wages, Price and Profit,* in Marx/Engels, *Selected Works in Two Volumes* (Moscow: Foreign Languages Publishing House, 1958), vol. 1, p. 446.

8. *The Unfolding of Faith in Progress after 1850*

The famous nineteenth-century French painter Gustave Courbet lived from 1819 to 1877. Once, when busily working on a canvas, someone asked him what he was really painting. Only after he had stepped back a certain distance from his canvas could he come up with the proper answer, namely, a faggot— a bundle of twigs. While he was actually painting, he had been concerned merely with how he could reconstruct on a canvas with his paintbrush what he observed with his eyes. What he saw with his own eyes was sufficient for him.

Until now we have hardly touched upon the history of art. Yet it is precisely from this field that we can often learn a great deal about a certain period. This also is true for the period around 1850. Not only did capitalism, which was still of recent date, show several new symptoms, but faith in progress itself entered a new phase: the phase of objectivity.

THE CULT OF OBJECTIVITY

Courbet was a Realist, and was particularly opposed to conceptions of art characteristic of Romanticism. Romanticism is a very complex phenomenon. On the one hand it clearly showed elements of resistance against an industrialized society and glorified the emotional unification of man with nature. Such traits remind us more of Rousseau than of Voltaire or an ode to industrial expansion. Nevertheless, Romanticism also contained an element essential to the beginning of Enlightenment faith, namely, the glorification of passionate, individual heroic deeds. It was characterized by what René Huyghe coined "the cult of energy." In many French romantic paintings, such as those by Géricault and Delacroix, the diagonal lines which dominate express energy and élan. These compositional devices were used, for instance, to emphasize the revolutionary pathos of Napoleon on horseback. At the center of Romanticism stands personal power of imagination and consequently the will to create new, nonexistent, imaginary worlds. The paradise images of Enlightenment faith were thus recovered and expressed in Romanticism.

Over against this, the Barbizon school and an artist such as Courbet represented a new trend in art, opposed to the world of the imagination. "Courbet, in talking to his students, wanted to destroy even the word 'imagination'."[52] In another context Courbet stated:

> I hold that painting is an art which is essentially *concrete* and can only consist in representing *real* and *existing* things. Painting is a physical language and deals with the visible world. Things which are abstract, invisible or non-existent do not belong to the domain of painting.[53]

It is fascinating to note that this new direction in art paralleled the development of faith in progress. This does not mean that by this time faith in progress decreased in significance or power; to the contrary, it was accepted in ever-broader circles and with ever-wider implications. "The culminating point in the history of the belief in progress," writes Morris Ginsberg, "was reached towards the end of the nineteenth century. . . . It owed its wide prevalence to the optimism inspired by the triumphs of applied science, made visible in the striking advances made in the technical conveniences of life. . . ."[54] Bury confirms this: "Thus in the seventies and eighties of the last century the idea

52. René Huyghe, "Art Forms and Society," in *Larousse Encyclopedia of Modern Art from 1800 to the Present Day,* ed. by René Huyghe (New York: Prometheus Press, 1961), p. 148. Charles Dickens shared this thought. "What he wanted were the facts and that the word 'imagination' should be banished for ever." See Bernard Dorival, "The Realist Movement," in *Larousse Encyclopedia of Modern Art,* p. 160.

53. Quoted by Huyghe, "Art Forms and Society," in *Larousse Encyclopedia of Modern Art,* p. 148.

54. Morris Ginsberg, *Essays in Sociology and Social Philosophy,* vol. 3: *Evolution and Progress,* p. 8.

of Progress was becoming a general article of faith."[55]

However, faith in progress does change in character. Confronted with what meanwhile was accomplished in the areas of technology and economics, it began to direct itself increasingly to this concrete reality. The beautiful images of paradise were regarded as too imaginary. Is it not sufficient simply to look around you and to observe that progress is right there, concretely and visibly, and that it will continue to be there? Why not, just like Courbet, be satisfied with what is directly before your eyes?

In the light of these concrete facts, the pathos glorifying the energetic, heroic deeds of the reformers and innovators of the pioneering stage seems to pale. Élan, geniality, and imagination belong to the vocabulary of Romanticism. Sobriety, systematic research, respect for the facts, and objectivity belong to Realism. They carried the day in the second half of the nineteenth century.

PROGRESS AS OBSERVABLE AND MEASURABLE FACT

Courbet's first concern was to represent real, existing things, simply and exactly. Accurate observation and recording of factual reality form the background of his art. The objectivity of Courbet's art and the commonly accepted factual realism were expressed in the realm of *science* by Auguste Comte (1798–1857), the founder of modern sociology and one of the fathers of *positivism.* He succinctly expressed his conviction in these words: "Since the time of Bacon the most brilliant brains have repeated again and again that real knowledge can only be founded on observed fact."[56] Comte was a pupil of Henri de Saint-Simon and stands in the tradition of the Enlightenment thinkers Turgot and Condorcet. In his own philosophy, however, he went far beyond these forerunners of positivism. In typical modernist fashion he divided the history of culture into three stages of which the last and highest one is of course the positivist phase.

55. Bury, *Idea of Progress,* p. 346.
56. Cited by Huyghe, "Art Forms and Society," in *Larousse Encyclopedia of Modern Art,* p. 148.

Positivism strives after positive progress in society by attributing an indispensable role to modern science which is characterized by strict natural-scientific observation of facts and by systematic prediction *(prévision scientifique)* based on such observation. Comte founded sociology, which he considered as the *theory* of progress based only on observed facts and embracing all of human society. "The human mind," he claimed, "has conceived astronomical and terrestrial physics and chemistry and organic physics relating to plant or animal life. There only remains, in order to complete this system of science by observation, for man to establish social physics. This is, in many ways, the most urgent problem to be solved."[57]

In summary we can say that after 1850 faith in progress gradually turned away from the paradisiacal and speculative images of the future typical of the Enlightenment era[58] in order to turn to concrete, factual evidence of progress daily observable in the areas of economics, technology, and science. "The future," according to Fred Polak, "is no longer a separate entity, but is squeezed into the day-to-day movement of the present."[59] That "day-to-day movement of the present" is subject to continual control and guidance from the new positivist "scientific" approach which wants to observe, register, and measure only the bare facts of reality.

> We are now at the hey-day of scientific materialism. Everything that can be experimentally confirmed, that can be seen, touched, measured, registered and controlled, is given a high value. This has led to the specifically modern habit of matter-of-factness and

57. *Ibid.* In the history of art this same desire for strict natural-scientific observation ultimately leads to *Impressionism* which finds its starting point in observation during a fleeting but reconstructable moment. Impressionism went one step beyond Realism; namely, the idolization of "the present moment and the immediate surroundings." Cf. Dorival, "The Realist Movement," in *Larousse Encyclopedia of Modern Art,* p. 159.

58. Cf. the title of Carl Becker's study, *The Heavenly City of the Eighteenth-Century Philosophers.*

59. Fred L. Polak, *De toekomst is verleden tijd,* 2 vols. (Zeist, the Netherlands: W. de Haan, 1958). English translation by Elise Boulding, *The Image of the Future,* 2 vols. (Leyden: Sijthoff; New York: Oceana Publications, 1961), vol. 2, p. 31.

to the narrowing of awareness which Whitehead has termed "the fallacy of misplaced concreteness."[60]

Does this mean that technological innovation and economic expansion must surrender their dominant role in society at this time? No, but a different appreciation does set in. They are no longer looked upon in the first place as means to be used or guides to be followed because in the future they might lead humankind to paradise. Rather, they have become objects of appreciation *in themselves* because of their concretely observable and measurable daily manifestations. The actual enjoyment of present progress takes precedence over possible future progress. The present reality of technological and economic growth has become central precisely because it is so real, tangible, and measurable.

This new orientation of progress toward measurable expression in the present has remained characteristic of western faith in progress ever since. One can readily provide examples of this from our own time. For instance, when we are asked how well off we are as a nation, our first reaction usually is a reference to the GNP—the gross national product. When we think of progress, we no longer think of the future but of what is taking place today. Moreover, economic progress is often entirely defined apart from qualitative criteria; it is reduced to what is directly and quantitatively measurable. Welfare in the West today is not only expressed in figures; it is nearly equated with figures—those of the annual GNP. This type of response to the question of welfare and progress reveals less about the issue than it does about ourselves. It is an expression of persons for whom the future has shrunk to a day-to-day advance of the present,[61] and for whom truth is equated with the observable, and essence with the measurable. Whoever is interested in discovering to what level of cultural and spiritual poverty the West has sunk need only ask after its welfare!

60. *Ibid.,* p. 33.
61. Cf. in this context the statement by Adolph Strasser, one of the leaders of the powerful American Federation of Labor: "We have no ultimate ends. We are going on from day to day. We are fighting only for immediate objects—objects that can be realized in a few years." Quoted by Ronald Segal, *The Americans: A Conflict of Creed and Reality* (Toronto/New York/London: Bantam Books, 1970), p. 94.

PROGRESS AND EVOLUTION

As we have just seen, realism and positivism after 1850 force faith in progress toward the sober, observable everyday facts in which this faith can see itself confirmed and mirrored at any time. However, to understand the unfolding of this faith in western culture up to the present, and with it the development of capitalism, other influences must be mentioned as well. The most important one is the theory of evolution, particularly since the appearance of Charles Darwin's *Origin of Species* in 1859.

On first sight the concept of *evolution* hardly adds anything to the concept of *progress*. What else is progress but evolution in a desired, ascending direction? But this interpretation is too simplistic and therefore untenable. A fundamental change takes place in the progress motif as soon as it is joined in one way or another with the theory of evolution.

In the first place, it is significant to note that Darwin described evolution as a process in which man develops from the animal world; in fact, man is regarded as an advanced specimen of the animal kingdom. The importance of this is immediately evident when we remember that the Enlightenment philosophers invariably regarded progress as a process started, controlled, and directed by man himself. By means of his rational insight, his critical ingenuity, and his technical and economic ability, man sets the wheel of progress in motion; only through this motion does he himself also develop toward perfection. However, in the concept of evolution we encounter a process that has already begun apart from human intervention. Man himself, whether he likes it or not, has been taken up in this process as a dependent element. In the theory of evolution man does not propel progress forward; he is being propelled toward progress by time. Instead of being the subject of progress, in evolutionary thought man has become first of all an object of progress.

It is beyond dispute that in this approach the glory of humanity has been greatly diminished. Human reason, once acclaimed as the absolute source of meaning in the world and the essence of human dignity, becomes in Darwin's theory "merely an organ that has been developed by man's effort to adapt himself to his environment. . . ."[62] Man becomes "the product and

62. Dawson, *Progress and Religion,* p. 19.

plaything of a 'Nature red in tooth and claw'."[63] Ultimately, civilization is no more than "a part of nature, being a development of man's latent capabilities under the action of favourable circumstances. . . ."[64]

A second element which the theory of evolution adds to the idea of progress concerns the notion of an unavoidable process of *natural selection.* The term "evolution" is not a colorless concept. It entails a view of human history as a process in which every form of life is won only after a *struggle* in which ultimate victory is best gained through *adaptation* to one's environment. The English philosopher Herbert Spencer (1820–1903) tried to apply the dogma of evolution to socioeconomic life. In *Social Statics* (1851) he drew the conclusion that the law of "the struggle for life" applies equally to the competition between industrial enterprises, and that the principle of charity should under no circumstances be the starting point for the development of socioeconomic life. For, says Bury, according to Spencer "the ultimate purpose of creation is to produce the greatest amount of happiness. . . ." That requires the elimination of "inferior creatures" who do not possess faculties enabling them "to experience the highest enjoyment of life."[65] In Spencer's own words: "Always towards perfection is the mighty movement."[66] This ascending development requires the sacrifice of the weak to increase the chances of life—and thus the utilities to be enjoyed—for the strong.

Evolution theory with its principle of "conquest through struggle" apparently also appealed to Marx, for he asked Darwin's permission to dedicate the first volume of *Capital* to him. However, the latter refused this honor.

Even more important than what Spencer and Marx thought about Darwin is the fact that the evolution motif lodged itself ever deeper into the western faith in progress. Around the turn of the century it had, in fact, become almost universally accepted. It was then believed that progress was based on the unavoidable process of natural evolution. This, according to

63. *Ibid.,* pp. 20, 21.
64. Bury, *Idea of Progress,* p. 338.
65. *Ibid.,* pp. 338, 339.
66. Cf. *Ibid.,* p. 340.

Bury, was the decisive factor which established the reign of the idea of progress at the end of the nineteenth century and the beginning of the twentieth.

SUMMARY

In recapitulating the main characteristics of faith in progress after 1850, we encounter the following elements: a shift in interest toward factual, observable economic and technical progress of the moment; the application of "positive" science as measure and aid in this process; an assessment of this process as a necessary, constantly present, and inexorable process in which man has been taken up; and finally, the recognition that in this process man must accept the struggle for survival for which he can best equip himself by a constant adaptation to his environment.

All of these elements are perhaps best summarized in Comte's motto: *progrès et ordre*—progress and order. *Order* or *system* is a prime requisite in a society in which progress itself, or rather, in which *making progress* has become a constant factor, considered by everyone to be an established fact and a firm necessity. Such order is not only required to protect progress as such; it is also necessary, in view of this new social constant, to prevent the loss of the mutual coherence of the whole. We can compare this with the flight of a spaceship which can, as a "system," move forward only when a definite purpose has been established for every one of its parts, and when all parts are mutually related in a balanced manner. In the same way the daily presence of constant economic and technical progress demands a *social system* which is permanently geared to this evolution; in which man himself is adjusted to this new life and work situation; and in which science functions to make the internal equilibrium of the progress system as stable as possible.

In other words, during the second half of the nineteenth century and the beginning of the twentieth we witnessed a transition from the duty to *effectuate desired progress* to the duty to *adapt to existing progress* present in all its concrete manifestations. This adaptation required the transformation of the whole of society into a system of survival with a single focus. The forces of economic and technological progress are related to the social system in a manner comparable to the relationship between a queen bee and her hive. The queen bee can only make progress in her work—egg production—if she is surrounded by a hive in which everything is functionalized and instrumentalized with respect to her task.[67]

---

67. Within the context of the present discussion we can only make brief reference to the change which occurred in the development of economic theory around 1870—a change prepared by John Stuart Mill with the publication of his main work *Principles of Political Economy* (1848). Nearly every trait of this new conception of progress also appears in economic reflection since 1870. Economics becomes a matter of arriving at conclusions on the basis of natural-scientific methods and therefore with the aid of observable and measurable quantities. In this process it is presupposed that the entire system of economic quantities tends toward an equilibrium (of the market) under the pressure of everyone's striving for a maximum of individual utilities. The system itself is completely closed because of the choice of relevant data which have to be quantifiable. One of the few worries which remained for the economist in this entire system concerned the question whether "utility" is objectively observable and above all *measurable*. Economic theory has been uninterruptedly and diligently preoccupied with this question until today!

9. Changes Within Capitalism Since 1850

If capitalism owes in large measure its origin and its very existence to faith in progress, then we must be able to trace evidence of that throughout the history of its development. As a matter of fact, we can expect to trace even more than that. If faith in progress has indeed been the major source of inspiration and the main propeller of western society during the last two centuries, then this must also be clearly visible within its diverse *sectors*. We can test this hypothesis by investigating whether in these diverse sectors parallel developments occurred which can indeed be explained only in terms of a common source.

In view of this we shall trace the development of capitalism from 1850 to the present by investigating—in bird's eye view—changes that took place in at least three sectors of society:

1. the sector of the internal life of an enterprise, including the relations between an enterprise and its management, its workers, and its investors;

2. the sector of relations among enterprises themselves and between the enterprise and its customers; and

3. the sector of the relation between industry as a whole and government, as well as the relationships between national states.

If my assumption is correct, then changes in each of these sectors should reveal close parallels with respect to each other as well as to the changing character of faith in progress itself after 1850.

89

CHANGES WITHIN THE ENTERPRISE

1. Size, legal structure, and mass production

We must be careful not to entertain an exaggerated picture of the size of enterprises at the beginning of the industrial revolution. A few employed a thousand or more workers, but most were of more modest dimension. This is not surprising if we consider that the enterprise at that time was first of all a typical individual undertaking. Moreover, the required capital often had to be gathered together from friends and acquaintances of the entrepreneur. This was the case even with the development of Watt's steam engine. "Without years of substantial financial assistance from Dr. Black, Roebuck, and Boulton," according to the historian Earl J. Hamilton, "Watt's steam engine might never have pumped a gallon of water or turned a factory wheel."[68] In other words, invested capital was still in the hands of only a few people who, because of the risk they took, were usually both owner and director of the enterprise. The establishment of a new enterprise, oriented to a specific goal, was often an adventurous and hazardous undertaking usually occasioned by a new technical invention, the industrial application of which might provide adequate return on capital investment.

This primitive picture of early business enterprises changed rapidly because some of the first projects proved to be so profitable that money began to pour in. An interesting example of such success is the story of Richard Arkwright, who started his career as a wigmaker but whose possessions at the time of his death were valued at £500,000. His wealth increased so quickly that he boasted he could pay off England's entire national debt if only he would live long enough.[69] Of course, nothing succeeds like success, and many of the well-to-do yielded to the temptation—with a great deal of hesitation at first—to risk part of their own wealth in similar undertakings. This did not mean that they always demanded proportional authority in the enterprise. Thus, a distinction gradually developed between entrepreneur and investor.

This change, of course, took place more rapidly as the

68. Earl J. Hamilton, "Profit, Inflation and the Industrial Revolution, 1750–1800," *Quarterly Journal of Economics* 61 (1942), 264.
69. Cf. Richard T. Gill, *Economic Development, Past and Present* (Englewood Cliffs, N.J.: Prentice-Hall, 1973), p. 55.

average size of the industrial concern expanded. Tempted by the possibility of producing at a lower cost per unit by means of enlarging the size of the undertaking, many entrepreneurs tried to increase the capital investment in their firms. However, the amounts required soon became so large that they could be provided only by bringing many investors together. For quite some time these attempts were realized within the legal structure of the limited liability company. In this organization the capital investment of the corporation was obtained from various shareholders. Their participation in the daily affairs of the company was indeed limited, but they could lose the value of their own capital input only in the event that the enterprise failed. As early as 1800 three hundred and fifty business corporations in the United States operated on this principle of limited liability. In England this type of distribution of liability and participation first became popular after the Companies Act of 1844 was adopted.[70] One result of this still rather limited separation of authority from ownership was the increasing independence of the business enterprise. It became less subject to the whims of the individual owner who in the earlier stage was the sole supplier of capital.

This trend intensified markedly during the second half of the nineteenth century because of the rise of mass production. The technology of production advanced so rapidly that the time had come to profitably manufacture products of only a few varieties in such great quantities and consequently at such low cost that the masses of society could afford them. In the United States "the number of manufacturing establishments jumped from 140,000 in 1859 to over 200,000 in 1900 and accounted for an increase in the index of manufacturing production from 7.5 in 1863 to 67.6 in 1900."[71] Thus, although the number of factories increased by less than 50 percent, because of growth in mass production the total industrial output multiplied nine times in less than forty years!

70. Cf. Oscar Handlin and Mary F. Handlin, "Origins of the American Business Corporation," in Frederic C. Lane and Jelle C. Riemersma, eds., *Enterprise and Secular Change: Readings in Economic History* (Homewood, Ill.: Richard D. Irwin, Inc., 1953), pp. 104, 105.
71. George A. Steiner, *Government's Role in Economic Life* (New York: McGraw-Hill, 1953), p. 82.

2. Internalization of science, management, and technology

This stormy process of industrialization, mass production, and large-scale growth of the individual enterprise was accompanied by a number of incisive shifts within the enterprise itself.

In the first place, along with the expansion in size, the internal division of labor began to be subjected to scientific analysis. Work in factories was expertly and theoretically split into an increasing number of basic operations. Moreover, the organization of the production process as a whole was also made the object of scientific scrutiny. Shortly after 1900, Frederick W. Taylor introduced his scientific analysis of the time and movements necessary for the performance of all partial functions within an entire mass production system. Science increasingly became an indispensable auxiliary instrument in the building and maintenance of ever more complex enterprises in which the systematic exploitation of all factors of growth was advocated, including the division of labor and assembly-line production.

Secondly, another internalization process was taking place within the enterprise. While on the one hand the separation between ownership and management continued, the function of the entrepreneur, on the other hand, became more closely tied to the undertaking. Gradually the business enterprise began, as it were, to have a life of its own. It developed its own system of life and work, and as a *system* it was in need of continuous management. In the early years of the industrial revolution the enterprise could be regarded as a dependent extension of the sovereign will of individual entrepreneurs and investors. However, after 1850 this was less and less the case. Business corporations developed into independent life systems—independent "beehives"—which in turn required management and capital for their continued independent existence. What happened to the enterprise was no longer determined by the will of the individual entrepreneur but by the law of social evolution. While the business undertaking was first established by the sovereign role of the entrepreneur, after 1850 the undertaking started to *internalize* this role. It assimilated this function into its own system as a vital but nonetheless replaceable part. The modern term for this internalized role is *management*. This term betrays the fact that the individual entrepreneur also was forced to obey the laws of evolution and henceforth had to accept the role of a derivative function in a system of life and work oriented to progress.

As a third facet of internalization we can point to a similar development in the relation of enterprise to technology. The first industrial enterprises were usually organized to utilize new inventions. As a rule, technology was brought into industry from the outside, for instance via patents. But since 1850 this also changed. For the sake of its own growth and continuity an industrial corporation had to be assured of the presence of *continuing technological innovation.* It acquired this certainty by making such innovation an essential part of its own industrial operation. In other words, technology was also *internalized.* In this connection Whitehead correctly observed that "the greatest invention of the nineteenth century was the invention of the method of invention."[72] "Research and development" became standard departments in modern industrial corporations. The first private American industrial research laboratory dates from 1900, and belonged to General Electric. It was followed by a host of others. "Managers and technologists became employees, not owners. Employed to solve technical problems, managers and technologists in a sense automatically become hired inventors."[73]

In summary, during the second half of the nineteenth century and the early part of the twentieth a process took place in which science, management, and technology, instead of independently contributing to economic progress in society, were increasingly assigned the role of internalized aspects of the daily operations of industrial enterprises. They became vital parts— *vital* to be sure, but still only *parts*—of the system of life and work which is called the modern corporation, in which the evolution of progress manifests itself daily to the fullest degree.

3. From profit maximization to system maintenance
When we proceed further into the twentieth century we witness first of all an intensification of the above-mentioned tendencies. The owner has become an even more anonymous investor. He is often treated by the large corporation as a kind of second-class creditor who must resign himself to wait and see what dividend will be paid to him by the board of directors. The boards themselves, however, have become an ever-stronger part

72. Alfred N. Whitehead, *Science and the Modern World* (Cambridge: Cambridge University Press, 1926), p. 120.
73. Jacob Schmookler, "Technological Progress and the Modern American Corporation," in Edward S. Mason, ed., *The Corporation in Modern Society* (Cambridge, Mass.: Harvard University Press, 1959), p. 143.

of the total system of the enterprise. Instead of being the owners of the corporation, as was the case earlier, it seems that the corporation now owns its board members and controls their personal lives, their ethics, as well as their circle of acquaintances.

Moreover, along with these changes, the goals of the enterprise also gradually undergo a change. As long as the undertaking was a direct extension of the individual will of the investors, profit maximization within a relatively short time span was considered a corporation's central purpose. However, when the business enterprise emancipated itself from the influence of individual investors and developed into a "going concern," the goal of a maximum profit also had to be surrendered. In its place we encounter a new dominant goal, namely, securing the continued existence of the corporation or—to employ current jargon—system maintenance. Profit maximization as a rule becomes of secondary importance except in situations where a certain minimum profit level is threatened.[74]

What does this tendency toward continuity and self-preservation mean in a society in which economic and technological progress has become a routine assumption of everyday existence and has been promoted to a kind of "social constant"? In such a society continuity on the part of the enterprise can only imply adaptation to economic progress. A business which does not grow economically and does not renovate itself technologically at all times, does not have a chance to survive the "struggle for life" in a progress-oriented society. In such an environment even a weakening in the growth of production and sales and a relaxation in technological innovation can be fatal. In this environment a real standstill means decline because progress is viewed as normal.

SUCCESSIVE CHANGES IN COMPETITION

Capitalism is not a static social system which holds for all times. Over the years it has clearly undergone changes and its character has been transformed. This is also apparent from the development of reciprocal relations among competitive enterprises. Following Heilbroner we can distinguish four phases in this development.[75]

74. Cf. John Kenneth Galbraith, *The New Industrial State* (New York: New American Library, 1968), chapter 10.
75. Heilbroner, *Making of Economic Society*.

1. Pure and perfect competition

In the early stages of the industrial revolution much competition took place, especially between new firms and traditional production units still using antiquated technology. "At any rate, the industrial capitalists," according to Gras, "prospered enormously in their competition with the survivors of the older régimes which still used older techniques."[76] However, competition gradually became stiffer because various newcomers lodged themselves in the same branches of industry. Soon so many new entrepreneurs were present in each branch that keen price competition was unavoidable. In this manner the first phase of competition set in—the phase of nearly *pure and perfect competition.*

During this period some of the ideals of classical economists such as Adam Smith and John Stuart Mill seemed to have become part of reality. The entrepreneurs were forced to match one another in a continual competitive struggle while consumers benefited in the form of price reductions. A kind of "equilibrium" between "antagonistic interests" came about; the invisible hand was in operation so that unhampered competition created benefits for the entire population. The client had become king. As consumer he could be seen as sovereign in his choice of products and producers, and to a large extent his needs were decisive for the orientation of production. In addition, at this stage a solution seemed to have been found for the problem of income distribution and power relations in socioeconomic life. Free competition balanced the power of one business enterprise by that of another. In their competitive struggle these powers neutralized each other to such an extent that in the end the large mass of individual consumers reaped the fruits. Moreover, high corporate incomes were systematically leveled off through competition, as a consequence of which the consumers, via price reductions, experienced a constant improvement of their real income.

However, this supposedly harmonious world of deism in practice soon began to come apart at the seams. The so-called paradox of free competition appeared: competition often tends toward its own elimination. The stiffer the competition, the more the elimination of the other competitor is desired. Thus,

76. N. S. B. Gras, "Capitalism—Concepts and History," from *Bulletin of the Business Historical Society* 16 (1942), reprinted in Lane and Riemersma, eds., *Enterprise and Secular Change,* p. 76.

the process of free competition frequently resulted quite naturally in monopolistic situations. This was especially the case when, because of a steady increase in the average size of enterprises, it became more and more difficult for new entrepreneurs to start afresh in a particular branch of industry.

2. Robber baron phase

Free and unfettered competition implies "instability" with respect to the form and structure of relations among enterprises. This soon became evident in practice during the so-called *robber baron phase* of capitalist competition. During this phase, which lasted until 1880, the entrepreneurs became shrewd strategists. Like medieval robber barons they set out to surprise their competitors by means of unexpected attacks, after which they withdrew to their fortresses with the spoils. One of the most intriguing examples of this method of competition is the battle between Jim Fisk and J. P. Morgan for the control of the Albany-Susquehanna Railroad. "Morgan held one end of the line in his own hands, and the other terminal was a Fisk stronghold." Like their feudal predecessors, they decided to settle the dispute with a fight "by each side mounting a locomotive on its end of the track and running the two engines, like gigantic toys, into one another."[77]

This period of cutthroat competition is still covered by a veil of rugged romanticism. Competition was a matter of daring and impudence, as well as unbelievable swindle and deadly combat. This style of competition, especially as found in the United States, still reveals distinct characteristics of the romantic "cult of energy" which belonged to the era preceding the victory of the "new objectivity." However, the "new objectivity" soon took over, even in the area of economic life.

3. Voluntary cooperation

As a result of the fact that in certain branches of business increasingly fewer competitors survived, businessmen began to realize that more profit and certainty could be attained through mutual cooperation and agreement than by means of surprise tactics and cutthroat competition. Thus the third phase of competition emerged—that of *voluntary cooperation*. Concentration in business increased; numerous trusts and cartels were formed.

Around 1900 the situation had changed to such an extent

77. Heilbroner, *Worldly Philosophers*, p. 194.

that, according to data provided by J. S. Bain, the 300 largest corporations in the United States directly affected four-fifths of the nation's important branches of industry.[78] At that time it was said that American citizens were born for the benefit of the milk trust and died for the benefit of the trust of undertakers. Governments also began to realize that uncontrolled free competition did not always lead to the most desirable results. Thus, from 1880 onwards an extensive antitrust legislation, as was found especially in the United States, accompanied the growing cooperation and collaboration in industrial life as systematically as possible. However, the effects of this legislation were limited. It did not accomplish the elimination or drastic reduction of power concentration which had taken place across the board in industrial life. Nevertheless, the gradual introduction of a certain degree of *stability* in the trend toward concentration was a notable achievement of the first half of the twentieth century. This marked the fourth phase, which lasted approximately until the second world war.[79]

4. Oligopoly, innovation, and advertising

Competition in branches of industry in which a few large corporations control at least half of the total production is essentially different from competition in branches in which production is distributed more or less equally over a large number of corporations. In the latter situation intense price competition can easily occur. However, in the former—the so-called *oligopoly* situation, in which the number of producers is small—such competition is an exception. Industries within such a branch keep close track of each other's prices. If one tries to increase its market share by a sudden price reduction, its competitors usually follow suit immediately. As a result, the intended increased profit from such a reduction is largely nullified. The initiator is forced to be satisfied with the original market share. Having learned from these mistakes, the leader will in the future think twice before starting another price war. It is much wiser and more profitable in the long run to accept price stability and, upon the signal of the so-called price leader in the particular

---

78. Quoted by Heilbroner, *Making of Economic Society,* p. 110.

79. Today we live in a phase which is characterized again by increased concentration. See our discussion under "Cooperation and identification," pp. 105ff.

branch of industry, to join in price increases of the branch as a whole.

As capitalism continues to persist and the oligopoly form becomes entrenched, price competition becomes less weighty. This is quite a different picture from what Adam Smith could have imagined! But this does not mean that the competitive struggle itself is abandoned. It is continued with equal intensity in two different areas, that is, *technology* and *consumer tastes*.

Technological competition is the attempt to get ahead via new techniques of production and organization, and via new products or new versions of existing products. If an industry advances in one of these areas, it may increase its market share. This type of competition fits perfectly in the total pattern of a progressive economy in which economic expansion and technological innovation are firmly tied together. Moreover, technological innovation is an excellent sign of adaptation in the struggle for the survival of the fittest in the process of social evolution.

Influencing consumer tastes is the second new type of competition. In some ways it is even more interesting since it represents an all-out effort to change the tastes or preferences of consumers with respect to a particular product by means of sales and advertising techniques. An industry which is able to persuade a body of consumers to buy its product faithfully has acquired a secure foundation for survival and continuity.

The rise of this type of competition is not, of course, an isolated phenomenon. It is related to the expansion of scale which requires ever greater investments. Investment risks are considerably reduced by consumer dependability. Furthermore, this "planning of consumer demand" becomes all the more urgent as the consumer acquires a higher income and gains in so-called discretionary purchasing power. The higher the income, the less stable the choice of products. It is dangerous to rely entirely on the fickle nature of the consumer when building one's industry. There must be additional certainty that he will indeed continue to buy the products manufactured by the particular industry. For that reason his tastes must be modified consistently.

This attempt at the manipulation of consumer tastes by means of advertising should be seen in a still larger context. Earlier we spoke of the internalization of technology and management. We can now add consumer tastes, which are also being internalized, as far as is possible, in the planning of industry. They are therefore made a part of the survival system of the corporation. There is definitely a parallel with respect to the changing role of technology and management. At the beginning of the industrial revolution the consumer was sovereign, like the entrepreneur. But as the process of human-directed progress was transformed into a process of predetermined economic evolution, the consumer lost a great deal of his early sovereignty. Now, to a great extent, industry—instead of the consumer—decides what products should be available in society and what "needs" should be met. "Progress and order"—Comte's motto—also aptly describes the new relationship between industry and the consumer. *Progress* in production demands a planned *ordering* of the manner of consumption. The content of consumption can no longer be solely a matter of free choice. Instead, according to the laws of social evolution, consumption—as a malleable, dependent entity—must be adjusted to the existing system of economic progress.

CHANGES IN GOVERNMENT-INDUSTRY RELATIONS

A historical sketch of the relationship between government and industrial life from the beginning of the industrial revolution usually starts with a description of the shifts in sociopolitical *powers* and *convictions* in the nineteenth and twentieth centuries. This often serves as the background for an explanation of the increasing government intervention in the economic process. Such an approach certainly has its merits. In the area of social legislation and social welfare in particular, the influence of different political conceptions and relationships of power has been decisive. As examples of this we can point to the rise of revisionist socialism, the emergence of reform movements in conservative parties, and the formation of social consciousness in the Roman Catholic Church and Protestant churches during the nineteenth century.[80] An illustration of the latter is the *Réveil* movement which started in Switzerland around 1820 and spread to various Protestant churches on the European continent, and in the second half of the nineteenth century helped foster the

80. Cf. Michael F. Fogarty, *Christian Democracy in Western Europe: 1820– 1953* (London: Routledge & Kegan Paul, 1957).

rise of a Christian social and political movement.[81] Together with the start of active labor movements—in England, for instance, the so-called coalition prohibition against workers was abolished in 1824—the climate was prepared for the realization of a concrete social policy, especially on the European continent.

1. A structural shift: from enemy to friend

That kind of historical sketch at best reveals only a half-truth. The change in the relation between government and industry during the nineteenth and twentieth centuries was of such a radical character that it cannot possibly be accounted for merely on the basis of an increasing desire for government intervention. During this period the very *structure* of this relation changed. Therefore, the causes for the intensive increase in government intervention can hardly be explained in terms of typical political circumstances. This intervention usually was a result of pure necessity; it was related to structural developments taking place within economic life itself.

This interpretation can be illustrated readily by the structural change in the role which the government assumes as soon as the scale of production in industry is substantially enlarged. As we have seen above, because of this expansion in scale, competition between industries in several branches ended in oligopolistic concentration of power and conspiracies against the public. At that point the government often interfered and, especially in the United States, introduced extensive antitrust legislation.

The most important motive for this more intensive government interference is not to be found in the rise of a totally different political outlook which renounced the ideal of free and full competition. To the contrary, most politicians of that time still adhered closely to the principle enunciated by John Stuart Mill: "Laisser-faire ... should be the general practice; every departure from it, unless required by some great good, is a certain evil."[82] However, it was precisely because they adhered

81. Cf. M. Elisabeth Kluit, *Het Protestantse Réveil in Nederland en daarbuiten: 1815–1865* [The Protestant Revival in the Netherlands and Western Europe: 1815–1865] (Amsterdam: Paris, 1970). Guillaume Groen van Prinsterer was one of the major links between this spiritual *Réveil* and the political developments in Holland. See Part One, note 91.

82. John Stuart Mill, *Principles of Political Economy* (1848), 2 vols. (Harmondsworth: Penguin Books, 1970), vol. 1, p. 314.

to this principle that interference was a must. The market economy itself and the continuance of free competition were threatened by scale expansion and power concentration. If left to itself, the process of competition might have resulted in self-destruction. Therefore the government, *for the sake of the continuation of the "free" market economy,* had to interfere.

This brief account illustrates the change in nature of the relationship between government and industry around the turn of the century. This new type of government intervention was not merely corrective; it was foundational and system-supporting. To clarify this, let us use the image of two circles—one for the government, the other for industrial life—each of which represents its respective sphere of influence. At the beginning of the industrial revolution, the two circles barely touched one another. That was the time of unspoiled *laissez-faire,* when the government's task was limited to the protection of the formal civil rights of the participants in economic life, especially of their private property and freedom of contract. This was followed by a phase in which both circles partially overlapped one another. Social legislation was introduced to correct some of the unpleasant consequences of industrialization in the work and life of the laborers and their families. However, beginning with the period of antitrust legislation, the circle of the government partly shifted below that of the industrial sphere. If this sphere was left completely to itself without support, free competition in industrial life would lead to disintegration and self-destruction. Its survival made government support and protection a new imperative.

Thus, from being a threat to the free market during the beginning of the industrial revolution, the government's role gradually evolved into one of a vital condition for the existence of the free market. Industrial life was as much in need of governmental care and intervention in its evolution and advance as it was in need of scientific management and innovative technology.

In other words, then, insofar as the evolutionary law of progress demands its own *system of progress* in society, even the government cannot escape the strictures of that system. Thus, the policy of the government has become one element in the magnetic pull of the technological and economic system brought into motion in society.

Perhaps an even more striking illustration of this process is the emergence of new goals of governmental economic policy during the twentieth century. These goals—such as full employment, the battle against inflation, and balance of payments—have all become quite familiar to us. They belong to a set standard package of government services in every modern western country. Again we must observe that these new government services and goals amount to much more than mere corrections of economic practice. Moreover, they are based only in a very limited way on conscious shifts in political and social convictions on the part of the citizenry and its political parties.

2. The end of laissez-faire

In order to clarify this further, we will briefly turn to the content of a booklet published in England in 1926. Its title is significant—*The End of Laissez-faire*.[83] Its author, John Maynard Keynes, was a relatively young British economist. At present he is justly famous for being the "father" of the full employment policies pursued by nearly all of the western governments today.

This publication is especially fascinating because in it Keynes looked back on the history of more than a century of modern capitalism and tried to draw up its balance sheet. Keynes was firmly convinced that, in spite of its faulty operation, capitalism still offered the best opportunities for the future. "For my part," he wrote, "I think that Capitalism, wisely managed, can probably be made more efficient for attaining economic ends than any alternative system yet in sight."[84] Since capitalism did not function perfectly, however, it had to be overhauled.

We must first discover what Keynes meant by referring to the faulty operation of capitalism. He was not really preoccupied with objections of an ethical or political nature. When he looked at capitalism in this booklet, he looked at it, as it were, with the eyes of a mechanic. He discovered that something was wrong in the "mechanism" itself, but he was certain that with a few technical adjustments it could be made to run for years to come. To use a contemporary expression, Keynes discussed the matter from the point of view of a systems analyst. He knew where the "system" of capitalism revealed its shortcomings and thus where it needed to be revised, like the mechanic who knows how to repair a machine. Hence for him the pronouncement "the end of laissez-faire" was not an emotionally-loaded political demand.

83. John Maynard Keynes, *The End of Laissez-faire* (London: The Hogarth Press, 1926).
84. *Ibid.*, pp. 52, 53.

It was a factual statement by an economic "expert" of the predicament in which capitalism gradually found itself as an adjustable *system* of progress.

In the early 1920s this predicament was marked by a large expansion in the scale of production—"the efficient units of production are large relatively to the units of consumption"[85]—by the formation of monopolies, and by high operating expenses. It was also marked by recurring depressions, unemployment, and a poor distribution of welfare. Moreover, since decisions with respect to savings on the one hand and investments on the other hand were made by different parties, Keynes argued, imbalances between savings levels and investment levels could easily arise. In such circumstances it is absurd to assume that "individuals pursuing their own interests with enlightenment in conditions of freedom always tend to promote the general interest at the same time."[86] In other words, in Keynes' time the deity of Adam Smith's invisible hand had failed to fulfill many of his lofty promises. As a representative of his own era and confronted with hard economic facts, Keynes was open to the idea that individual behavior and the public interest can at times be harmonized only by drastic revisions in the economic system itself.

In 1936 Keynes published his principal work *The General Theory of Employment, Interest and Money.*[87] At that time the industrial countries suffered more than ever before from massive unemployment, stagnating production, and acute differences in wealth. For Keynes this was not only a confirmation of his insights presented in *The End of Laissez-faire;* it also offered an immediate occasion to refine his conclusions and to provide concrete recommendations. He did this on the basis of a fundamental theoretical analysis of potential unemployment situations in a market economy.

Keynes concluded his analysis with the assertion that, as a result of a divergence in savings and investment decisions in a modern capitalist economy, situations of unemployment not only *arise very readily* but also display a tendency of prolonged and *nearly unlimited duration.* Unemployment situations, in his

85. *Ibid.,* p. 32.
86. *Ibid.,* pp. 10, 11.
87. John Maynard Keynes, *The General Theory of Employment, Interest and Money* (London: Macmillan & Co., 1936).

view, arise quite naturally as a kind of by-product of the market equilibria between savings and investments. His conclusion, therefore, is self-evident. If we want to maintain capitalism as the ordering system of our society—and Keynes wanted this— then it is inevitable that the government itself must interfere in the relationships between savings and investments. In the context of a positive employment policy, the government *itself* must make such investments so that employment opportunities are restored and the growth of welfare is revitalized.

Keynes attempted to show the indispensability of additional *protective supports* for the market economy. Left to its own devices, the free market economy via an expansion of scale not only leads to the end of competition (unless the government prevents this with its own antitrust policy), but results also in chronic unemployment (unless the government prevents this as well). For that reason, according to Keynes, the government should not hesitate to add a distinctly new policy to its program, namely, an all-out effort toward full employment, which apparently cannot be expected as a normal by-product of the existing market economy.[88]

This, in fact, also happens in actual practice. Directly confronted with the predicament that the market economy is incapable of getting itself out of the rut of chronic unemployment, the governments of western industrial countries are forced to adopt a separate and continuous policy which aims at full employment. In this way they lend support to the market economy. At the same time they become more deeply involved in economic life as a whole. To return to our earlier image, the circle representing the government now shifts even further under the one representing industrial life.

---

88. It is very revealing that in Keynes' analysis a lopsided unemployment situation is characterized as an economic *equilibrium*. This proves that Keynes had broken radically with the deistic conception of economic equilibrium as harmony. In Keynes' case economic equilibrium can easily imply social disharmony. He replaces the deistic idea of economic order—"the natural order"— by a conception of economic engineering. For him the economic order is a system that can and must be improved by certain technical interventions. He claimed this as early as 1926, as we saw before, when he said: "For my part, I think that Capitalism, *wisely managed* can probably *be made more efficient* for attaining economic ends than any alternative system yet in sight. . . ." *(The End of Laissez-faire,* pp. 52, 53; italics added.) Capitalism in Keynes' view is a mechanism that can be overhauled and needs continual professional care from economic experts.

Thus, the policy of full employment has in a certain sense come into being in a forced manner. The course of the market process imposed it on the government; it was not a decision made for political reasons. The same is true to a large extent for the other goals of contemporary government economic policy, such as the battle against inflation and the pursuit of a satisfactory external equilibrium of the economy (balance of payments). These are not the kinds of goals which a government likes to add to its policy programs. They are really a result of inadmissible gaps, defects, and disturbances in the practical functioning of every "progressive" market economy.

In conclusion, it has by now become quite clear that a large-scale market economy is not, so to speak, a plant which can grow outdoors. Instead, it appears to be a greenhouse plant which bears sufficient fruit only when it is surrounded by an artificial climate of permanent government care. This diagnosis sounds like a paradox but is true nevertheless: the protective interference of the government in the functioning of the market economy increases in order to guarantee the latter's continued existence; at the same time this market economy continuously shrinks in size precisely as a result of governmental intervention. Because this *system* of growth is based on the market economy, the government has no choice but to cooperate in providing the proper *climate* for growth. Using another analogy, the government becomes the indispensable protective wall of the spaceship Progress. This wall surrounds the whole of society and protects it against every harmful influence from outside.[89]

3. Cooperation and identification

A further development in the relationship between government and industrial life occurred in particular during and after the second world war. This phase, so to speak, moved like a new layer over the existing "corrective" and "supportive" layers of government interference. From that time onward the relations between government and industrial life became increasingly characterized by mutual *cooperation* as well as by a partial *identification* of their respective purposes.

During this period, which extends to the present day, the scale of industrial life is still expanding considerably—but not nearly as much as earlier with reference to mass production and

89. For a further discussion of this theme, see John Kenneth Galbraith, *Economics and the Public Purpose* (Boston: Houghton Mifflin Co., 1973).

the technology thereby required. The optimum in mass production had been achieved by many industries; so scale expansion had to occur in other outlets. These were found especially in the extension and spread of corporate activity in diverse areas of production and distribution on the part of a single concern. In other words, the *conglomerates* came into existence. Moreover, we are confronted with an increasing spread of production activities on the part of the same concern in diverse countries. The *multinational* corporations began to develop. Richard J. Barber, in his study *The American Corporation*,[90] which gives a lively description of industrial development toward conglomerates and multinationals, illustrates this double shift by pointing to *U.S. Rubber*. This American corporation is less than half "rubber," since most of its activities are focused on other products and services. At the same time it is less than half "U.S.," for more than half its production plants are located outside the United States. This is not an exceptional case; it is one of many.

It is obvious, of course, that at a time when industrial life—partly for reasons of self-aggrandizement, partly to distribute risk—increasingly orients itself toward a variety of countries and toward a combination of conglomerate activities,[91] its interest in what happens in the sphere of government also intensifies sharply. In this sphere decisions are made about the weal or woe of all power combinations which affect the public interest. From the other side, it is also obvious that the government, in the face of enormous tasks in the areas of defense, environment, urban renewal, and so forth, more than ever before feels the need for cooperation with industry. It needs to call on industry's know-how, research capacity, and organizational ability to solve its own problems. In this way the idea and reality of *copartnership* between government and industrial life have become commonly accepted during our lifetime, both in the United States and elsewhere. Government and industry are reciprocally interdependent; they need one another continuously. To return to our analogy, the respective circles of government and indus-

90. Richard J. Barber, *The American Corporation* (New York: Dutton & Co., 1970).

91. For example, the well-known Ogden group in the U.S.A. is simultaneously involved in banking, insurance, agribusiness, fruit plantation, hot dog sales, sales of various other consumer articles, and is at the same time one of the most important undertakers in America. Cf. Barber, *American Corporation,* especially Part I:3: *The Industrial Octopi.*

try not only touch and support each other; they gradually and profoundly interpenetrate each other in every area of economic life.

The identification of the goals of business and government increasingly fits this total picture. To a large extent this identification has already taken place, as becomes apparent from a comparison of the goals and aims of some forty years ago with those of today. In the sphere of government policy, for example, the conscious promotion of economic growth has become a normally accepted goal; it is no longer a debatable matter. A government policy oriented to economic expansion has now taken its place alongside an industrial policy directed toward the same goal. This growth mentality is partly dependent on the awareness that a government attempt to achieve full employment has little chance of succeeding without forceful economic growth. If productivity increases, forceful economic growth is imperative for everyone to remain employed. This growth mentality is also dependent on the political efforts to establish *the welfare state,* that is, to surround every citizen with an abundance of social and economic provisions from the cradle to the grave. Of course, such a welfare state—or "great society"—needs an adequate economic basis. This basis can be provided only by a continual expansion of production.

Forceful economic growth, however, is not the only goal which points to increasing identification of the aims of government and industrial life. The modern state itself has also become vitally concerned with the promotion of technology. Only a few decades ago it would have been unthinkable that a government should regard continual advance in the area of applied technology as one of its most important tasks. As a prime example of this changed attitude we can point to the area of space travel. In 1870 the government protected the man in the street; in 1970 it launched man on the moon.

4. North-south and east-west relations

International considerations also play a role in this emphasis on rapid economic growth and intensive technological progress. This is especially so in the relationship between the rich western world and the poor "third" world and in the relationship between the free world and the communist countries.

The history of the relationship between the western countries and what we now have come to call the third world has from the outset been dominated by the self-interest of the West. At the time of the Renaissance, the nations of western Europe were primarily interested in the extension of their own political power and in the acquisition of the goods produced in Asia, Africa, and the Americas. Gold was one of their prime objects. But when in the process of time the entire structure of western society became increasingly directed to the pursuit of material expansion and production, the relationship between the rich western countries and "their" colonies began to reflect that pursuit and assumed a more permanent, structural character. This structure of *economic imperialism* arose as the expression of the intense desire on the part of the western nations to have a guaranteed import of enough raw materials from their own "safe" and "dependable" colonies to maintain the uninterrupted continuity in their own economic expansion. And it should be noted carefully that this economic imperialism is still the dominant factor in the structural relationship between the western nations and the third world. This is the case even after the phase of decolonization following World War II when nearly every colonized area, in its striving for political independence, managed to shake off the colonial grip of the "free" western nations. This imperialism is present in the continued economic dependence of the third world upon the western nations. The dependence is evident in a variety of relations, such as the marketability of third-world products in the protected western markets, the function of the third world as a market for western products, the availability of sufficient capital for development in the third world, and the access of the third world to technology and managerial know-how which is largely controlled by western multinational corporations. The entire program of development aid, as promoted by the western countries themselves, is therefore quite ambivalent. On the one hand, it is doubtless an expression of genuine concern and a sincere willingness to help in the face of existing misery. But on the other hand, development aid fits excellently in the western model which requires the use of as many factors as possible—here the third world—as dependent variables serving its own system of economic expansion. The emergence of the powerful urge for economic self-reliance in the third world can therefore be viewed as a protest and defense on the part of the third world against further "internalization" efforts on the part of western capitalism. The third world increasingly recognizes that the imitation of western economic growth, sustained by development aid, is radically in conflict with its own culture. This growth demands large-scale industrialization, expresses itself in an exhibitionistic style of consumption, reduces human relations to a monetized common denominator, urbanizes an uprooted population, and impoverishes the stability and quality of familial ties in the nation. Moreover, the third world is becoming more and more conscious of the fact that its imitation of western growth patterns entails the continuation of an inescapable economic dependence upon the West and the international market dominated by the industrialized nations.

This north-south relationship is paralleled and also complicated by the east-west relationship. It is striking that here again the emphasis is increasingly placed on the necessity of economic growth and technological advance. Direct rivalry in many respects has existed between the western bloc of democratic countries and the eastern bloc of communist countries, particularly since the second world war. But it is remarkable how onesided the issues in this exchange have become. They are largely focused on the question of (1) which system shows the largest increase in the gross national product per capita and (2) which system advances most rapidly in technology—that is, in industry, arms, and space travel. It appears that the East as well as the West considers an answer to both of these questions decisive for the future. The best system is the one which can prove to the entire world that with respect to both technological and economic progress it is ahead of its opponents.

As for the communist countries, this focus should not really surprise us. Following Marx's and Lenin's line of thought, these countries are still sincerely convinced that only on the basis of a correctly organized economic substructure, which entails the inclusion of all productive forces, can the best superstructure of society be built. Only in that way can total human well-being enter the social order. Leaving China out of the picture for now because it is much more selective with respect to economic growth than Russia and its satellite states, it is emphatically clear that the emphasis on the significance of a rapid economic and technological growth is nowhere more pervasive than in the countries behind the iron curtain. Here this emphasis, as professor H. J. Lieber of the Free University in Berlin once remarked at a conference in Germany, even takes on the form of a *Vergöttlichung der Wachstumrate,* a deification of growth remedies. It should therefore not surprise us in the least that in Russia the transition from "socialism" to communism is formulated in economic terms. "Communism" will have been achieved when every form of poverty within the communist countries has been eradicated, when public transportation is available to all at no cost, and so forth.

But shouldn't the West know better? In our confrontation with communism, what do we think is the heart of western culture? Is it our ability to achieve a more rapid economic and technological expansion than the communist countries? Or is it our respect for the rights and dignity and freedom of human personality? By concentrating all our efforts on accomplishing the former, the capitalist western world can perhaps win this race. But in doing so it stands to lose its own distinctive value and dignity as a culture. Against the force of economic and technological expansion, freedom and justice do not have a single chance of survival. They have become like cut flowers which, separated from their roots, will soon wither.[92] The West might win this race but in the process lose its soul.

CONCLUSION: TRACING PARALLEL TRENDS

We have traced the development of capitalism since 1850 within three areas: the internal structure of the enterprise, competition among enterprises, and the relationship between industrial life and the government. In the latter context we discussed very briefly the development in relations between East and West. Does this overview of the development of capitalism confirm our basic hypothesis, that is, that faith in progress is the key factor which has given shape to the western social order in all its spheres?

1. Adjustment to social evolution

In our search for an answer to this question we are struck by two developments which run closely parallel in each of the areas described above. The *first parallel development* in each of the sectors concerns a diminution of individual sovereignty and an increasing adaptation to the demands of the evolution of progress. At first the industrial enterprise was little more than an extension of the will of the individual entrepreneur and investors.

92. W. A. Visser 't Hooft, "Moet het Westen worden verdedigd?" [Must the West be Defended?], *Wending*, 1956.

However, within a few decades it grew into an independent system of progress which required—to maintain its self-sufficiency—continuity in *self-management,* a reliable supply of *capital* (the investor's participation and authority were minimized), and constantly improved *technology* (research became a standard department in industry). Hence, we spoke of a process of internalization. At the same time, the enterprise itself could maintain its continuity only by constantly adapting to the given social, economic, and technological progress in society as a whole. An industry which is not innovative and is unable to increase its sales is soon mercilessly eliminated. In short, the enterprise itself as a distinct entity demands its own management, technology, and capital; but in turn it has become a dependent factor, an instrument of the underlying system of progress at work within society as a whole.

In the area of competition we encounter a similar development. In the beginning the entrepreneur was sovereign. As a "robber baron" he tried to impose his will on his competitors. But gradually competitive relations shifted toward the situation of oligopoly, which forced industries to obtain power by means of innovative technology and of advertising. The latter form of competition, as we saw, is particularly interesting because it pulls consumer preferences within reach of industrial planning. Also, the consumer has to sacrifice at least a part of his former almost unlimited sovereignty so that society as a whole can be assured of secure and expanding markets.

However, most marked in all this is the *government's* surrender of part of its sovereignty and its adaptation to the system of progress. Time and again it has to support the market economy to save it from disintegration and destruction. It does this by means of its policy relating to competition and by combating unemployment and inflation. As a result of this forced accommodation to the demands of social evolution, the government's dependency grows, and the road is paved toward increasing identification of government purposes with those of industrial life. At first only the market economy exists in a situation of dependence; that is, it constantly requires the support and protection of the government. But then the government itself becomes increasingly dependent on the market economy: the government cannot realize the goals of its own policies without economic growth which in turn comes about only via the market economy. In this way the goals of both government and industry become ever more identical in a predicament of mutual dependence on a societal system which is entirely geared to guaranteed progress.

2. Narrowing of cultural perspective

In addition to this increase in dependence and adaptation on the part of persons and institutions within society, we can detect a *second parallel development* in the course described above, namely, a persistent narrowing of human relations and purposes to technical and economic achievements as ends in themselves. To begin with, we encounter this in the internal changes in industrial life. The goals of the enterprise shift from short-term profit to continuity in growth as such and to primacy of technical innovations. Secondly, an analogous change occurs in competition, with respect to both the production of ever new products and the control of consumer preferences, both of which serve to enlarge material growth. And finally, we notice a shift in purposes of government policy from *Rechtsstaat* (law-state) to welfare state, and an accompanying shift from independence to a high degree of governmental involvement in the day-by-day routine of technical invention and innovation. Questions as to the ultimate goal and final destiny of this economic and technological progress are seldom—if ever—raised. Whether or not human happiness is served is a minor issue, discussed only as an afterthought. A century ago Groen van Prinsterer commented on this shift in outlook when, in the context of personal responsibility in a changing society, he recalled that Luther in his time had said, *"I* cannot do otherwise" while today it is said *"It* cannot be otherwise."[93]

These parallel and simultaneous developments in different sectors of society indeed point to the penetrating impact of a single cultural force. In this entire evolution of western society the presence of faith in progress is tangible and observable even at a distance. It is a faith in the beneficial social effects of daily, concrete economic and technological advance, even if this demands continual adaptation and inescapable adjustment on the part of all members of society.

Here I am reminded of a book by Andrew Carnegie, first published in 1900, with the challenging title *The Gospel of Wealth.*

---

93. Guillaume Groen van Prinsterer, *Unbelief and Revolution: Lectures VIII and IX* (Amsterdam: The Groen van Prinsterer Fund, 1975), p. 2, n. 2.

This book contains a call to such accommodation and obedience. The author exalts "our wonderful material development, which brings improved conditions in its train," and he speaks of the law of competition "as being not only beneficial, but essential to the future progress of the race." Then he concludes his eulogy with the sermonic words: "Such, in my opinion is the true gospel concerning wealth, obedience to which is destined some day to solve the problem of the rich and the poor, and to bring 'Peace on earth, among men good will'."[94]

Western man has learned to accept this obedience to the law of modern progress as a matter of course. This requires persistent efforts toward greater material gain and more advanced technology in all man's social functions, relations, and decisions—as consumer, producer, laborer, voter, and trade unionist. Through this very obedience he has obviously called forth and consolidated a society which in all its parts and institutions has oriented itself to these limited goals.

94. Andrew Carnegie, *The Gospel of Wealth and Other Timely Essays* (Cambridge, Mass.: Harvard University Press, 1962), pp. 16, 16–17, and 29 respectively. Compare in this context also the cutting observations by Burckhardt in his letter to Von Preen dated July 2, 1871: "In the meantime, the idea of the natural goodness of man had turned, among the intelligent strata of Europe, into the idea of progress, i.e. undisturbed money-making and modern comforts, with philanthropy as a sop to conscience." Jakob Christoph Burckhardt, *The Letters of Jacob Burckhardt,* trans. Alexander Dru (London: Routledge & Kegan Paul, 1955), pp. 147, 148.

10. *Progress, Political Parties, and the Labor Movement*

At least one question remains which we must still answer in the context of this discussion: what has been the role of the political parties and the labor movement in the development of capitalism since 1850? We have seen how the governments in the western democracies have, almost inevitably, become increasingly involved in economic life. At the same time we are fully aware of the fact that in these same democracies various political parties and currents have been continuously active, each of which has tried to force the "ship of state" into its own course. Moreover, the labor movement, in its broader social concerns, attempted to influence not only industrial life but also the formation of government policy. How then is it possible that in a calculation of the final outcome we encounter so little of its direct impact on the shaping of society? Certain influences from this side can, of course, be detected. But these are considerably less than one would expect in view of the intense differences in political conviction and social position. In this connection it is noteworthy that the differences with respect to the social systems within the diverse western countries are relatively minor, even though these countries have been guided by very divergent governmental regimes and coalitions over a period of time.

LIBERALISM AND SOCIALISM

With reference to the intense differences in political outlook, we are immediately confronted with the important distinction between liberalism and socialism. This distinction applies primarily to politics, but has also—especially in western Europe—

profoundly influenced the character and composition of the social organizations of employers and employees.

What is the nature of this contrast between liberalism and socialism? For the origins of *liberalism,* we should recall the link between deism and the resultant conception of the state. In this view, it is precisely by abstaining from direct interference in economic life that the state serves the natural and providential development of society. The liberal principle of justice is the conception of relative natural law, which requires the state to protect rights and civil liberties based on private property. In contrast, *orthodox socialism* has the tendency to regard the state as an instrument of exploitation, an extension of the ruling class. For that reason it aims at the elimination of the state. The principle of justice of original socialism is the conception of absolute natural law, which can be realized only on the basis of a return to communal property. Hence, absolute natural law is characterized by the absence of class distinctions and by a community of people which renders to each in accordance with his or her economic need.

The differences are indeed striking. Liberalism gives primacy to the individual; socialism to the community. Liberalism defends the natural right of the status quo; socialism looks ahead to the realization of absolute natural law. Liberalism emphasizes the protection of civil rights, especially those of property; socialism proclaims the vision of the liberation and exodus of humankind out of every situation of economic coercion. In spite of these differences, however, we are struck by the common moorings of both sociopolitical movements. Whether primacy is given to the individual or the community, in either case it is given to autonomous man who—alone or in community with others—in a sovereign way determines his own destiny. Furthermore, in either case the modern conception of natural law is basic. This conception looks upon human happiness as a result of man's interaction with nature, and regards certain institutional forms of property—private property or communal property—of decisive significance for the weal or woe of society as a whole. Moreover, the distinction between the liberal stress on civil rights and the socialist emphasis on economic welfare is not quite as pronounced as it seems. Both the maintenance of civil rights by liberalism and the acquisition of economic welfare by socialism point to the potential for and the necessity of the same unhampered technological and economic progress.

Thus it is not very surprising that liberalism and socialism grew ever closer together with respect to their practical policy. Socialism became revisionist socialism. It accepted an advance "payment," as it were, on the advent of a future and better society, and for that reason today attempts to realize a measure of economic equality for all. The modern socialist-oriented labor movement, in the first place, fights for higher wages; and, even though on paper the radical reform of society is highly praised, for this purpose it seldom resorts to its most important weapon—strikes. During the same period liberalism gradually developed into neo-liberalism which accepts the fact that a successful market economy needs the continual care and sustenance of a definite government policy with respect to social legislation, antitrust legislation, and unemployment. The economist Abba P. Lerner formulated what happened during and as a result of this development of liberalism and socialism as follows:

> So close indeed is the *rapprochement* between the two that the differences are to be sought outside of the institutional order that is advocated by both the pragmatic collectivist and the liberal capitalist. The former suggests that collective organization be applied except where competitive enterprise works better in the social interest. The latter favors the restoration of free competition wherever possible and would permit collective organization when for technical reasons this should prove impossible. Both come to the same thing.[95]

To say that both come to the same thing is to claim too much. But apart from that Lerner's comments are undeniably correct and significant.

In view of this it is quite easy to explain why we encounter so little of a direct shaping influence of modern liberalism and modern socialism on the final societal structure of capitalism. The struggle between liberalism and socialism has been narrowed down to the question of *who* is entitled to the fruits of technological-economic progress and *from whom* they should be derived. Meaning, manner, and tempo of this progress are hardly ever discussed. Only questions with regard to the *distribution* of income, welfare, knowledge, and economic power still mark the

95. Abba P. Lerner, *The Economics of Control* (New York: Macmillan, 1944), p. 4.

differences between these two sociopolitical movements, rather than questions as to the nature, orientation, and destination of welfare, knowledge, and power.

ABSENCE OF CHRISTIAN DIRECTION

Unfortunately, it must be added that with respect to these matters Christian political parties and the Christian labor movement—both of which were common phenomena in Europe during the last century[96]—often hardly differed from liberal and socialist parties and labor organizations. Of course, certain differences of approach and intent existed. For instance, the Christian social movement in the Netherlands was always of the opinion that an enterprise was to be considered neither an object of private property nor an object of pure class struggle; instead, it looked upon an industrial unit as a cooperative work community of co-responsible people. We can also point to Abraham Kuyper's challenging view with respect to the relation between government and industrial life. Influenced by the Reformation, he connected this relation with the specific calling to man in the respective social spheres which had to prevent the subjection of the state to industrial life as much as the subjection of industrial life to the state. This is the principle of sphere sovereignty or sphere responsibility.[97] However, it would be incorrect to claim that *in dealing with progress* Christian political and social organizations, with respect to their practical policy, have displayed a style of their own, or that, in distinction from other such organizations, they occupied themselves intensively with the question of the *direction* of progress. Synthesis with the entire development of society is the mark of modern Christendom. For this reason both Christians and humanists are responsible for the presence of good and evil in the unfolding of the western social order.

96. Cf. Fogarty, *Christian Democracy in Western Europe.*
97. Abraham Kuyper, *Christianity and the Class Struggle* (Grand Rapids, Mich: Piet Hein, 1950); and F. VandenBerg, *Abraham Kuyper* (St. Catharines, Ontario: Paideia Press, 1978). Cf. L. Kalsbeek, *Contours of a Christian Philosophy* (Toronto: Wedge Publishing Foundation, 1975), pp. 91f.

PART THREE: DISAPPOINTMENTS OF PROGRESS

11. *The Vulnerability of Progress: Introduction*

"Progress itself goes on progressing; we can no longer stop it or turn it around."[1] This statement by the contemporary philosopher Karl Löwith reveals quite a different view of human progress from that held during the Enlightenment. At that time progress was regarded as a confirmation of the sovereignty of man who in an autonomous process of creative reflection and action subjected nature to himself. Löwith, however, expresses the notion that man has been forced to abdicate his sovereignty once and for all. Progress itself apparently has assumed sovereignty and has subordinated man to itself. Martin Buber expressed similar feelings in *I and Thou,* where we read:

> the stokers still pile up coal, but the leaders merely *seem* to rule the racing engines. And in this instant while you speak, you can hear as well as I how the machinery of the economy is beginning to hum in an unwonted manner; the overseers give you a superior smile, but death lurks in their hearts. They tell you that they have adjusted the apparatus to modern conditions; but you notice that henceforth they can only adjust themselves to the apparatus, as long as that permits it.[2]

Instead of being the creator of progress man has increasingly become its servant.

This was evident even in our discussion in Part Two. Eco-

1. Karl Löwith, *Nature, History, and Existentialism and Other Essays in the Philosophy of History* (Evanston, Ill.: Northwestern University Press, 1966), chapter 9: "Fate of Progress," p. 160.
2. Martin Buber, *I and Thou* (New York: Charles Scribner's Sons, 1970), p. 97.

nomic and technological progress indeed began as a process of sovereign determination by the human will. But it soon appeared that progress itself, in order to continue, was in constant need of managerial services, of technological innovation, of a planned market, and of government support. The law of industrial evolution gradually held all of society in its sway. In this way a societal system unfolded which is permanently in the service of progress, comparable with the organism of a beehive unfolding around the queen bee who is constantly and wholly busy with the production of eggs.

Can a societal system in which everything is directed to uninterrupted progress indeed continue to exist? That question must be asked because, with respect to at least three points, such a "system of progress" appears to be distinctly vulnerable.

This is true first of all for the *environment* in which economic and technological expansion takes place and which in the final analysis furnishes the material possibilities for such expansion. We can employ an analogy here: a spaceship may be equipped with the most reliable rocket engines and its internal system may function perfectly, but to make its journey it needs adequate fuel which has its source outside of the spaceship. It is not a self-sufficient system. In one way or another it puts a strain on its environment. With respect to our larger problem we must ask: can the finite earth upon which we live tolerate in the long run the strain of our unbridled progress?

Secondly, the functioning of the *system itself* is vulnerable. We noted earlier that the market economy required government support; at times it was even in need of fundamental revision. Still, the economy in most countries does not function smoothly at all. To the contrary, certain problems of economic policy, such as unemployment and inflation, now seem quite unsolvable.

Last but not least, the vulnerability applies to *men and women,* the passengers who travel the road of progress. Will they always be prepared to play the role assigned to them? Will not the adaptation this requires ultimately be unbearable?

In these three forms of vulnerability we encounter almost all the problems posited in the Introduction as challenges to our present-day western culture. We will discuss them successively in the next three sections, and will discover that these problems are not isolated but indeed are rooted largely in a common nurturing soil.

12. *The Vulnerability of the Environment*

Concern for the earth's "tolerance" has grown markedly in recent years. This is apparent from the extensive literature about pollution of soil, water, and air, and about the extinction of many kinds of plants and animals. Similar concern is expressed regarding the adequacy of raw materials and energy and the availability of cultivated soil sufficient to feed a growing world population.

The occasion for this concern, at least in part, was the rapid increase of production and welfare in the rich countries. For instance, it appears that the average yearly per capita consumption of energy in the United States is about fifty times higher than it is in India and three times the consumption per person in western Europe. The consumption of raw materials and the level of pollution of the environment in the West is thirty to fifty times higher than in the developing world. While in 1950 the total consumption of primary raw materials in the United States was two billion tons, in 1972 it had increased to four billion tons, amounting to twenty tons per capita each year. According to W. Uytenbogaardt, professor of geography at the Free University of Amsterdam,

> It has been calculated that in the first forty years of this century more minerals were used than in all previous centuries combined. Further, that the total use of minerals after the second world war has meanwhile surpassed the total of all previous use. Finally, that the United States by itself has consumed more raw materials,

121

including fuel, in the past thirty years than the entire world before that.[3]

From 1946 to 1971 the gross national product (GNP) of the United States increased by 126%. At the same time the pollution of the environment increased by a staggering 1000%. According to Barry Commoner, the average American's

> food is now grown on less land with much more fertilizer and pesticides than before; his clothes are more likely to be made of synthetic fibers than of cotton or wool; he launders with synthetic detergents rather than soap; he lives and works in buildings that depend more heavily on aluminum, concrete, and plastic than on steel and lumber; the goods he uses are increasingly shipped by truck rather than rail; he drinks beer out of nonreturnable bottles or cans rather than out of returnable bottles or at the tavern bar. ... He also drives about twice as far as he did in 1946, in a heavier car, on synthetic rather than natural rubber tires, using more gasoline per mile, containing more tetraethyl lead. ...[4]

Only 20% of the world's population reside in the rich, noncommunist countries of the world, but their share in total world consumption amounts to no less than 65%.

A growth percentage of only 3½% of the gross national product in the rich countries doubles their GNP in a period of twenty years and exhausts the still available raw materials, energy, space, and environment at least in the same proportion. In view of these figures it is quite proper, indeed imperative, to ask whether the spaceship of progressive economic technological expansion could explode because of certain external limits. During the Romantic period it was customary to paint ruins of stately castles of a former era overgrown with wild nature as a sign that human civilization was powerless in the face of the eternal strength and dignity of nature. In our own time, however, the paintings depict the ruins of factories and highways lost in a landscape which itself has also been surrendered to total destruction.

This image of expansion which collapses because of external *physical* limits is not related only to an approaching exhaus-

---

3. W. Uytenbogaardt, "De grondstoffenverdeling in de wereld als mogelijke oorzaak van konflikten" [The Distribution of Raw Materials in the World as a Possible Source of Conflicts], *Transactie,* February 1973.
4. Barry Commoner, *The Closing Circle* (New York: Alfred A. Knopf, 1971), p. 145.

tion of raw materials and energy, and to the threat to the world's ecosystem via pollution of its weakest links, such as ocean environments and the atmosphere; it is related equally to *political* limits. In fact, these limits will quite likely play a more incisive role than the external physical limits.

Uytenbogaardt has pointed out that the countries which began the second world war—Germany, Italy, and Japan—were motivated partly by the assumption that they were the "have-nots" in the area of raw materials and energy. They aimed at obtaining more *Lebensraum* (living space) for themselves and therefore attacked other countries. However, according to Uytenbogaardt, the "have-nots" of our time are predominantly the *rich* western countries. That is the case not because their own production of raw materials and energy is so low but because their demand for these has become so great that they can no longer fill it from their own sources. Today the United States is forced to import at least one third of all its raw materials. In other words, the rich western countries need the entire world in order to continue their own economic expansion. Just like the have-nots of the second world war, they will probably be prepared to take forceful action if raw materials and energy are not readily made available to them. However, will this be tolerated with impunity by these other countries, some of which possess nuclear weapons—that monstrous product of modern technology?[5]

The paradox is even more evident when we consider the element of power associated with it. The rich western countries have enormous technological and economic power. They are first both in scientific ability and in the strength of their defense. However, it is precisely as a result of this progress that they have become more and more vulnerable. Their capacity is phenomenal, but they cannot accomplish anything without a guaranteed supply of raw materials and energy. This *powerlessness* of the industrially advanced nations may well determine the political future of the world more decisively than their *power* has done until now.

---

5. Cf. W. Uytenbogaardt, "De grondstoffenverdeling in de wereld als mogelijke oorzaak van konflikten."

LIMITS AS CHALLENGE

We have seen that capitalism is an extremely *flexible* system of progress. Progress itself is not so flexible, for it is an indispensable and firmly accepted *presupposition*. But in relation to that given presupposition, capitalism has until now displayed an amazing adaptability. It was capable of internalizing technology for its own continuity, of acquiring government suppport for its own protection, and of incorporating consumer preferences— at least partially—within the system of progress. For that reason it is not surprising that, seen from the point of view of the system, this new confrontation with limits is regarded as a challenge to be solved directly within the contours of the system itself.

Such a solution is not necessarily impossible. At least two trumps can be played which give it a good chance. The first trump is mobilization of *technological ability* to avoid or defer the limits in the areas of energy, raw materials, and environment. With respect to pollution, better purification techniques can be developed. As to scarcity of raw materials, exploration and exploitation methods can be improved or new methods can be devised. Finally, alternative energy sources can be tapped, varying from atomic energy to solar energy or even tidal energy. On the surface there seems to be no limit which cannot be removed or at least avoided by means of our advancements in technology.

The second trump is the *price mechanism* of the market economy which can be used directly as a conservation policy with respect to environment, raw materials, and energy. In part this happens spontaneously, for when the demand for raw materials, energy, and so forth is greater than the supply, their price goes up. Rising prices in turn cause a decline in demand. With reference to the environment a similar effect can be obtained by introducing levies and fines for those not complying with pollution regulations.

Thus with respect to both *supply* (by improved techniques and applied research) and *demand* (by the brake effect of the price mechanism), the "solutions" to this new challenge appear to be readily available. And both "solutions" fit perfectly *within* the existing system of progress.

However, both trumps can be countered with weighty arguments. As to the first trump, used to avoid or defer the approaching limits, we face the problem of the *interdependence* of those limits. For instance, when natural raw materials are replaced by synthetic raw materials, we shift to a manufacturing process involving considerable environmental pollution and usually energy consumption. Furthermore, when the depth levels of ore mining increase, we are again faced with new energy and environmental problems. Moreover, with respect to alternative energy sources, it is clear that the exploitation of nuclear energy is accompanied by harmful effects on the environment because of radioactive rays and thermal pollution. Again, the production of solar energy takes a great deal of space, which is scarce in densely populated areas. Finally, purification of a polluted environment usually consumes energy and raw materials.

One could compare all of this to life in a room with mutually connected partitions. When you move one partition further away, the other partitions automatically come closer. Of course, this does not mean that every move of one of the partitions causes an equal or greater loss of space for the others. Recycling of materials, for instance, can make such a considerable contribution to existing raw materials and the environment that possible energy loss can be almost disregarded. In other words, to use the terminology of the modern "game theory," it is not necessarily a matter of a zero-sum game. The gains can be greater than the losses. This interdependence of the limits does teach us, however, that the image of near *infinite* room for material expansion can hold only for persons with a blind faith in technology. In the final analysis man will not be able to escape natural limits, including those of space. He can only try to defer a fatal collision with one of those limits as long as possible. But this is not a definitive solution.

We can conclude, then, that modern man is indeed changing from a *God-fearing* being to a *time-fearing* being. This is how F. L. Polak describes what is now taking place.[6] The future seems to have doom in store for us rather than paradise.

The second trump—the price mechanism of the market economy—also offers little comfort. This is due, in the first place, to the fact that prices of raw materials and energy appear to be only partially sensitive to future depletion. The time span

6. Fred L. Polak, *De toekomst is verleden tijd,* 2 vols. (Zeist, the Netherlands: W. de Haan, 1958) English translation by Elise Boulding, *The Image of the Future,* 2 vols. (Leyden: Sijthoff; New York: Oceana Publications, 1961) vol. 2, p. 108.

of speculative price changes hardly exceeds five years, according to the investigations of Jan Tinbergen, Nobel prize winner in economics. The current prices of raw materials which might be exhausted in ten to twenty years often reflect little if anything of this possible depletion. Moreover, every price increase has two sides: increased costs for the consumer and increased income for the producer. Therefore, higher prices for raw materials and energy involve not only higher costs but also higher revenues. Thus, they result in higher incomes for persons and countries producing them. When, in turn, these higher incomes lead to increased expenditures, the original brake effect of the price increases on consumption is countered by these new stimuli on total world consumption.

Even more important than the two preceding counterarguments is the response from the population of the western countries to all these price increases. Is it realistic to assume that they will, without complaint, accept the resultant slackening or cessation in the growth of their own real consumption? Galbraith correctly observes: "That social progress is identical with a rising standard of living has the aspect of a faith."[7] As long as this disposition dominates, every price increase will be followed by a demand for compensating income and wage increases. As long as the battle against material growth occasions this type of response, it is an illusion to expect any real reduction in the consumption of raw materials and energy by means of the price mechanism. The battle seems lost even before it is begun.

This should not surprise us, though, for it is rather foolish to expect a *mechanism* to permanently check and channel the impulse of human desire, will, and faith. This expectation becomes even more paradoxical when we consider that the price mechanism—the word *mechanism* in this context is very significant—has until now been an instrument toward progress, no less than has technology and the role of the government. It has become one of the elements of the social system which progress demands as its environment. In that capacity it has assumed the task of immediately translating all claims for a higher standard of living into concomitant price and cost increases. In this way the price mechanism profoundly affects society. This particular function can hardly be eliminated without affecting the essential

7. John Kenneth Galbraith, *The New Industrial State* (New York: New American Library, 1968), p. 174.

core of the price mechanism itself. In other words, as long as the price system continues to function as a mechanism, part of its very nature will be to serve material progress, no matter how much society as a whole might be endangered by that service. Therefore, if an attempt would nonetheless be made to use it as a check against the excesses of material growth, it might behave like a dog confused by utterly conflicting orders.

THE INPUT OF THE CLUB OF ROME

In the reports issued by The Club of Rome[8] a fascinating effort has been made to examine the tension between growth in production and population in diverse parts of the world on the one hand, and existing supplies of raw materials and energy and limits of space and environment on the other hand. It is correctly assumed that the solution to these problems cannot be found via the free market mechanism but that we must look in an entirely different direction. The first report suggests a halt in the growth of production in the rich countries and a limit in family size of a maximum of two children. Both suggestions result from a computer model which supposedly indicates that problems of environment, raw materials, and energy for global society as a whole can become controllable in the future, and that a massive mortality rate due to starvation can be avoided. The second report adds that massive financial aid from rich countries to poor countries is an indispensable condition in accomplishing this aim, perhaps even more than a standstill in the growth rate of western material production.

Scientific analyses such as these can be greatly helpful in understanding the extent of the problematics. However, these reports do not touch upon the essential core of the issue. In fact, the manner in which the new global problems are dealt with fits in with the very climate of thought which produced these problems and which allowed them to reach such enormous proportions. This is especially the case with the first report.

For example, economic and population questions are approached in terms of a so-called dynamic world model, even consisting, in the second report, of various geographically de-

8. First report: Dennis L. Meadows *et al., The Limits to Growth* (New York: New American Library, 1972); second report: Mihajlo Mesarović and Eduard Pestel, *Mankind at the Turning Point* (New York: Dutton, 1974).

limited subsystems. In this mathematical context the problem raised is whether and to what extent the entire world system is threatened by possible destruction. In this world model present trends of economic growth and population are projected into the future and evaluated with respect to the economic and ecological capacity of the earth. One should not, of course, argue against this as a scientific method. However, it becomes a different matter when the compilers of the reports also attempt to suggest concrete *solutions* by means of the same method. These solutions aim at preventing a clash between economic and population expansion on the one hand and the economic and ecological capacity of the earth on the other hand.

Of course, the solutions are proposed in a scientifically modest manner. From computer calculations it *appears* that the fatal clash can be avoided—or in any case postponed—if an attempt is made toward zero growth in production and population. However, we are confronted here with a suggestion of an *ethical* nature, for it implicitly expresses an opinion about desirable human conduct. But the ethics implied in this suggestion is clearly an ethics of system maintenance and system survival. Human beings can remain quite as they are, provided they are prepared from now on to follow these concrete directions for the sake of their own survival. This is an ethics derived from a scientific model—an ethics based on goals rather than on principles or starting points. Such guidelines for human behavior are not derived from universally valid norms; rather, they result from the desire to prevent an unwanted ultimate condition. From that undesirable condition these guidelines are "calculated" back into the present so that we can incorporate them into our immediate personal conduct. In this context the title of the second part of the public relations film which The Club of Rome produced about its first report is typical: *Let our goal be our new beginning!*

But has anything of substance changed if an ethics of progress has merely been transformed into an ethics of survival? This question is decisive because in both types of ethics it is a *system*—either of progress or of survival—that provides the norms for good and evil. Moreover, the guidelines for human behavior which this system ethics produces are offered on the basis of the same standard which once served as the decisive criterion for the entirety of human "progress," namely, rational-scientific human knowledge. In an earlier context[9] we spoke of the "new objectivity" as a stepping-stone in the evolution of the belief in progress. The "ethics of system survival" underlying the reports of The Club of Rome also radiates the stark coldness of this "new objectivity." It is, so to speak, a computer ethics which hardly transcends the level of a few mathematical quantities: *zero* (for growth) and *two* (for the number of children).

Finally, this type of ethics disregards what fundamentally drives a culture. It must be clear—and the compilers of the reports admit this to a certain extent—that in the magnetic field of faith in progress as it is still present, continual economic expansion cannot possibly be reduced to zero by the magic formula of a computer. This is true all the more insofar as the western economic order is founded on that faith in progress and has organized itself in all its institutional aspects in terms of the realization of the hope in economic expansion.

My ultimate and most essential objection to these reports, therefore, concerns their basis; that is, their ethical foundation. This basis can be summarized in one sentence: The "measure," the size of the earth, really appears to be too small for man; so for our own sake we will have to learn to restrain ourselves. However, confronted with the crisis of western faith in progress, it seems that the decisive issue lies elsewhere. The decisive question we face is whether we ourselves, as the bearers of western culture, have met our *human* "measure," the measure of responsibility, of stewardship of an earth entrusted to us. This question, based on an ethics of a given principle rather than of a humanly determined goal, is left out of consideration in the conclusions of the reports of The Club of Rome. Essentially, those conclusions demand nothing more from humankind than a renewed adjustment to the changed data of our existing societal system.

9. See Part Two, section "The cult of objectivity," pp. 80ff.

13. *The Vulnerability of the System*

In recent years most western countries have been startled by the combination of two problems, each of which by itself is difficult enough to solve. These are inflation and chronic, structural unemployment. Double-digit inflation has become a common phenomenon lately, while unemployment has worsened markedly in most countries, often amounting to more than five percent of the total working population. The classic prescriptions to cure both ills appear to be hardly effective anymore. As a matter of fact, they seem to counteract each other. For instance, a reduction in the money supply (for example, by means of a decrease in the creation of money by the government) can combat inflation, but at the same time it also aggravates unemployment. Conversely, a forceful effort against unemployment (for example, by means of an increase in public expenditures) can easily stimulate inflation. The recovery of the world economy from the recession of 1975 is greeted with joy by many economists and politicians, but it is also viewed with considerable concern, for this economic restoration will certainly entail the aggravation of inflationary tensions.

This is not the place to discuss the technical suggestions proposed by diverse professional economists for the solution of this ticklish "stagflation" problem. In view of the structural undercurrent of both unemployment and inflation, it remains to be seen whether these "solutions" will indeed help. The word *structural* here—in distinction from *cyclical*—implies that the problems we face are integrally connected with the structure of the western economy. Temporary and provisional countermeasures in the area of monetary and budgetary policy do not elim-

130

inate these structural problems, despite the claims of Keynesians or Friedmanites. The depth of these problems becomes apparent in a further investigation concerning the question of *money supply* in a society oriented to continual economic expansion.

THE GOLD STANDARD AND LAISSEZ-FAIRE

In order to maintain economic expansion in a market economy, a reliable money supply is required. Money is necessary for the production and marketing of goods, for the formation of capital, and for the maintenance of reserves in the sphere of production and consumption.

For centuries the money supply in western society was tied to production of precious metals: silver and gold or an alloy. The gold standard was introduced in England in 1816 and was maintained—with a few interruptions—until the economic crisis of the thirties. It implied that every nation tied the extent of its internal money supply to the quantity of gold deposited in its central bank. It was, in fact, obliged to do that because each of its subjects had the right to exchange his currency for gold at the central bank against a guaranteed price. Thus, money supply in society was not an arbitrary matter but was based on a set external standard—the quantity of gold which each country had at its disposal. Wage and price levels also had to be adjusted in terms of this standard. For instance, if a particular country profited greatly from trade with another country and thus imported extra gold which increased its internal money supply, this would directly result in a rise in wage and price levels. Of course, this created a new equilibrium, for rising wages and prices at home imply greater difficulties in exporting abroad. In turn, it meant that the influx of gold from abroad would gradually come to a halt. The equilibrium was restored automatically via the free market operation and the accompanying transfers of gold.

The gold standard, therefore, was a typical element of the laissez-faire doctrine which as a whole focused on the equilibrium effect of the market. "The gold standard was a laissez-faire institution because it was supposed to function automatically, in self-regulating fashion, in accordance with private market transactions at home and abroad."[10]

10. George Dalton, *Economic Systems and Society* (Harmondsworth: Penguin Education, 1974), p. 49.

As is well known, the gold standard crashed during the crisis of the thirties. As a "laissez-faire institution" it shared, so to speak, in "the end of laissez-faire." It is noteworthy that one of the most important causes of this crash lay in *the absence of "downward flexibility" of wages and prices*. Because of this, countries losing gold and with a shrinking money supply appeared to be particularly vulnerable; instead of causing a fall in prices and wages, the reduction in money supply resulted especially in decreased production and growing unemployment. Consequently, one country after another abandoned the "automatism" of the gold standard and decided henceforth to regulate its own money supplies.

There are certain aspects to this process which are seldom mentioned in textbooks on economics but which for our purposes are of essential significance. In the first place there is the close relationship between the fall of the gold standard and the changes which capitalism as a social system had undergone. In Part Two of this book an attempt was made to describe and analyze these changes in a general manner. We noted that at the beginning of the twentieth century capitalism had moved a long way from the system of "free competition." As a result of industrial expansion in scale, monopolies and oligopolies began to dominate the market economy. Meanwhile, the power of labor unions had made a significant impact in the labor market. Prices and wages by that time were largely determined outside the sphere of "perfect competition." They were no longer established in one way today and in another way tomorrow; rather, to a great extent they were *being determined,* either by the price leader in a particular branch of industry or—with respect to wages—through negotiations with the labor unions. For that reason it is not surprising that during the crisis of the thirties prices and wages generally appeared to lack the downward flexibility required by the gold standard, and that consequently a decrease in a nation's gold supply only increased unemployment. In other words, before the gold standard as an "institution of laissez-faire" declined and fell, the pure laissez-faire situation in economic life itself—that is, free and perfect competition—had largely disappeared. In view of this, the fall of the gold standard can be regarded first of all as the outcome of a historical process. It was the final, unavoidable consequence of a predicament.

Therefore, the occasional expression of the wish to reinstate the gold standard clearly reveals an insufficient historical understanding. A money supply in the tradition of a laissez-faire conception of the economy presupposes a society based on the same principle. However, this principle has evidently become—as Eugen Schmalenbach had observed in the 1940s[11]—a practical impossibility in today's society because of technological expansion in scale and increasing overhead costs.

FROM THE GOLD STANDARD TO THE LABOR STANDARD

A second important aspect of this entire development must be noted here. After the fall of the gold standard, money supply became permanently *internalized* in the *progress system* of society. What happened here is similar to what occurred with respect to technology, the entrepreneurial function, and the role of the government. As we observed in Part Two,[12] all of these factors played an external role at first: they provided a platform from which progress could be launched. But after a certain period the roles were reversed so that technology, management, and the government were called upon to fulfill an indispensable role in the service of progress. Analogous to this, money supply also first appeared as an external given in the development of economic expansion. However, during the crisis of the thirties this expansion came to a halt and even reversed itself, causing massive unemployment. When this occurred, the monetary authorities resorted to what seemed the only solution, that is, to place the manner and extent of money supply in the service of salvaging economic expansion and employment. Thus, money supply became a *dependent instrument* in the societal system that demanded continued economic progress.

At first this step in a fundamentally new direction gave great cause for relief. A new "magic formula" seemed to have been found to rid western economies of unemployment. Instead of burdening the economy with the need for continual adjustments to a limited quantity of gold, it had now become possible to expand the money supply *by choice* so that a sufficient, effec-

---

11. Eugen Schmalenbach, *Der freien Wirtschaft zum Gedächtnis* [In Memory of the Free Market Economy] (Köln und Opladen, 1958; originally published 1949). It is a noteworthy peculiarity that a convinced liberal like Schmalenbach delivered this "funeral oration" about the free market economy!

12. See the section "Changes within the enterprise," pp. 90ff.

tive demand could always be created to guarantee a market for an expanding quantity of products of a fully operating production apparatus. Not surprisingly, these "Keynesian" budgetary policies were commonly accepted in western countries, particularly after the second world war. These policies required that governments choose such a relationship between their revenues and expenditures that sufficient purchasing power in society was maintained to guarantee full employment in all circumstances.

However, one has to be careful with "magic formulae." We remember this from Goethe's poem *Der Zauberlehrling,* in which a magician's apprentice had learned the magic word from the sorcerer to produce water from nothing. But he did not know how to make it disappear, and he nearly drowned in the flood which he had launched. Today's tempo of inflation in most western countries reminds us of just such a flood. What happened when the supply of money was unleashed by the "magic formula"? The English economist J. R. Hicks gives perhaps the most penetrating answer to this question. He asserts that "it is hardly an exaggeration to say that instead of being on a Gold Standard, we are on a Labour Standard."[13] Each social group demands its own share of progress by claiming a certain percentage in wage or profit increases (with resultant higher prices),[14] while comparable increases in governmental expenditures and subsidies also take place.

If the money supply is no longer dependent on any external ties, only one thing can be expected: it will be adjusted to increases in costs, prices, and wages (negotiated via the collective bargaining process, or "settled" in some other way). Hicks even goes beyond this. He claims that the value of money has become a by-product of wage negotiations. He regards this as a complete reversal of the rules of the gold standard by which wage and price levels were adjusted to a given money supply based on the presence of gold. Instead, at present the money

13. J. R. Hicks, "Economic Foundations of Wage Policy" (1955), *Essays in World Economics* (Oxford: Clarendon Press, 1959), p. 88.

14. In oligopolistic power situations the theoretical possibility exists of fixing prices in such a way that industrial expansion is wholly financed by private corporate means. Charles Levinson is even of the opinion that the most important cause of inflation today is to be found in this manner of price fixing on the part of the large corporations, especially of the multinationals. See Charles Levinson, *Capital, Inflation and the Multinationals* (London: George Allen & Unwin, 1971).

supply is adjusted to wages and prices, established by means of "bargaining" processes. In short, the monetary system has become the dependent servant of economic progress and its way of distributing benefits over a variety of groups in society.

This reversal is clearly one of the most important causes of the present spiral of inflation. The brake effect of a restrictive money supply is lost and for that reason *rigid claims have the final say.* This entire development cannot, of course, be undone by a simple intervention. Advocates of a return to a restrictive money supply tied to set rules—such as Milton Friedman, who proposes a fixed annual percentage increase[15]—will be confronted with the same problem which hampered the functioning of the gold standard: wages and prices increase—not decrease— as a result of the rigid claims. In such a predicament a "restrictive" monetary policy will again, in the first place, affect existing levels of production and employment.

Everything considered, it seems as if we have reached the point of no return on the road of economic progress; it is as if every bridge behind us has collapsed.

THE UNEMPLOYMENT PROBLEM

The magic formula of money supply has eliminated the brakes, unleashing an inflationary deluge in western society. But as a magic means money supply has shown its limitations also. At first it appeared to be a forceful remedy against every type of unemployment. Later, however, it became increasingly clear that there are certain types of unemployment—especially the so-called "structural" or "technological" types—which are hardly affected by this remedy. They persist even during periods of severe inflation. As a matter of fact, it is quite possible that today's tenacious unemployment exists, at least in part, precisely because of an oversupply of money.

To what does the conscious transition from the gold standard to a labor standard lead? As has been noted earlier, in that situation the claims made—including those in the area of wages— are given a chance to harden and become ever more severe. The flow of money adjusts itself to these claims in a very flexible manner. In a society in which everything centers around money

15. Cf. Milton Friedman, *A Program for Monetary Stability* (New York: Fordham University Press, 1961).

and improved living standards and in which considerable differences in income continue to exist, a hardening in wage demands is clearly to be expected. But these claims can easily turn out to be so great that they exceed the growth rate in production and productivity.

Of course, this situation can be a stimulus to increase the rate of productivity per laborer, for example, by means of more capital-intensive machinery. In other words, firm wage claims may lead to increased productivity. But if that occurs, such claims effectuate a quicker replacement of labor by capital. Here we are confronted with a typical case of *technological unemployment* which Keynes, as early as 1930, described as follows: "This means unemployment due to our discovery of means of economising the use of labour outrunning the pace at which we can find new uses for labour."[16]

The tempo and direction of technological innovation naturally play an essential role in this entire transition. This innovation, internalized in industrial life itself, makes possible a steady increase in productivity. At present an industrial laborer can produce more in one day with his improved, refined, and mechanized apparatus than his colleague in 1900 could in an entire week. This explains the enormous rise in the standard of living, but it also explains the economy's inability to guarantee work for everyone. The economy has become less manageable; it is imbalanced and top-heavy.

Steady technological innovation indeed calls forth real problems. These become apparent first of all when a minor stagnation in national or international demand occurs. Even when the rise in demand decreases only slightly, the result can be increased unemployment. If through continuous technological innovation the productivity of each laborer would increase an average of four percent while the number of workers remains the same, it is clear that—in order to keep everyone employed—the total production as well as the total sales must also continue to increase at least four percent per year. However, if sales opportunities decrease to a mere two percent, then, in a short time, we are unavoidably confronted with elimination of workers from the production process. Their dismissal must bridge

16. John Maynard Keynes, "Economic Possibilities for Our Grandchildren" (1930), *Essays in Persuasion* (New York: Harcourt, Brace & Co., 1932), p. 364.

the difference between the four percent rise in production possible with the existing labor force and the two percent rise in production required to meet the market demand. If this slump in the growth of sales continues for several years, a considerable decline in national employment can result. This is the case in particular for those sectors in the economy in which the rise in productivity of labor is greatest, such as in the industrial sector. Thus in the United States industrial production between 1953 and 1960 increased by 17%. During the same period, however, the number of factory workers decreased by approximately 5%.[17]

Here an analogy with a cyclist can be made. As long as the cyclist maintains his speed he remains balanced on his saddle. But if he tries to stop, he loses his balance. Similarly, the western economy is only in balance as long as economic progress persists, as long as a *growing* market for its products is present. If the tempo of economic growth declines only slightly, however, then a threat to the internal stability of society emerges. *No stability exists other than the one based on progress.* Every part of the social system is directed and geared to this stability.

With respect to the problems arising from continual progress in society, it is interesting to observe in the second place how much more government money and effort are involved today to keep a single laborer employed compared with forty years ago. In the thirties a laborer worked with machines which in value often did not equal and seldom exceeded his yearly wages. Because of continual mechanization, today's worker operates machinery which represents a value equal to several annual incomes of the operator. Consequently, when employment has to be created for the contemporary laborer, considerably larger expenditures are required than in the past. As a matter of fact, because of the trend toward increasing mechanization and automation, this amount is still climbing. We could compare this process with the effects of the use of penicillin. When used for the first time it is very effective. However, with continued use ever greater doses are needed to guarantee the same results. In view of the many doses of "purchasing power" required today to reemploy one unemployed laborer, the popularity of a policy of increased employment opportunity declines visibly in the western economies. Is it not much cheaper to keep workers

17. Cf. Robert Heilbroner, *The Making of Economic Society* (Englewood Cliffs, N.J.: Prentice-Hall, 1968), pp. 165f.

unemployed and to provide them with a decent yearly income? This is a typical symptom of a top-heavy economy which cannot cope with the problem of increasing productivity.

Keynes maintained in 1930 that he knew what to do with this increasing productivity of labor. In spite of his own predictions with respect to technological unemployment, he regarded this growing productivity as the precursor of a happier society in which the economic problem would be solved definitively. As a result of the enormous rise in the standard of living, according to Keynes, humankind would be provided with the opportunity to spend its energy on noneconomic purposes for the first time in history. For that reason he urged his readers to regard potentially increasing technological unemployment as "only a temporary phase of maladjustment." And he insisted: "All this means in the long run *that mankind is solving its economic problem.*"[18] In order to reach that goal, we should not be altogether too scrupulous in the means of attaining it. Says Keynes: "Avarice and usury and precaution must be our gods for a little longer still. For only they can lead us out of the tunnel of economic necessity into daylight."[19]

The title of Keynes' essay of 1930 is "Economic Possibilities for Our Grandchildren." One wonders whether those grandchildren, who are the children of today, would want to repeat Keynes' assertions. Or will it be apparent to them that by "solving" their "economic problems" they have been rewarded with even more complex problems? Can a society in which many people no longer perform meaningful tasks maintain its stability? Keynes seemed to waver about this question: "For we have been trained too long to strive and not to enjoy."[20] Nevertheless, this did not prevent him from unhesitatingly following the road to the ultimate solution of the economic problem, despite the dangers connected with it. Thus he proclaimed:

> I see us free, therefore, to return to some of the most sure and certain principles of religion and traditional virtue—that avarice is a vice . . . and the love of money is detestable, that those walk most truly in the paths of virtue and sane wisdom who take least thought for the morrow. We shall once more value ends above means and prefer the good to the useful.[21]

18. Keynes, "Economic Possibilities" p. 364.
19. *Ibid.,* p. 372.
20. *Ibid.,* p. 368.
21. *Ibid.,* pp. 371, 372.

Isn't the revival of religion and ethics, which is to follow in the track of progress, most remarkable? To attain that revival, all we seemingly have to do is to please the gods of avarice and money a little longer. "For only they can lead us out of the tunnel of economic necessity into daylight." With these assertions Keynes clearly does not transcend the level of a naive twentieth-century imitation of eighteenth-century Enlightenment philosophy.

THE VICTORY OF UTILITARIANISM

This complex of nearly unmanageable inflation and chronic unemployment can be traced back to the dominant place in our society given to technologically founded economic progress, measured in terms of maximum production of consumption goods. Inflation is a natural by-product of a societal system which is so strongly oriented to *economic* progress that it is in permanent need of additional monetary injections. At the same time structural unemployment is a spontaneous by-product of the sovereign penetration of *technological* progress, which continually augments the productivity of labor. The connection between these two social ills and our cultural progress also can be illustrated by the relationship between these ills and the profound influence of utilitarianism on the entire western style of life.[22]

We have already discussed utilitarianism in Part One of this book.[23] Utilitarianism is a type of ethics which neglects the motives underlying human action and pays attention exclusively to the effects of such action in terms of increased or decreased utility. Actions resulting in increased utility for the individual as well as society are considered morally good. We have observed how utilitarianism provided strong moral support for the initial start of the industrial revolution. It was an ethics *placed in the service of economic expansion.* If the most important form of utility or happiness is the availability of consumption goods, and the most important disutility the "pain of labor" performed to obtain these goods, then of course every effort to provide society with the prospects of more products and more leisure time becomes useful and is declared ethically good.

22. To my knowledge, Dr. A. B. Cramp of Cambridge University is the first economist who pointed out this relationship. Cf. his publication *Notes towards a Christian Critique of Secular Economic Theory* (Toronto: Institute for Christian Studies, 1975), Provisional Paper.
23. See section "Utility and Morality," pp. 29ff.

Persons and groups engaged in economic activities always have a certain *horizon of happiness* in view. By this I mean the level of aspiration or the range and intensity of well-being which persons and groups pursue by means of their actions. The horizon of happiness constitutes the frame of reference for the search of meaning and joy in life.

It cannot be denied that our horizon of happiness, particularly since the industrial revolution, has clearly been reduced to a typical utilitarian one. Western man was led to believe that he was capable of obtaining well-being for himself by means of the greatest possible surplus of "utilities" over "disutilities." This constitutes the framework of action of the labor organizations in their battle for higher wages and better working conditions. It also forms the pattern for industrial operations, and it shapes the activities of modern governments which can establish a welfare state only on the basis of "utilities" or consumption possibilities which they provide for their citizens from the cradle to the grave.

A consistently maintained utilitarianism, constituting the horizon of happiness for all people and groups, produces a particular kind of society. It is a society oriented to progress in utilitarian terms, that is, the greatest possible surplus in "utilities" compared with sacrificed "disutilities." That, according to the rules of utilitarianism, is the only progress ethically justifiable. This means concretely that society has to be structured in such a way that its members are enabled to acquire the most in goods (utilities) for the least in labor (disutilities).

Against this background we can better understand basic trends in our society. In the first place, the continual growth in productivity of labor in western economies becomes more comprehensible. Increased productivity guarantees that with a given labor effort (disutility) more goods (utilities) can be produced. In this way true happiness for all, in the utilitarian sense of the word, is promoted and secured. In the second place, from this vantage point it is efficient, useful, and therefore good to make industrial decisions in terms of only one criterion: the productivity of labor. The application of this criterion will not prevent the mind-numbing repetition of piecework nor the utter monotony of the assembly line, since the net result of such practices may still be most useful in terms of income obtained (utility) and labor saved (disutility). Thirdly, in this light the problem of growing inflation and increasing unemployment can be understood afresh. Inflation is, of course, directly related to the general pursuit of more buying power necessary to acquire "utilities" for the individual or for the group to which he belongs. But increasing technological unemployment also is clearly a natural result of the utilitarian horizon of happiness. This limited horizon teaches individuals—and therefore society—to regard labor in every circumstance as a disutility to be avoided as much as possible.

In this light today's increasing structural unemployment is exactly what we should expect. It is direct evidence of the enormous "progress," in utilitarian terms, which enabled us to produce large quantities of goods with a minimal "sacrifice" of labor as a whole. In this technological unemployment we are therefore, however painfully, directly confronted with the consequences of our *own* horizon of happiness. It is a mark of the victory of a culture which is utilitarian both in thought and life, a culture which we obviously continue to promote daily with our economic activities.

14. *The Vulnerability of Western Man*

SCYLLA OR CHARYBDIS

In the preceding sections we have discussed a variety of problems each one of which by itself is difficult to solve. But in mutual combination they become a nearly unbearable burden. On the one hand, we noted that western society is threatened by the danger that its expansion can collapse because of external limits. The limits of environment, raw materials, energy, and space reveal their contours ever more clearly on our horizon. In addition, we are now also confronted with the limits of the political readiness of the so-called third world to make its own resources fully available to the western industrialized nations. From this it can be concluded that the western world, if it wants to survive, will have to learn to control its economic expansion. Otherwise it will be forced to do so by these limits. On the other hand, the societal system of the western countries is so deeply rooted in unlimited growth that any reduction in its tempo of expansion quickly results in fatal dangers for the internal stability of this society.

For the moment it seems that the problems of inflation and unemployment can be mitigated by increased production so that people at least keep their jobs, and the rigid economic demands of employers, employees, and the government can temporarily be reconciled. As soon as the tempo of expansion is slowed down, however, the threat of inflation and unemployment becomes acute. Furthermore—and this is far more serious—such a stagnation in the tempo of growth will in due time derail the *entire* system of society, for every aspect of this system

142

is oriented to continuity in progress. That is true for the purposes of government and business, the mutual relationships between enterprises, the institutions in the area of money supply, the manner in which wages and prices are determined, the institutionalized innovation of techniques, the relations between industrial life and the state, and, finally, it holds for the interdependence between business and consumer. Continuity in progress is the great constant in relation to which all major aspects of the societal system in the course of time have become dependent variables. Progress, so to speak, is the magnetic north toward which all compass needles are always drawn. As soon as this magnetic pull is eliminated, the compass needles spin in confusion. Thus, any hint of pursuing a direction without this magnetic pull of progress appears as an invitation to sail toward chaos, toward a fundamental disintegration of the entire societal system.

Progress has put society in its bind. Hence, we must ask whether society is still in charge of this progress. An alarming dilemma seems to face us here. The spaceship of progress in which we are all caught either seems to run up against unmovable external limits or to come to ruin because of internal disintegration. It looks as if the world will fall to pieces because of persistent faith in the dream of progress, or else the dream may go to pieces because of the world surrounding it. A third alternative seems excluded; thus, we must choose between Scylla and Charybdis.

For all that, only part of the weight of the present challenge to the West has been touched upon. Until now the position of western man himself, who is faced with this challenge and to whom it is in fact directed, has hardly been discussed. Western man—in a sense that means all of us—is certainly not that "unmoved mover" as at times he is depicted. He is no longer that autonomous subject who can sovereignly set processes in motion and who can also sovereignly, at a moment of his own choice, stop these processes again. To the contrary, western man, as a result of the process of progress which he has initiated, is now caught in the predicament of being managed rather than of being the manager. Progress, the work of our own minds and hands, is not a neutral entity that stands outside of our life and thought; it is a force that has penetrated profoundly into every fiber of our existence. In the following section we will look at a few phases of our life which show that western man, at least in part, has indeed become the adjusted man, the person fitted into the mold prescribed by progress.

THE ADJUSTED PERSON

In a society in which progress sets the tone to which all human institutions and relationships are tuned, it is to be expected that all of its members are fundamentally influenced by this progress in their thoughts, words, and deeds. How could man remain untouched while technology, the government, the wage and price system, and the managerial function are intensely affected by this force? Without a doubt, human personality itself has also been pulled inescapably into the magnetic field of progress.

1. Adjustment at work

This is the case, first of all, for today's *entrepreneur* or *manager* who daily has to "relearn"; that is, to think and act in terms of keeping up with economic growth and technology. This fosters a mentality which in its total effect does not remain limited to the sphere of business. The fact that the modern corporation itself makes ever greater demands on its managerial staff, not only with respect to its time but its entire disposition toward life, accentuates this. It may even entail a kind of totalitarianism, a claim on body and soul. From the point of view of the business enterprise the proper "ethics" for the manager is unlimited loyalty to the corporation; his faith must consist of complete dedication to his work, and his hope for the future lies in the certainty that all's well with his enterprise! Whoever is incapable of endorsing this ethics and faith may be an excellent person but is a failure as a manager. In this context Galbraith correctly analyzed the modern manager's predicament, whose "family, politics, sometimes even alcohol and sex, are secondary."[24] His entire life is claimed by and for the sake of progress.

But the ordinary *industrial laborer* in a modern factory can hardly escape this "law of social adjustment" either. In Part Two we hinted at the loss of a human dimension in much of today's work because of the excessive emphasis on the utilization of every factor of economic growth.[25] As a result, the division of labor has led to extreme fragmentation of operations, and the

24. Galbraith, *New Industrial State,* p. 165.
25. See the section "Progress and economic growth," pp. 68f.

process of mechanization at times reduces labor to monotonous and uncreative repetition of stereotyped movements. When people engage in such work daily, in which even mutual communication—the physical movement of people to and fro—is taken over by the technical substitute of the assembly line, they cannot but be affected by this in their personal existence—their spirit, thoughts, and social relationships.

Statistical research has shown that often only a minority of industrial laborers dislikes this kind of work. Most workers are of the opinion that they would not want any other job. When asked for their reasons they point to the fact that they are not required to think in order to perform their task; that they are not burdened with worries once they go home; and that their wages are often higher than in many other jobs.

Are these reactions reassuring? Not really. Of course, it is good that there are differences between people, which are also expressed in a healthy variety of opinions concerning the work they do. But this acceptance of monotony is not a healthy response. Moreover, we don't get much farther with the argument of some that, after all, simple work is not necessarily meaningless. This is certainly true, but much more is at stake in the uncreative repetition of stereotyped movements in a great deal of mass production. We must get to the root of the matter. If labor lacks every element of choice, every opportunity for creativity, every possibility of personal cooperation and mutual contact during its performance, then elements other than simplicity of work and healthy differences between people are at stake. Positive appreciation of repetitious monotony on the part of the laborer points to a reversal in relations between man and technology. Instead of technology being adjusted to the humanity of the workers, we are obviously faced here with a situation in which the workers, in body and soul, are being adjusted to technology. Because of this they do not mind their inhuman type of work.

Managers as well as laborers experience the pressure of required adjustment, both inside and outside the sphere of work. But its effects are broader; for this adjustment penetrates the personal lives of all of us, even in the manner in which we appreciate sports, in sexual life, and in our way of spending leisure time. Because the influence of faith in progress on our personal lives is often underestimated, a brief illustration of this in each of these areas can be helpful in understanding how we, at least in part, have been shaped by this faith.

2. Sports

When we compare our involvement in sports today with that of a hundred years ago, a number of marked differences strike us. In the first place, we note that sport has become an independent activity, an "enterprise" or "business." There is a production side to it—with paid employees—as well as a consumption side— the "passive" recreation on the part of the public. The practice of sport in many ways has become an independent economic sector, subject to the same driving force of technological and economic progress affecting the other economic sectors in society.

To begin with, a good sportsperson has his or her own "manager." This is the person whose task it is to sell his "product" as well as possible. He can be regarded as the representative of economic progress in the world of sports. Besides a good "manager," the sportsperson also needs a coach who teaches and trains him or her in all the technical know-how of the trade. This person can be looked upon as the representative of technological progress in the realm of sports. He "measures" his client's progress daily, for even in sports it is a measurable phenomenon.

In origin, sport is a healthy competitive relationship between people, in which the element of play accentuates mutual friendship. But as an extension of the cultural choice of western society, in which a person's worth is expressed in the manner in which he or she relates to things, the bond between people in many sports is gradually pushed to the background. The most fundamental relationship in various branches of sport no longer consists in competition between two persons but between one individual and the clock. In terms of records established only two things are important: the person and the time he or she has made. The most basic accomplishment in these sports is one that improves upon previous records. In this way progress in sports also becomes perceptible and quantifiably measurable.

A very important part of every sport is steady conditioning by patient training. Success requires a good physical condition right at the outset, but this is certainly not always the final outcome. Much conditioning comes down to an overemphasis on certain physical qualities. The best results are obtained by the athlete who is prepared to train with the intensity and regularity of a machine. This was confirmed, for instance, by the spectacular results on the part of the East German athletes during the Olympic games of recent years. They were in the best condition to break records. "Wound up" like machines, they could run and swim like machines and complete their programmed tasks before the eyes of an excited public. But had they perhaps already become mechanical puppets, preadjusted playthings in the prison of technological progress and thus artificially perfected?[26]

3. Sexuality

Today no subject seems to be discussed more frequently than sexuality. Perhaps that explains why it was abbreviated to the three-letter word *sex,* as short as *war, man,* and *God,* and even shorter than *labor, bread,* and *love.* Fortunately, sexuality no longer is regarded as something to be ashamed of, something sinful, belonging in the realm of secrecy. In that respect we have made true progress. However, the other side of that coin reveals less positive facets. In the context of our discussion we will point to three changes which have taken place with regard to our appreciation of sexuality.

In the first place, sexuality as "sex" has gradually become an independent, detached, urgent human "need" demanding satisfaction. The personal relation between husband and wife which forms the context for authentic sexuality—in other words, the most profound expression of permanent and mutual love—has become secondary.[27] Sex is an end in itself. Love is a mere byproduct: we "make" love. A parallel change can be observed in the manner in which contact is sought between members of the opposite sex. Today this contact has to be open and direct so that no time is lost. Sexuality becomes a quick, often impersonal play of sudden impulses. Moreover, sexuality increasingly is transferred from the private to the public sphere and is even accompanied by public symbols of demonstration—"sex bombs." These can be compared with the public symbols in the world of sports—the sport heroes. Of course, this development is closely

26. With reference to the relation between technique and sports, see Jacques Ellul, *The Technological Society* (New York: Alfred A. Knopf, 1964), pp. 382–384.
27. For a more extensive treatment of sexuality, love, and marriage, see James H. Olthuis, *I Pledge You My Troth* (New York: Harper & Row, 1975).

related to the objectification of sexuality, for if sexuality is independent and detached, then it can easily be expressed by independent human "symbols." It was precisely this notion of sexuality that caused Marilyn Monroe's distress, as is evident from one of her last interviews in which she commented: "That's the trouble, a sex symbol becomes a thing. I just hate to be a thing."[28]

Thirdly, this public objectification of sex is greatly promoted by the rise of the pornographic industry, one of the new economic sectors of modern society. This industry manufactures the most impersonal sexuality which, consequently, is for sale. Hence sexuality has become, more than ever before, an independent economic object, caught up in the advance of technical progress. Sex manuals teach us how to advance in the technique of sexual fulfillment and how to obtain maximum satisfaction by following the prescribed "variations."

4. Scarcity of time

Nearly everyone in western society suffers from a frightful shortage of time. A new saying has it that in the past people perished from lack of food but today they perish from lack of time. This lack of time is apparent not only from the quick tempo of our lives and from our crowded schedules, but also from the manner in which the modern family spends its time.

The Swedish economist S. B. Linder deals with this problem in a fascinating book pointedly called *The Harried Leisure Class*.[29] According to the author, economic science has always claimed that increased welfare will offer more leisure time. But today nothing seems to be as scarce as time. One of the causes for this miscalculation by economists, says Linder, is their neglect of the time aspect of consumption. Every consumption product automatically takes our time. We need time to buy it, to maintain it, and to replace it. For that reason, he argues, a culture which becomes richer materially becomes poorer in terms of available time.

Linder also explains how this scarcity of time affects our life styles. The appearance of time-saving household appliances can in part be explained as a result of this situation. That also is true with regard to disposable articles. We no longer have the

28. *Time,* July 16, 1973, cover story.
29. S. B. Linder, *The Harried Leisure Class* (New York: Columbia University Press, 1970).

time to maintain our possessions or to return items like empty bottles. Furthermore, a direct connection seems to exist between the growing shortage of time and the changes in methods of advertising and sales. Only a few decades ago advertisements were of a decisively informative nature. They informed the consumer about an article so that he could compare it with others in order to make a choice. However, since we no longer have time to compare the quality of various items—a situation aggravated by the quantity and variety on the market—modern advertising has become suggestive in nature. Advertisements often merely aim at creating the illusion that the consumer will feel better and happier after he or she has acquired a certain article. The act of purchasing has increasingly become more impulsive—a situation which modern advertising exploits by orienting itself more and more to the consumer's subconscious. Clearly, the "helplessness" of today's consumer has sharply intensified. The possibility to mold and manipulate his tastes runs parallel with his shortage of time.

An even more incisive consequence concerns our relationship to one another. Because of the demands on our time by the material welfare we experience, our time and our reflections are increasingly determined by our preoccupation with material goods and decreasingly by our personal association with fellow human beings. Thus, here also the bond between man and fellowman is secondary to the link between man and things. For that reason there is undoubtedly a direct connection between the growing material welfare and the growing loneliness in modern society. In particular, of course, this affects people living outside the bonds of the immediate family. But it also affects the life of the family itself. A modern western family takes on the image of a miniature society in which each child has his or her own room and enough money to meet his or her needs. In this "society," watching TV and listening to records, which are technical objects, fill the void with respect to genuine personal contacts.

CONCLUSION: THE DILEMMA OF WESTERN MAN

This list of changes in the life and thought patterns of western man is far from complete. We could point to the nonchalance and recklessness in our handling of material goods as well as to the urge for excitement, sensation, and thrills. But we have a sufficiently clear picture of the measure in which we are affected by the pressure of continual adjustment. It is striking that these changes in our attitudes and actions reveal such great similarity in orientation. It is not only in the area of sports and sexuality but also in that of work and leisure that we are struck by the same shift from lasting *personal* bonds toward hasty, impulsive, and fleeting ties with *things*. Moreover, in nearly all cases this link with things is immediately subjected to the rules of economic and technical progress.

The more we reflect on it, the more bewildering this process of adjustment becomes. Humankind does not seek after adjustment as such, as if this will provide us with happiness. Of course, many persons accept these developments and changes, seemingly without objection. They are apparently still caught in the naive idea of progress which holds that increased personal income and luxury is the best guarantee for happiness in life. But there are also countless others who suffer under the fleeting character of human relationships, under the lack of meaning in their work, under the hurried pace of life, and under the obtrusive character of advertising. Indeed, there are numerous men and women who sense that they are *being* lived.

Nevertheless, today this awareness of the failure of progress does not lead to what one might expect in such a situation, namely, a conscious and carefully considered redirection of the entire course of life and society, a new reflection on how we could act differently, coupled with an intent search for a different work and life style, with an appeal to social organizations and political parties to work toward such radically reconsidered ends. It appears as if western man is paralyzed with respect to his own position; as if he—the maker of progress—is more and more persuaded of his own powerlessness with respect to this progress. Apparently he can only think in terms of this dilemma: either to participate in a *revolutionary resistance* to everything connected with the economy, science, and the overwhelming technology of modern society, or to accept *continual adjustment* to the external and obtrusive demands made on his life—its style, tempo, and direction. What is the origin of this bewildering cultural schizophrenia of western man? What is his deepest motivation as the architect of his *own* happiness and as the creator of his *own* progress?

15. *The Dialectic of Progress*

It is no easy matter to provide a satisfactory explanation of the cultural schizophrenia of western man. But it is clear that the bewildering phenomena which are the symptoms of that cleavage are somehow related to his faith in progress. In Part Two of this book we saw faith in progress, so to speak, in action. It became apparent that the progress motive was not just one out of many possible motives for action, but that it revealed definite religious overtones. The West has learned to live by *faith* in progress, in *hope* of progress, and out of *love* toward progress, as Eberhard Ernst once formulated it.[30]

A faith and a religion never leave their adherents unaffected. They put a stamp on them, shape them into image bearers. A religious choice is the most profound and decisive choice men and societies can make, shaping and affecting their entire existence. To begin with, this is true for so-called primitive cultures with their idol worship. Even though the images of idols are made of wood or stone, their adherents attribute to them a sovereign power and an independent existence. This belief in idols has a deformative effect on the thoughts and actions of its adherents. As the psalmist put it: "Their makers grow to be like them, and so do all who trust in them."[31]

But is this also true of modern societies? Here we are reminded of Keynes' comments about the worship of modern

30. Eberhard Ernst, *Die Fortschrittsidee in Wirtschaftslehre und Wirtschaftswirklichkeit* [The Idea of Progress in Economic Theory and Economic Practice] (Ph. D. Dissertation, University of Mannheim, 1951), p. 8.

31. Psalm 115:8 (N.E.B.).

151

gods: "Avarice and usury and precaution must be our gods for a little longer still. For only they can lead us out of the tunnel of economic necessity into daylight."[32] Undoubtedly Keynes' observation contains a large measure of irony. But for western man much more than irony is involved. Insofar as western man attributes divine stature to the forces of progress, we might well be confronted with a situation parallel to that of idol worship in primitive cultures. These forces are given divine prerogatives as soon as man puts an unconditional *trust* in them; that is, as soon as economic and technological progress are depended upon as the guides to the good life and as the mediators of our happiness. We already detected this religious faith and trust in Carnegie's *Gospel of Wealth*. As in primitive cultures, powers that are regarded as gods and saviors can gain a dominant influence over our lives from which we cannot readily extricate ourselves. Keynes suffered from the illusion that this extrication is an easy affair: as soon as the "gods" have led us out of the dark tunnel of economic necessity into daylight we can discard them, since they have then finished their service.

But will the gods in turn let us loose? One cannot choose one's own masters in life without accepting the status of servant. It appears therefore that the sense of powerlessness present in western culture may well be closely connected with the *faith dimension* of the progress motive. Powerlessness results when one's own power is delegated; but it is precisely a *faith* (in progress) that can elicit such a delegation of power.

SIGNS OF POWERLESSNESS

This sense of powerlessness has now become a reality in the lives of many people. We can most clearly illustrate this with a number of citations from contemporary writings.[33]

Charles A. Reich observed that "Technology and production . . . in our country . . . pulverize everything in their path:

32. Keynes, "Economic Possibilities," p. 372.
33. Some of the more popular publications dealing with this theme are these: William Barrett, *Time of Need: Forms of Imagination in the Twentieth Century* (New York: Harper & Row, 1973); Theodore Roszak, *The Making of a Counter Culture* (New York: Doubleday & Co., 1969); Theodore Roszak, *Where the Wasteland Ends* (Garden City, N.Y.: Doubleday, 1972); and William Irwin Thompson, *At the Edge of History* (New York: Harper & Row, 1971).

the landscape, the natural environment, history and tradition, the amenities and civilities, the privacy and spaciousness of life, beauty, and the fragile, slow-growing social structures which bind us together." He adds to this: "Thus a true definition of the American crisis would say this: we no longer understand the system under which we live . . .; in turn, the system has been permitted to assume unchallenged power to dominate our lives, and now rumbles along, unguided and therefore indifferent to human ends."[34]

Ralph Lapp expresses a similar conviction in his analogy between today's society and a train. "We are aboard a train which is gathering speed, racing down a track on which there are an unknown number of switches leading to unknown destinations. No single scientist is in the engine cab and there may be demons at the switch. Most of society is in the caboose looking backward."[35]

Thirdly, one can quote Karl Löwith, who dealt with "the *fate* of progress" in an impressive article by that title. "An uncanny coincidence of fatalism and a will to progress presently characterizes all contemporary thinking about the future course of history. Progress now threatens us; it has become our fate." To this he adds that we are *"set free* and yet *imprisoned* by our own power. . . . Progress itself goes on progressing; we can no longer stop it or turn it around."[36]

What strikes us in each of these quotations is that the power of progress is depicted as a superior force which merely evokes helplessness and insecurity in us. Reich speaks of the "unchallenged power to dominate our lives," and Löwith states that "progress itself goes on progressing." This creates a feeling of inability to "stop it or turn it around." According to Lapp we are as helpless as passengers in a "train which is gathering speed" and controlled by "demons at the switch," while the entire social system, in Reich's words, "rumbles along, unguided." We encounter the same sense of impotence in the words of Kurt Schiller, West Germany's former federal minister for economic affairs, who once compared our efforts toward further economic

34. Charles A. Reich, *The Greening of America* (New York: Random House, 1970), pp. 7 and 14 respectively.

35. Cited by Alvin Toffler, *Future Shock* (New York: Random House, 1970), p. 382.

36. Löwith, *Nature, History, and Existentialism,* pp. 159 and 160 respectively.

progress with riding a tiger. The tiger simply goes his own way and might lead us to a fatal destination. However, to jump off would be even more dangerous. Therefore, we continue our uncontrollable ride, clinging to the back of what might become our ruin.[37]

Powerlessness easily leads to fear. This happens especially with those people who, in the face of the great impersonal powers of our time—technology, economics, and science—experience their own helplessness so profoundly that they are firmly convinced that these powers lead an independent existence outside of us from which they can consciously control us. At that point the decisive question is no longer how we ourselves look upon science, economics, and technology. The question rather is how these powers look upon us. What else—so we read in the "underground press"—are we in the eyes of science but objects for experimentation, a multitude of copulating rabbits! And technology—can it treat us differently from a digit in a computer? Finally, economics—does it know that we are more than caged consumers, endlessly manipulable? Fear is a reaction which we must take seriously. One ought not to play games with it. It is a reaction in people who sense that they are caught in a labyrinth from which there is no escape.

Such paralyzing fear has been illustrated brilliantly in the haunting horrible images of the English artist Francis Bacon. In his painting entitled *Head VI*,[38] he has depicted a man seated in an empty box indicated by a few straight lines. Apparently the man designed his own box. He screams helplessly, for the upper half of his head is already dissolved and has disappeared in the vacuum in which he finds himself. Evidently he is caught in a process of total dissolution. His mouth is wide open and his scream will last until his mouth will disappear and the sound will dissolve into nothingness. It looks like the image of a man who knows that the gods he has made with his own hands have turned into deceivers, but who—precisely because they are his gods—no longer has the power to free himself from them.

37. Kurt Schiller, "Stability and Growth as Objectives of Economic Policy," *The German Economic Review*, vol. 5, no. 3 (1967), p. 178.
38. For a discussion of this painting see H. R. Rookmaaker, *Modern Art and the Death of a Culture* (London/Downers Grove: Inter-Varsity Press, 1970), pp. 173f.

FREEDOM VERSUS DOMINATION

By establishing a connection between the powers of the modern age, the contemporary sense of powerlessness, and the terrorism of idols, we have introduced an extremely loaded subject. For that reason it makes sense to approach the theme of modern man—at once threatened and helpless—from a new angle, namely, from the reciprocal relation between the motive of domination and the motive of freedom in the unfolding of western humanism since the Renaissance. This seems like a detour, but may be worth our while.

In Part One we saw that Renaissance man ventured into the world around him to discover it and to subject it to himself.[39] This *domination* ideal of western humanism—the will to rational knowledge and domination of the world in every respect: scientific, artistic, political, technical, and economic—was already at that time inextricably linked with what Herman Dooyeweerd[40] calls the *freedom* or *personality* ideal of humanism, that is, the effort to develop an absolutely free, autonomous personality. Pico della Mirandola described this conception of human personality at the height of the Italian Renaissance in these words: "O highest and most marvelous felicity of man! To him it is granted to have whatever he chooses, to be whatever he wills."[41] The domination and personality ideals belong together. What would express the freedom of the human personality better than man's knowledge, control, and domination of the world? How else could the domination ideal be realized except on the basis of the free, unfettered development of human personality? For Renaissance humanism these two ideals are an extension of one another. They are each other's complement, each other's proof, and each other's expression.

However, it soon became evident that this new vision of man and the world was not quite as harmonious as it first seemed.

39. See the section "The ground motive of the Renaissance," pp. 12ff.
40. See Herman Dooyeweerd, *In the Twilight of Western Thought* (Philadelphia: Presbyterian and Reformed, 1960), pp. 46–52. For a more extensive treatment of the early Renaissance idea of freedom, the rise of modern science, and the synthesis of Kant and Fichte, see Dooyeweerd, *A New Critique of Theoretical Thought*, 4 vols. (Amsterdam: Paris; Philadelphia: Presbyterian and Reformed, 1953–58), vol. 1 (1953), pp. 169–495.
41. Giovanni Pico della Mirandola, *Oration on the Dignity of Man* (1486), in Ernst Cassirer *et al.*, eds. *The Renaissance Philosophy of Man* (Chicago: University of Chicago Press, 1948), p. 225.

Certain tensions and even conflicts developed between these two ideals, particularly because of the rise of the natural sciences. For instance, this was the case when certain scientists, completely in line with the ideal of rational domination of the world, arrived at the startling conclusion that, in essence, thinking is nothing but a material, cellular process in the human brain. For a sincere humanist, however, thought is the seat of human dignity and grandeur, the very source of human freedom and personality. Thus, a direct tension between these two ideals was the result. This dichotomy only intensified as the natural-scientific method was applied more systematically. This method threatens the unique value of the human being by making him the plaything of associations in psychology, or by depicting him as the ultimate product of determined processes in the mechanics of the new social sciences. Dawson correctly observes:

> From the 17th century onwards, the modern scientific movement has been based on the mechanistic view of nature which regards the world as a closed material order moved by purely mechanical and mathematical laws. All the aspects of reality which could not be reduced to mathematical terms . . . were treated as mere subjective impressions of the human mind. . . ."[42]

It is no wonder that protests were voiced against this development, and that the humanists of the so-called school of idealism, in reaction, began to base their philosophical reflections on the absolute priority of the personality ideal.

THE DIALECTIC OF PROGRESS

Is this conflict between the two ideals of personality and domination within humanism a coincidence, a mere unfortunate accident? Of course not. As Dooyeweerd's penetrating analysis has shown, an indissoluble *inner* tension exists between them. They have stood in a relation of *dialectic contradiction* with one another from the very beginning. Thus, it is neither possible nor consistent on the one hand to subscribe to the rational-scientific character of all processes in the world, and on the other hand to stop in your tracks the moment you reach the realm of free human personality. Moreover—and this is the other side of the same coin—it is neither possible nor consistent

42. Christopher Dawson, *Progress and Religion: An Historical Inquiry* (London: Sheed & Ward, 1929), p. 219.

first to declare the entire world to be the great arena for the exercise of the personal human will (as, for example, Fichte did) and then to stop suddenly when you realize that this results in the elimination of rational knowledge and control of this world. Both the humanist domination ideal and the personality ideal by nature lay claim on the *entire* person and the *entire* world. For that reason, within the humanist world picture, they struggle continually for *supremacy.* The history of western thought since the Renaissance has been marked uninterruptedly by this struggle. In this process the pole of the rational domination motive has tried to annex that of human personality and, vice versa, the pole of human personality has almost continuously revolted against that of the rational domination motive.

Of course, there have also been attempts at reconciliation, at synthesis. Best known is the attempt of Immanuel Kant who tried, so to speak, to create a division of property. He reserved the sphere of natural phenomena for the area of science, while the world behind these phenomena, the *Dinge an sich,* as well as self-knowledge were reserved for free human personality. In the context of our theme, however, it is of greater importance to understand the ideas of *progress* of the Enlightenment philosophers as efforts toward synthesis and reconciliation. Human *progress,* as they conceived it, was the indispensable bridge between the domination ideal and the personality ideal. By putting the dynamic vision of progress into practice, they were convinced that man, precisely by means of his control of this world, would reach the greatest fulfillment of his own personality. This, of course, completely legitimized all efforts toward progress. For thus, they believed, it would some day be shown to full advantage what it meant to be integrally human with respect to both the domination of nature as well as the realization of human personality. In this way the progress ideal indeed provided the deepest meaning of life. It became the legitimate principle and starting point of their thoughts, words, and deeds.

But what has happened to all these "solutions" and "syntheses" in the ups and downs of modern thought? As to the *Kantian and neo-Kantian divisions of reality,* they were soon fundamentally undermined by the development of philosophy itself. They simply could not be maintained in the face of the irresistible urge for unobstructed continuity and consistency demanded by the humanist personality ideal. So after the reign of positivism we see the rise, especially in Europe, of various counter-philosophies like existentialism. The neatly established neo-Kantian distinctions, such as the one between the realm of necessity (or facts) and the realm of freedom (or value), are systematically cut to pieces by the incisive critique of these protest-philosophies. However, the critique is not of a kind that leads to genuinely new perspectives. What is left after the battle between the dialectic camps is mainly a heap of ruins. The science ideal is dismantled, and little remains of the once so elevated personality ideal. The existentialist philosopher is left with its remnants, namely, his personal desperation, his disgust, and his suffering from the world and from his fellowmen. The personality and domination ideals have, as it were, destroyed each other in present humanist thought precisely because each ideal laid claim on the entire world and the entire human being.[43]

If this is the final outcome of humanist *philosophy,* one can hardly expect a more harmonious result with regard to *practice,* in the concrete efforts to realize faith in human progress in the social order. This faith has the same dialectical origins; it suffers the same tensions inherent in the humanism from which it was born. As soon as the humanist domination ideal took on flesh and blood during the industrial revolution in the capitalist efforts toward progress—and thus shifted from the sphere of philosophy and science into the center of concrete social reality—then this domination ideal could not rest, because of its very nature, until it tried to subject the whole person and the entire world to itself. It is impossible and inconsistent to strive toward complete domination and total progress without also involving the entire human personality. Once the force of progress is set in motion, one cannot prevent the treatment of the human person as an *object* by this very force. The opposite is of course also true. When the humanist ideal of freedom and personality is threatened by this objectification of man and the world, it begins to protest against the dictatorship of the domination ideal by establishing a total counterclaim on man and the world. This can be illustrated from the rapid and restless succession of counter-movements, not only in philosophy but also in literature, art, and life styles. In this way expressionism in painting succeeded impressionism; in complete reaction to impressionism, its start-

---

43. For an analysis of these dialectical tensions in twentieth-century European thought, see S. U. Zuidema, *Communication and Confrontation* (Toronto: Wedge, 1971), especially "Man in Contemporary Philosophy," pp. 129–148.

ing point became the will toward full and uninhibited expression of one's own free personality. In the same way, the positive pictures of a dawning future, characteristic of Enlightenment influence from Voltaire through Marx and beyond, have gradually given way to distinctly negative images which, in violent colors, depict a threatening future for humanity in a society abandoned to the domination urge.

As a rule, however, genuine alternatives are lacking in these reactions and counterimages. In reaction to the objectification and mechanization implicit in the realization of progress, the alternatives frequently suggest a society without domination and authority and with complete personal liberty and equality. This is the alternative of anarchism. Or we are offered a future society in which every technical and economic advance is radically rejected. But it should be noted carefully that these proposed solutions—there are indeed those who no longer want to think in terms of "solutions"[44]—also do not transcend the inexorable dialectic between the ideal of domination and the ideal of personality, no matter how faded and colorless these ideals have become in our time.

SOME CONCLUSIONS

At least four conclusions can be drawn from the above considerations.

1. Western society has patterned and adjusted itself into a consistent and goal-oriented system for the promotion of economic and technological progress. As a result, it exerts permanent pressures of adjustment on our lives. This "objectification" of western man as "object" of progress is inseparably connected with both his aims at rational dom-

44. Cf. in this context for instance the publications by H. G. Wells. In *Men like Gods* (Toronto: Macmillan, 1923; originally published 1912), one of his earliest books, he is still of the opinion that man is capable of directing progress—a task which he calls a project for more than giants: it is a task for gods. In *The Camford Visitation* (London: Methuen, 1937), protest and critique begin to play an essential role. His last book, *Mind at the End of Its Tether* (London: Heinemann, 1945), is an open confession on the part of the author that human progress is doomed to end in chaos; man and his "palace" are trampled under foot by technology. See also Paul Gerhard Buchloh, "Vom 'Pilgrim's Progress' zum 'Pilgrim's Regress'" ["From 'Pilgrim's Progress' to 'Pilgrim's Regress'"], in Erich Burck, ed., *Die Idee des Fortschritts* [The Idea of Progress] (München: Verlag C. H. Beck, 1963), pp. 153–178.

ination of the entire world as well as his faith in progress which moves its adherents to utter dependence upon the guides and sovereign powers which they themselves have chosen. To speak of the "fate" of progress is, therefore, an incorrect assessment of the true position of western man, as if he were pursued by an external calamity in spite of his own good will. What will befall him was brought into motion by himself. "Thus the survival of the fittest may be replaced by the fitting of the survivors."[45]

2. The diverse reactions to the dictates of progress, from activist rebellion on the part of the "counterculture" to the most passive resignation and even fear, often display an unwillingness to search for concrete alternatives and solutions. Behind this lies the belief in man's own powerlessness—a belief which is really only a special variant of an internally disintegrated faith in progress. But there is also another factor that lies behind this, namely, that in reaction to the overwhelming societal presence of the humanist domination ideal—in organization, technology, bureaucracy, scientific management, and manipulation—the opponents and critics know of no way out but to flee or crawl into the culturally dead-end road of the temporarily revived personality ideal.[46] Viewed from the vulnerable position of that ideal in the contemporary situation, the luminous seraphs of technology, science, and welfare are degraded to little more than infernal demons.

3. The behavior and activities of western man are still consciously or subconsciously controlled by both ideals. For that reason his conduct with respect to the challenge to western culture can be expected to reveal a *split* nature: he is tossed to and fro between his urge to take his chances with progress and to renounce it at the same time; between his love and his hate for progress. "An uncanny coinci-

45. Quoted by William Irwin Thompson, *At the Edge of History,* p. 167, from Herman Kahn and Anthony Weiner, *The Year 2000: A Framework for Speculation on the Next Thirty-Three Years* (New York: Macmillan, 1967), p. 347. For another recent discussion of this entire problematics see Barry Commoner, *The Poverty of Power* (New York: Alfred A. Knopf, 1976).

46. Daniel Bell describes this dead-end road as the "exhaustion of modernism" evidenced especially in the counterculture of the sixties. See Bell, *The Cultural Contradictions of Capitalism* (New York: Basic Books, 1976), especially chapter 3.

dence of fatalism and a will to progress presently characterizes all contemporary thinking about the future course of history."[47] It is very clear that western man, who is torn by inner tension and uncertainty, cannot be expected to navigate the ship of western society between Scylla and Charybdis[48] with a steady hand.

4. Capitalism is primarily the economic incarnation of humanist-oriented aims toward progress. It has followed and incorporated the changes in the evolution of trust in progress. For that very reason, however, capitalism is also intricately caught up in the dissolution and disintegration of this faith in progress. In principle, the dissolution started at the beginning of the twentieth century, but it seems only at this time to occur at a quickened pace. At any rate, it must be expected that capitalism itself will become increasingly involved in the tension between the two primary humanist ideals of domination and of freedom—a tension which has penetrated the social order more than ever before so that no member of society can escape it. The crisis of capitalism is, therefore, not only a crisis of the capitalist *system;* it is at the same time a crisis of the *culture* which has nurtured this system until the present day.

47. Löwith, *Nature, History, and Existentialism,* p. 159.
48. Cf. pp. 142ff.

PART FOUR: TOWARD THE DISCLOSURE OF SOCIETY

16. *A Miscellany of Responses*

The problems we encountered in the preceding sections are overwhelming. They affect not only the breadth of the entire western social order but also penetrate that order in depth. They touch our bodies as well as our souls. They affect not only our own lives but also the lives of our children.

In view of this it is not surprising that, at least in many cases, the reactions to this complexity of problems are of a penetrating nature and reflect existential choices. For instance, we are confronted with the profound, existential choice of *revolution.* This choice is based on the conviction that only a radical overthrow of the present social order, even if necessary by means of violent protests, can help us. Another choice is the one of *escape* by developing a *counterculture.* This choice is rooted in the personal conviction that we must shun society with its misery and unceasing manipulation of the human mind, and that we must create new life possibilities for ourselves. Another group opts for *revision.* This choice is made by those who regard a conscious transformation of our societal structuration as the only meaningful solution to its problems.

Before presenting my own reflections on this matter, it is appropriate to take note of a few of these reactions. It is impossible here to achieve a complete presentation; rather, my only purpose is to illustrate briefly a number of alternatives that have been suggested, and to add a few critical comments where necessary.[1]

1. With respect to the role of technology, Egbert Schuurman's *Techniek en toekomst* [Technology and the Future] (Assen, the Netherlands: Van Gorcum,

REVOLUTION: HERBERT MARCUSE

Herbert Marcuse is not a typical representative of the attitude of resistance or revolution, but he certainly is one of the more interesting ones. He belongs to the circle of neo-Marxists of the so-called Frankfurt School.[2] From this perspective he had deeply concerned himself with the issue of the influence of the "capitalist" social order on the thoughts and acts of western man. He regards this influence—which he calls *conditioning*—as so incisive that it is capable of almost completely wiping out human personality and individuality, that is, of reducing man to a one-dimensional entity. "Contemporary industrial society tends to be totalitarian," according to Marcuse. For, he continues, "not only a specific form of government or party rule makes for totalitarianism, but also a specific system of production and distribution."[3] Marcuse regards the work assigned to the laborer in capitalist societies, the needs suggested to him, and the language he daily absorbs via newspapers and television, as mere instruments of manipulation. Their influence can reach so far that "individuals identify themselves with the existence which is imposed upon them and have in it their own development and satisfaction."[4] Thus "the subject which is alienated is swallowed up by its alienated existence."[5] As a result of industrial domination man has become one-dimensional. The term "one-dimensional" implies that Marcuse's view of man leaves open the possibility of more than one dimension. What are the other dimensions through which perhaps an escape from the present one-dimensional society might perhaps become possible?

At times Marcuse indeed speaks of the possibility of a two-dimensional culture. By the second dimension in culture he apparently means, in particular, the "greatness of a free literature and art, the ideals of humanism, the sorrows and joys of

---

1972) provides excellent information regarding these various attitudes. English and German summaries appear on pp. 399–455. An English edition of this detailed study is in preparation.

2. See Martin Jay, *The Dialectical Imagination: A History of the Frankfurt School and the Institute of Social Research, 1923-1950* (Boston/Toronto: Little Brown, 1973).

3. Herbert Marcuse, *One-Dimensional Man* (Boston: Beacon Press, 1964), p. 3.

4. *Ibid.*, p. 11.

5. *Ibid.*

the individual" or what he calls "the celebration of the autonomous personality."[6] This same motif returns in his critique of President Lyndon Johnson's conception of "The Great Society." The critique culminates in his accusation that contemporary society "releases the individual from being an autonomous person: in work and in leisure, in his needs and satisfactions, in his thoughts and emotions."[7]

In Marcuse's thought, therefore, the personality ideal and the domination ideal exist as two dimensions next to or even opposite one another. This immediately reveals the consistently humanistic character of Marcuse's thought. For, as we have seen, these are the two poles of the humanist world view which compete with each other for supremacy. In fact, Marcuse openly acknowledges the dialectic tension between these two dimensions, and in that tension he chooses as the only measuring rod for authentic humanity the pole which is fundamentally threatened under the capitalist system—the pole of *free human personality.*

Marcuse's approach is particularly interesting because he views the role of technology in modern society as perhaps the most serious threat to human personality. He claims that "by virtue of the way it has organized its technological base, contemporary industrial society tends to be totalitarian."[8] Moreover, in his critique of Johnson's "Great Society" he seems to suggest that alternatives for society can be derived from a different use of technology.

> The dynamic of endlessly propelled productivity is not that of a peaceful, humane society in which the individuals have come into their own and develop their own humanity. . . . Such a society may well reject the notion (and practice) of 'unbridled growth'; it may well restrict its technical capabilities where they threaten to increase the dependence of man on his instruments and products.[9]

Would not this approach, in principle, contain a real solution to the problems presently confronting western society?

From a closer scrutiny it soon becomes apparent that Mar-

6. *Ibid.,* pp. 57 and 56 respectively.
7. Herbert Marcuse, "The Individual in the Great Society," in Bertram M. Gross, ed., *A Great Society?* (New York: Basic Books, 1966), p. 63.
8. Marcuse, *One-Dimensional Man,* p. 3.
9. Marcuse, "The Individual in the Great Society," p. 59.

cuse is too convinced a Marxist to consider this as a realistic alternative within, or proceeding from, the existing capitalist structure of society. As he explains in *One-Dimensional Man,* the gradual completion of the process of automation within this society is a prime requisite. It is only on the basis of a completed industrial technology that one can expect the unfolding of the "realm of freedom" and the birth of an authentic two-dimensional society. He writes:

> Within the established societies the continued application of scientific rationality would have reached a terminal point with the mechanization of all socially necessary but individually repressive labor. . . . But this stage would also be the end and limit of the scientific rationality in its established structure and direction. Further progress would mean the *break,* the turn of quantity into quality. It would open the possibility of an essentially new human reality—namely, existence in free time on the basis of fulfilled vital needs. . . . In other words, the completion of the technological reality would be not only the prerequisite, but also the rationale for *transcending* the technological reality.[10]

The last sentence is particularly revealing. Marcuse foresees the future possibility of an alternative, better society only on the basis of continued automation within society. For him, because he is a Marxist, the "technical base . . . remains the very base of all forms of human freedom."[11] Therefore, the continued existence of the technical base must first of all and above all be safeguarded. Here we encounter unadulterated Enlightenment language: "All joy and all happiness derive from the ability to transcend Nature."[12]

But what must be done while technology has not yet been completed, and the capitalist societal structure therefore has not yet served its full purpose? In Marcuse's view the only stance one can take is to participate in the "Great Refusal"—"the protest against that which is."[13] The arts are particularly suited for that, as they can criticize, ridicule, break, and recreate while—driven by the ideal of free personality—they can refuse to be

10. Marcuse, *One-Dimensional Man,* pp. 230f. Marcuse's dependence on Marx is evident when one compares this statement with Marx's view of the relation between the realm of necessity and the realm of freedom. See Karl Marx, *Capital,* vol. 3, p. 820.

11. Marcuse, *One-Dimensional Man,* p. 231.

12. *Ibid.,* p. 237.

13. *Ibid.,* p. 63.

absorbed by the prevailing one-dimensional civilization. Apart from the necessity of waiting for the arrival of a completely mechanized society, Marcuse proposes no alternative but this protest.

Is this indeed a real alternative? It is quite clear, in fact, that everything remains as it is. This protest is really a split alternative, for Marcuse can only propose it by virtue of its lack of success. As he admits, the Great Refusal is "politically powerless" and ought to remain so. It may not endanger the fulfillment of capitalism's high mission: the completion of the mechanization of industrial technology. Marcuse expresses in this critical—and to some extent hypocritical—theory that only in this way can he "remain loyal to those who, without hope, have given and give their life to the Great Refusal."[14]

The conclusion drawn from this is eminently clear. We do not have to look to Marcuse—the neo-Marxist—for a positive contribution to help solve the crisis in western culture. His contribution is imprisoned in the dialectical interplay between the contradictory humanist ideals of personality and domination. In the final analysis, as a Marxist he continues to be a believer in technology in spite of his authentic concern for an endangered freedom and humanity in a capitalist society. He maintains his faith in the progress of production technology as the indispensable basis for the complete "pacification" of society, that is, for the decisive leap into the future realm of freedom and peace.

ESCAPE

The boundaries between an attitude of resistance and one of escape cannot always be drawn very sharply. Escape can be a form of quiet resistance while conversely—as is in part the case with Marcuse—the manner of resistance within society can approach escape. This is illustrated by what Theodor Adorno, perhaps the most profound philosopher of the Frankfurt School, suggests as the appropriate alternative to the dominance of the technological rational pride of western man. In his view there is no other real alternative than acceptance of the *inevitable fate of suffering*[15] as the most human protest which can be found. Adorno points to the victims of the Auschwitz extermination to show what

14. *Ibid.,* p. 257.
15. Theodor W. Adorno, *Negative Dialectics* (New York: Seabury Press, 1973), pp. 361ff.

he has in mind. These victims suffered as full human beings at the hands of their enemies who treated them in a "rational" manner, that is, as being no more than "samples" of a kind. Adorno's disturbing call for the conscious acceptance of suffering in effect constitutes an attitude of both passive resistance and escape.

The most striking feature of the more normally accepted attitude of escape is the will to withdraw from society, even in the physical sense of the word. The history of this attitude goes back many centuries. It was present in the mystical trends of medieval monasticism as well as in certain Anabaptist currents which arose shortly after the Reformation. Today's attitude of escape or withdrawal from the world is usually based on quite different motives. This does not mean that every element of mysticism—the yearning for union with God or with the divine—is absent. But today mysticism is expressed first of all in a pantheistic glorification of man's union with nature, and of the union of one human being with another. This type of mysticism is the basis for many communes founded in this generation.Their members regard them as oases of mutual love and of respect for nature in the midst of the wasteland of a society which depersonalizes human beings and exploits nature.

Despite the wholesome intentions behind many of these communes, we must ask whether they represent a real alternative, a real solution to the problems of western society. In the first place, many communes are characterized by a split morality. Their members often silently assume that other people are prepared to stay within the society they themselves shun, thereby enabling the members of the commune to purchase clothing, to make use of available equipment, and, in case of illness, to fall back on the medical care provided by society. Much "escapism" therefore reveals an élitist double morality: "the rules for my life naturally cannot hold for your life." Because of this it is difficult to believe that the "commune system" can provide a meaningful alternative for society.

More importantly, escape as an expression of reaction reflects a *negation* of the existing problems. The question of what would be a responsible use of the existing possibilities of economic and technological development is usually disregarded by this attitude. As a rule, the yearning for union with nature prevents an honest confrontation with this issue. For that reason this escapism usually does not result in a single solution to any problem. Rather, it is mainly an effort to eliminate social and cultural problems from one's horizon.

COUNTERCULTURE: CHARLES REICH

Another attitude which shows a certain affinity with the attitude of escape, though it cannot be wholly identified with it, is one which expresses confidence in the emergence of a so-called counterculture.

Theodore Roszak, Charles Reich, and William Irwin Thompson, whom we discussed in an earlier context,[16] are proponents of a counterculture. These writers consciously repudiate the adoration of "big technology" in our materialist society, and take up a position against what Roszak labels "religion of science"—that which makes us reduce life to physical and mathematical categories. Their answer does not lie in a conscious political or social revolution. Instead, they hope for a breakthrough of an internal revolution of human consciousness. In that respect their alternative is comparable to the attitude of escape.

There are differences, however, for according to most countercultural thinkers this new consciousness will emerge almost automatically from *existing* society. This spiritual revolution is, in fact, fully present in embryo in the dynamically changing conceptions of modern youth who reject the materialistic assumptions of their predecessors. In this way a counterculture is born which goes back to the mythical and visionary sources of an authentic culture. The apologists of the counterculture, as Egbert Schuurman describes them,

> hailed other forms of knowledge, such as those provided by imagination, intuition, wisdom, mystery, inspiration, ecstasy, contemplation, meditation, myth, gnosis, passion, the unspeakable, the mysterious, and the holy. Their aim was not to know as much as possible, but to know as profoundly as possible, to move away from continual abstraction towards more deeply meaningful, "transcendental" knowledge.[17]

Charles Reich elaborates this approach in his own way in *The Greening of America.* In his analysis he distinguishes three successive forms of consciousness of the American citizen from the founding of the United States to the present, all of which to a certain extent still exist alongside of one another today.

16. See Part Three, section "Signs of powerlessness," pp. 152ff.
17. Egbert Schuurman, *Reflections on the Technological Society* (Toronto: Wedge, 1977), p. 50.

Consciousness I is the pioneer mentality, characterized by the desire to get ahead in society through one's initiative. Its stance is distinctly egoistic. Consciousness II is one of adjustment to modern industrial society, of complying with its wishes and of orienting one's self to its values. "Consciousness II . . . is an 'institution man.' He sees his own life and career in terms of progress within society and within an institution."[18] Today, according to Reich, a third type of consciousness is emerging—one which has the force of an inevitable social evolution. "It comes into being the moment the individual frees himself from automatic acceptance of the imperatives of society and the false consciousness which society imposes."[19] The most important principle of this new consciousness is to "be true to oneself" under all circumstances. The first commandment of Consciousness III reads: "Thou shalt not do violence to thyself."[20]

The rise of this new consciousness, according to Reich, can be seen in the contemporary style of dress. The basic principle for this style is that clothes, above all, serve one's own comfort—they are expressions of freedom. They need not be variegated to serve different purposes on different occasions. The way one appears in one place is the way one appears everywhere, and at all times: "As we are here, we are always."[21]

The new consciousness also implies change in personal relationships with others. The central concept of *togetherness* emerges here. This togetherness consists of mutual sharing of similar experiences in the most divergent ways on the assumption that no participant needs to feel himself or herself personally bound to others. On this basis the new consciousness requires endless experimentation. It expresses itself spontaneously in music festivals and "happenings" and in various types of communes. It also has implications for the manner in which authority and personal loyalty are experienced. "Authority and hierarchy are rejected because they represent the subjection of human values to the requirements of organization."[22] A Consciousness III person "should doubt his own teachers. He should be-

18. Charles Reich, *The Greening of America* (New York: Random House, 1970), p. 71.
19. *Ibid.,* p. 241.
20. *Ibid.,* p. 242.
21. *Ibid.,* p. 253.
22. *Ibid.,* p. 384.

lieve that his own subjective feelings are of value."[23] Finally, "personal relationships are entered into without commitment to the future; a marriage legally binding for the life of the couple is inconsistent with the likelihood of growth and change; if the couple grows naturally together that is fine, but change, not an unchanging love, is the rule of life."[24] The central guideline for life lies in acquiring experience of one's self and—without ultimate commitment—of others. "Consciousness III declares experience to be the most precious of all commodities. All experience has value."[25] Sensitivity to new or long-forgotten emotions must be restored. They must be experienced at the highest level of the human senses and spiritual capacities and, if possible, beyond these limits.

Reich expects that this new type of consciousness will present itself in an ever more pregnant form. Moreover, he expects that this will automatically effectuate a fundamental and profound change in the social *order,* as a result of which most of today's problems will melt like snow before the sun. The emergence of Consciousness III implies that technology is gradually losing its dominating grip on human conduct, that is, technology can and will be used by man only as he sees fit. "Consciousness III must create a culture that knows how and when to use technology."[26] Technology is not rejected, but is used only when relevant. "The hippie agricultural communes are not a rejection of technology, they are a choice, by people who have had too much plastic in their lives, to live close to the soil for a while. They are free to return to technology when they wish."[27] This new attitude toward life will necessarily be accompanied by a different social structure.

> To the realists, the liberals and radicals and activists who are looking for a program and a plan, we say: this is the program and the plan. When enough people have decided to live differently, the political results will follow naturally and easily. . . . The new consciousness will bloom, and whatever it gives life to, a university, a public school, a factory, a city, and finally the courts, the

23. *Ibid.,* p. 392.
24. *Ibid.,* p. 394.
25. *Ibid.,* p. 279.
26. *Ibid.,* p. 408.
27. *Ibid.,* p. 409.

Congress and the Presidency, will become responsive to human needs.[28]

We have not presented Reich's views so extensively because he is such a profound thinker. To the contrary, the superficiality of his argument is directly proportional to its journalistic flair. Nevertheless, what he expresses is what many young people hope for and experience. Does this hope indeed offer a path to a meaningful future, a path which rescues us from the incisive problems of contemporary society?

In trying to answer this question it should be noted first of all that Reich does not present a defense of the counterculture, but in effect proceeds to describe its very presence in our midst. The counterculture emerges more or less by itself. It is contained in the very law of social evolution which holds that one type of consciousness of necessity must be succeeded by another. Consciousness III, therefore, presupposes a technological society. It is only on this basis that it can emerge.

Thus Reich, like Marcuse, tends to stress the importance of *waiting* when it comes to a solution to the problems of western society. Thanks to the mental revolution which has taken place, the problems will be solved of their own accord. The counterculture presently developing will furnish all the required answers.

There is another striking feature in Reich's argument. His characterization of the type of human being now emerging is often very accurate. However, it is noteworthy that this new person can hardly be appreciated as an "improved" type. In fact, Reich's characterization reveals an uncanny resemblance to the "adjusted person" we encountered in Part Three.[29] The Consciousness III person is a type of human being who does not want to enter into lasting personal relationships. He only seeks out incidental, noncommittal relationships which leave him free. Moreover, his key purpose in life is "experience." The most prominent rule for his life lies in striving after continual expansion of his own possibilities toward satisfaction of ever new wishes and needs. But can such a person, whose life's fulfillment appears to be the endless experimentation with all forms of incidental pleasure, indeed exist and live outside the technological accomplishments of a thriving modern society? Of course

28. *Ibid.*, p. 377.
29. See pp. 144ff.

not; that would last only for a while, as Reich honestly admits. This type of person, despite his often rebellious disposition, belongs entirely to this society—of which he is, also in Reich's sketch, the very product.

Reich is correct in his assertion that a particular social order belongs to a particular form of consciousness. But it is not difficult to guess what kind of social order belongs to Consciousness III. The latter requires a society in which technology and economics, more consistently than ever before, are employed to satisfy every new human need. In such a society new *sensations* are endlessly produced, ripe to be experienced immediately.[30] Consciousness III's society also reveals an astounding disintegration of social life, for loyalty, justice, ethics, and compassion have receded as binding norms. These "values" may be pursued only for the "incidental" satisfaction of a personal or a collective need. It seems that we are confronted here with a social order in which one experience after another is artificially produced and reproduced for the benefit of individuals who will only feel more and more dissatisfied, until the last possible experience—no longer artificially induced—namely, death, disintegration, and personal desolation.

Reich's counterculture definitely is not the redeeming answer to the profound problems of our society. The appearance of books like *The Greening of America* are more a symptom of the crisis in which western society finds itself than a contribution to its solution.[31]

REVISION

In addition to resistance, escape, and the hope for a counterculture, a fourth solution to the contemporary problematics should be mentioned. This one aims at revision or transforma-

30. Cf. in this context Ronald Segal, *America's Receding Future* (London: Weidenfeld and Nicolson, 1968); published in North America under the title *The Americans: A Conflict of Creed and Reality* (Toronto/New York/London: Bantam Books, 1970). The author describes the rise of this "sensation culture," illustrated with numerous examples. See also Daniel Bell, *The Cultural Contradictions of Capitalism* (New York: Basic Books, 1976), chapter 2: "The Disjunctions of Cultural Discourse," pp. 85–119.

31. This assessment also holds for Reich's recent book *The Sorcerer of Bolinas Reef* (New York: Random House, 1976).

tion of the existing structure of society. We will briefly consider two representatives of this position: John Kenneth Galbraith and Dennis Gabor.

1. Revision of society: John Kenneth Galbraith

Galbraith's contribution is important for more than one reason. In the first place, it is clearly evident from various publications[32] that he is definitely not a supporter of unlimited economic and technological expansion. He deplores what he calls the "preoccupation" with rising production which is just as common among businessmen and politicians as it is among spokesmen for the labor movement. In *The Affluent Society,* for instance, he vividly describes the disadvantages associated with unlimited growth: increasing inflation, manipulation of consumer tastes, and a greater social imbalance. In spite of that he does not fall into the opposite extreme of rejecting every form of technological and economic development.

Secondly, it is to the author's credit that he points to the relationship between the problems mentioned and the structure of the western economic order. He has done this particularly in *The New Industrial State,* where he singles out the pursuit of economic and technological progress of the "industrial system"— that is, that part of society which is dominated by the large corporations—as the nucleus of contemporary society. It is intriguing to note that Galbraith believes that the government also is directly involved in this process of progress. Thus he writes that "if economic goals are the only goals of the society it is natural that the industrial system should dominate the state and the state should serve its ends."[33]

In the third place, it is significant that Galbraith not only believes in the possibility of curtailed economic and technological growth, but also believes in the positive consequences of such curtailment for all of society. He writes:

> If we continue to believe that the goals of the industrial system—
> the expansion of output, the companion increase in consumption,
> technological advance, the public images that sustain it—are co-

32. Cf. in particular his major publications: *American Capitalism: The Concept of Countervailing Power* (Boston: Houghton Mifflin, 1952); *The Affluent Society* (Boston: Houghton Mifflin, 1958); *The New Industrial State* (New York: New American Library, 1968); and *Economics and the Public Purpose* (Boston: Houghton Mifflin, 1973).

33. Galbraith, *New Industrial State,* p. 406.

ordinate with life, then all of our lives will be in the service of these goals. . . . Our wants will be managed in accordance with the needs of the industrial system; the policies of the state will be subject to similar influence; education will be adapted to industrial need. . . .

If, on the other hand, the industrial system is only a part, and relatively a diminishing part, of life, there is much less occasion for concern. Aesthetic goals will have pride of place; those who serve them will not be subject to the goals of the industrial system; the industrial system itself will be subordinate to the claims of these dimensions of life.[34]

Nevertheless, if we follow Galbraith's argument a bit more critically and pay particular attention to his practical suggestions for improvement, we cannot help but feel disappointed. This is not because Galbraith lacks courage, or because he is hesitant to make relatively radical proposals. For example, in *Economics and the Public Purpose* (1973), he goes well beyond his earlier proposals which centered around a heavier emphasis on public services and expenditures for education (which he considers the "major goal of society"), and which called for the "countervailing power" of the consumer. He now also argues for a socialization of medical care, housing construction, and public transportation, as well as for the nationalization of a number of very large enterprises. He also views strict wage and price controls and a tough environmental policy as unavoidable steps. Certainly all this contains much that is worthwhile, albeit less on the side of his proposals for socialization and nationalization than on the side of his policy suggestions on wages, the environment, and consumers. The disappointment which remains, however, concerns his assumption that the role which technology and economic expansion as such play in western society can hardly be corrected, especially as this concerns the advance of technology. If we penetrate a bit more deeply into his whole approach, we discover that this is no accidental circumstance.

Here we should take cognizance of Galbraith's dependence on Thorstein Veblen, the founder of the Institutionalist School of economic theory. For both men the core development of every modern society lies in technology and technologically determined organizational processes. Whether we like it or not, Galbraith asserts, technology makes its demands; and compared

34. *Ibid.,* p. 405.

with these demands, the formative influence in society of spiritual factors and ideas takes second place. "The imperatives of technology and organization, not the images of ideology, are what determine the shape of economic society."[35] More specifically with reference to our own society, the industrial corporation is determined by the dominating role of an expanding technology. The very core of the corporation lies in the so-called *technostructure,* that is, the form of organization within which the corporation's specialists, with their different types of technique, arrive at group decisions. In turn, this technologically directed existence of the industrial sector influences all aspects of society to a great degree. "The goals of the mature corporation will be a reflection of the goals of the members of the technostructure. And the goals of the society will tend to be those of the corporation."[36]

This is indeed the language of an adherent of Veblen's school of economic evolutionism. The inescapable law for society is that of self-preservation. This law imposes technological imperatives on us. Thus for Galbraith every economic system is a system of survival. In his view every institution and organization must develop appropriate technological and organizational methods in order to survive the struggle for existence. "For any organization, as for any organism, the goal or objective that has a natural assumption of preeminence is the organization's own survival."[37] This inescapable process of adjustment shapes and bends all social institutions into its mold. It even directs our cultural tastes and preferences.

For that reason, Galbraith argues, the real enemy of the market is not ideology but the engineer. Who is capable of resisting the onward march of technology?, he asks. Hence, he predicts that the economic systems on either side of the iron curtain will draw closer together, for they share the same "imperative" technology.

Galbraith's *Problemstellung*—his way of delineating the problematics—of course limits the range within which he can find solutions. This means that in his view no escape is possible from the technological imperative. His solutions invariably presuppose the continued existence of technostructures whose

35. *Ibid.,* p. 19.
36. *Ibid.,* p. 171.
37. *Ibid.,* p. 177.

technological core is unchangeable and irreversible from the outside. In view of this the best we can strive for is a *subordination* of the technologically qualified industrial system to higher (aesthetic) values present in society. Of course, this subordination does not really change or improve the industrial system, but it will muzzle or bridle the system sufficiently to prevent it from doing further harm. It is like pulling the fangs from a venomous serpent which still remains dangerous.

To bring about this subordination, Galbraith focuses his hope on the new intellectual élite of the future. This élite will be shaped by an educational system characterized by "systematic questioning of the beliefs impressed by the industrial system." Such "countering action is what helps the individual escape this subordination" to the industrial system.[38] This is the only indication of a proposed solution by Galbraith which goes beyond the application of a few new technical interventions. It is not surprising, therefore, that his only hope for the salvation of society is to be found in this intellectual élite, as we read in the final paragraph of *The New Industrial State.*

> We have seen wherein the chance for salvation lies. The industrial system, in contrast with its economic antecedents, is intellectually demanding. It brings into existence, to serve its intellectual and scientific needs, the community that, hopefully, will reject its monopoly of social purpose.[39]

When we compare Galbraith with Marcuse we encounter two worlds which at first sight seem to have little in common. Nevertheless, there is a significant link between them. Both start from the assumption that the force of advancing technology compels everyone to adjustment, and both conclude that as a result individual human personality is being threatened. However, Marcuse is a *revolutionary* who advocates the Great Refusal. Galbraith, instead, is an *evolutionist* who in the final analysis relies on the redemptive and critical power of a highly-developed educational system and increased academic excellence.

What makes Galbraith so confident of the validity of this hope and trust? Isn't education a part of the same society? And isn't it for that reason subject to the same dialectical tensions between rational domination and free personal development

38. *Ibid.,* p. 377.
39. *Ibid.,* p. 406.

which characterize the whole of modern society? Galbraith, though in a way quite different from Marcuse, also seems to place his confidence almost irrationally in what a critical scientific method (and an educational system shaped by this) can do for the society of the future. Our final conclusion on the contribution of Galbraith must therefore be a qualified one. His concrete proposals are worth consideration, and to some extent are definitely practicable. However, the question of whether they touch the problems at their root, and contribute toward their resolution, cannot be answered affirmatively.

2. *Revision of man: Dennis Gabor*

Dennis Gabor was awarded the 1971 Nobel Prize for physics. He is the author of *The Mature Society*—a diagnosis of society which, in a manner of speaking, continues at the point where Galbraith left off. He is not satisfied with making some vague references to the value of "education" without further specifics; neither does he come up with suggestions for merely technical adjustments and alterations of the existing economic system. He keenly senses that we cannot consider the future of society without a consideration of man himself—for what western man thinks, hopes, and believes will be decisive for the future of society. Hence, education and science must begin to focus on the predicament of western man in very specific terms.

Gabor's diagnosis of the condition of our culture is lucid and direct. He is convinced that we have won many victories in our battles with earlier "enemies." The science of medicine, for instance, has gained control over many illnesses. Illiteracy is being reduced over the entire world, and poverty is gradually being eliminated. Only one enemy actually remains: "There is no enemy left but man."[40] However, in a world with limited raw materials, a vulnerable environment and an increasingly complex society, this enemy will prove to be the most difficult to conquer. Man has learned to consider "growth" and "hope" as synonymous, and he is accustomed to perpetual increase in welfare and comfort. But such growth cannot continue endlessly, for the natural environment cannot bear this, and raw materials and energy are limited. Growth and hope have become identical in the mind of man. There is a limit to growth, but

40. Dennis Gabor, *The Mature Society* (London: Secker & Warburg, 1972), p. 1.

who can live without hope? Quite clearly, this dilemma is similar to the one discussed in Part Three of this book.

Faced with this dilemma, Gabor sees no other solution but a reduction in economic expansion, coupled with a reorganization of man's technological ability. Instead of accepting "technology autonomous," which is driven by the imperative that "if something *can* be made it *must* be made," technology is to be reorganized "for the good of society." "It must now be re-directed, from 'hardware' inventions towards social inventions."[41] At the same time, Gabor is correctly aware of the inadequacy of this change if man is to be reconciled to a situation without hope which, as we have seen, would be tantamount to a situation without economic growth. The salvation of our society is only possible if *man himself* changes.

Up to this point we can accept Gabor's analysis quite readily. But our attitude changes drastically when he proposes the "remedy" for this problem of changing man himself. His solution lies in the contribution of the modern social and life sciences. He argues that if these sciences should be directed consciously toward this goal, a change in human nature would be attainable. In the first chapter of *The Mature Society* Gabor confesses in all honesty where his hope for the future lies: "All my hopes and all my fears are in the future of this historical process; how by better social machinery better compromises may be made with an improved human nature."[42]

This statement provides much food for thought. In our discussion of the philosophers of the French Enlightenment in Part One, we saw how they believed that the "new social machinery could alter human nature and create a heaven upon earth."[43] Has Gabor perhaps returned to the thought pattern of the Enlightenment? It certainly looks that way, especially in the light of his own confession: "I *believe* in the perfectibility of man, because this is the only working hypothesis for any decent and responsible person."[44] This statement of belief indeed reveals a striking similarity with Enlightenment faith. But there is also a striking difference. Gabor, in distinction from the French phi-

41. *Ibid.,* pp. 43, 44.

42. *Ibid.,* p. 6.

43. John B. Bury, *The Idea of Progress: An Inquiry into its Origin and Growth* (London: Macmillan, 1920), p. 205. See *supra,* pp. 36ff.

44. Gabor, *Mature Society,* p. 6. Italics Gabor's.

losophers of the eighteenth century, knows that man has not really been perfected and forever continues to fall into corruption. Therefore he immediately adds: "But I *know* of the almost infinite corruptibility of man."[45] For that reason Gabor has to go beyond the French Enlightenment when it comes to his own conclusions. The French thinkers could still believe in the *spontaneous* flowering of human perfectibility on the basis of expanded education and new social institutions. But Gabor can no longer afford such naiveté. In view of man's ineradicable corruptibility, all that can be done is to *plan* and *organize* his future perfection, in a scientific manner and to the last detail. In order to accomplish the desired change in human nature itself, man's development toward the good and also his avoidance of evil must be promoted systematically and scientifically.

Gabor's conviction that man can be transformed by scientific means is underscored with the loaded terms he introduces. He speaks of the "engineering of hope," that is, the scientific art of navigation to restore the hope man has lost; of "social engineering"; of "bio-engineering," which involves influencing human hereditary qualities; and of the development of a "new anthropology." Our task, according to Gabor, is to "change 'human nature', as it now manifests itself, so as to fit into a system of which progress is not measured by the annual growth of GNP per capita."[46] For that reason Gabor, in distinction from Galbraith, makes very concrete proposals with respect to the education of the future, including elements of "hardship" and "competition." He also presents detailed suggestions for the future process of selection for positions in society. One should measure—note the word *measure*—not only a person's IQ but also his EQ (ethical quotient) to prevent stupid and immoral persons from making decisions for society. Fortunately, says Gabor, there seems to be a high positive correlation between intellectual and ethical qualities.

To get at the thrust of Gabor's approach succinctly and pointedly, one can say that he has made every effort to lock up western man for good in the prison of his own making. Western man, in Gabor's opinion, has clung to economic growth and technology in the hope for a better future. But now he tends to stand in the way of attaining this happier future and must

45. *Ibid.* Italics Gabor's.
46. *Ibid.*, p. 87.

therefore be adjusted to the new reality. Hence, western man must be transformed to such an extent that he will be able *"to understand our civilization, and to be at peace with it."*[47] To leave the future up to man himself as he is now is far too dangerous. For the sake of his own improved future he must be converted by science into a properly adjusted being who will be at peace and at home in the society surrounding him.

If there is one book that reveals the dangers of an erroneous choice with regard to the crisis of our culture, it is Dennis Gabor's *The Mature Society.* It is a radical expression of one pole of humanistic conviction. I do not want to use the adjective *humanistic* in a pejorative sense. Rather, I use it in a descriptive sense to indicate that Gabor's argument consistently and mercilessly draws the consequences of the ideal of domination by science. This ideal, as we saw in Part Three,[48] finds its spiritual origins in classical western humanism. Therefore it should not surprise us that within the confines of the same humanism voices of protest are heard against the scientistic pride present in Gabor's type of solution. At the opposite pole of the humanist dialectic the Great Refusal is advocated and a cry is sounded for the protection of the dignity of human personality. But will this voice of protest ever provide a remedy?

In spite of our radical rejection of Dennis Gabor—a moral obligation on our part—we may not forget that he is in fact thoroughly consistent in his argument. His basic thesis is that the western world knows no future unless man himself changes. The required change in the nature of man must be more than the will to refuse, as Marcuse demands; the readiness to escape into communes, as Roszak proposes; or the willingness to spend more public funds for unemployment payments and educational opportunities, as Galbraith advocates. If there is anything at all that speaks well for Dennis Gabor, it is his keen awareness of the need that more is required of man than a combination of the virtues his opponents advocate.

47. *Ibid.,* p. 74. Italics Gabor's.
48. See section "The adjusted person," pp. 144ff.

17. *No Easy Way Out*

It is one thing to critique the proposed solutions to the problems of our society. It is quite another thing to present an alternative solution that is indeed appropriate. It must be admitted in all honesty that the solution we need is exceedingly difficult to come by. In the first place, it should be eminently clear from the entire argument developed thus far in this book that isolated remedies for supposedly isolated problems will not suffice to solve the crisis confronting our society. The problems are not isolated. In origin each issue is closely intertwined with the other issues. To a great extent they are all outgrowths of a common base. It simply will not do to prune the branches; we will have to focus on the underlying root, for that is where the sickness of our society started.

Moreover, it should also be clear that the common root of the issues we face belongs to a different order than the framework of reference within which social and economic issues are customarily approached. For example, it belongs to the normalcy of politics to think and act in the framework which permits only a progressive ("leftist") or a conservative ("rightist") direction. But the problems we face have not arisen as a result of a policy which is either too conservative or too progressive. (For that matter, I can hardly think of another distinction which is as flat, as confusing, and as contradictory as that between conservative and progressive.) The common root must instead be sought in the nearly ineradicable tension between western man's will to dominate and his will to be free. That tension laid the foundation for, and was embodied in, the structure of our unique and closed society. To be sure, this closed society certainly has the noble aim to lead humankind to future *freedom*. But because of its spiritual moorings, the only avenue open for our society to pursue this freedom consists in the *domination* imposed by progress over every detail of our social life. In this way an attempt was made to unite man's urge to be free and his urge to dominate into one grand scheme. But it is not surprising that the cracks in this structure become increasingly evident since it was built on a split foundation. The house we have built is a house divided against itself.

TRAITS OF A CLOSED SOCIETY

One can describe this closed society by using two images which we have used on several earlier occasions: the image of a speeding spaceship and that of a buzzing beehive. In a spaceship everything is calculated and aimed at accomplishing only one great purpose, namely, to travel the planned route with a high-average velocity. Every part of this ship has been computed as accurately as possible and has an immediate functional relationship with that purpose only. A similar situation occurs in a beehive. It represents a strict organization of a living society around the queen bee engaged in producing eggs. The continuation of her activity, which is decisive for the survival of this species, is the nerve center and precept of all social activities taking place around her.

With this in mind we can describe a closed society as one which combines strict organization with all-encompassing and hence all-dominating concrete purposes. The term *tunnel society*[49] is perhaps even clearer since it evokes the image of a society in which everything—people, institutions, norms, behavior—contributes to the smooth advance toward the light at the end of the tunnel. But the end of the tunnel never appears to be within reach; the light shines forever *in the future.* Nevertheless, it keeps everything and everyone in the tunnel on the move. The closed or "flattened" character of such a society comes into prominence particularly in the *functional streamlining*

49. The image of a tunnel was suggested by Keynes in a statement we quoted earlier: "Avarice and usury and precaution must be our gods for a little longer still. For only they can lead us out of the tunnel of economic necessity into daylight." John Maynard Keynes, "Economic Possibilities for Our Grandchildren" (1930), *Essays in Persuasion* (New York: Harcourt, Brace & Co., 1932), p. 372.

imposed on the social order in each of its aspects. Nothing is of essential value in any social relationship unless it is a means to advance in the tunnel. Whatever does not serve that purpose is considered meaningless and valueless. Personal and social life is not considered meaningful in itself as it is lived *from day to day*. Today has meaning only if its achievement serves as a stepping-stone to reach tomorrow. But tomorrow will be another today!

Present-day western society is certainly not a fully closed "tunnel" society. It would be incorrect to make such an assertion. There is still a deep sense of righteousness alive in the West. The great majority of the population has a genuine respect for civil rights and freedoms, and for the principles of a democratic constitutional state marked by the rule of law. Hard materialism is characteristic of many, but not all. As for the structuration of society, it can be said that the state and industry, churches and families, are still recognized to a great extent as institutions with their *own* tasks and their *own* responsibilities. That would not be the case in a full-fledged tunnel society, in which independent norms of justice and a rich variety of societal relationships could no longer be tolerated. This is evident in the archetypical tunnel societies which we find in totalitarian countries behind the iron curtain.[50] But at the same time it cannot be denied that the West has moved alarmingly far on the road toward a real tunnel society. We have already pointed out how much the norms of justice and ethics have been bent to serve progress in society. We have also discovered a tendency to streamline; for example, in the trend to equate the tasks of

50. It is interesting to observe that the features of a closed or tunnel society are in fact essential components of all societies behind the iron curtain. Morality, justice, and ethics bear an ideological stamp which betrays in advance a subservience to the system and the all-embracing significance of the class struggle. The objectives of the economic sector in society have been completely identified with those of the state; economic and political power coincide. Finally, the "light" at the end of the tunnel—the transition from a "socialistic" to a "communistic" society—is the all-pervasive societal goal, which is considered attainable on the basis of sufficient technical, economic, and scientific achievements. It seems, therefore, that a convergence—the growing toward one another of the social orders of East and West—is unavoidable, at least insofar as the West does not escape the pressure pushing it toward a more complete tunnel society. Cf., for instance, Jan Tinbergen, "Do Communist and Free Economies Show a converging Pattern?," *Soviet Studies,* vol. 12, no. 4 (April, 1961), pp. 333–341.

government and business, whereby the original distinctions in tasks increasingly grow blurred. Moreover, the people themselves—in their habits, feelings, and behavior—are all moving in the same direction: toward progress, which pulls them the way a magnet pulls metal particles.

This has occurred while the guides of progress themselves—economic growth, technological innovation, and scientific advances—are raised above normative judgment to the status of "providers of meaning" for everyone who follows in their footsteps. Indeed, it cannot be denied that in several respects western society reveals the traits of a closed or tunnel society. Within two centuries it has crystallized into a closed, functional system of norms, values, institutions, and behavior patterns for the benefit of continued economic, technological, and scientific development which we equate with social liberty and cultural advance.

The tunnel character of western society is the source of many of today's problems. This claim can be defended particularly with reference to the peculiar nature of these problems. In the first place, they frequently reveal cancerous symptoms. In the second place, paradoxically, they often appear to be both the malady as well as the result of progress.

Social problems today are *cancerous* because they display an alarming persistence. They are largely immune to the solutions provided by progress. The problem of unemployment, for instance, has different implications today than it had during the thirties precisely because it can no longer be solved by means of more money, technology, and scientific ingenuity. Our problems have become *immune* to progress, but at the same time they weigh heavily upon us because they are *manifestations* of progress. Unemployment is not only a disease; it is also a clear manifestation of progress with respect to labor-saving techniques. Similar phenomena are present in the accelerated tempo of our daily life, in the proliferating intrusion of the media, and in the intensified consumption of energy and resources. Our progress has become our problem. The tunnel has become a trap. Our social maladies are immune to progress as well as directly bound up with progress. They are not incidental, corrigible side-effects; they are incurable expressions of progress itself.

DISCLOSURE OF SOCIETY

In view of this we must conclude that our most essential problems can be solved only when the place of progress itself in society is openly discussed. Only in open confrontation with that light at the end of the tunnel, that beckoning but forever receding and hence imprisoning goal, can we find real solutions. In order to contribute to this discussion I would like to introduce a new concept, namely, that of the *disclosure of society* or, to use a commonly accepted term, the striving for an *open society*.[51]

What is meant by disclosure? This term is intended to express a direction of human life quite distinct from that of a tunnel society. Disclosure implies the recovery of the meaning and value of human life outside of its subjection and service to progress. In the context of our entire discussion it means life's liberation from the closed horizon of a deadly servility to the narrow goals which we established for ourselves by accepting progress as the essence of western culture. Disclosure, therefore, is first of all a process in which the *norms* for human life—like justice, trust, and truth—regain their original validity for our decisions and acts, also with respect to that broad range of decisions and acts where at present the criteria of progress are of overwhelming importance. Secondly, in a process of disclosure, cultural *institutions* and societal forms—like governments, trade unions, and economic enterprises—regain opportunities to develop themselves according to their own distinct responsibilities. Finally, a process of disclosure removes the unbridled pressure on the individual *person* to adjust his or her habits and behavior to external demands. In an opened society the individual is no longer forced to exist as an anonymous object, a recepticle or plaything of economic, technical, and scientific progress. Disclosure implies that every day life is intended to have its own meaning; that today's significance is not exhausted in what it may contribute to tomorrow's needs and wants.

If we are to find a point of departure for the solution of

51. A discussion of the philosophical parallel of the concept of disclosure can be found in the writings of Herman Dooyeweerd and some of his associates. For Dooyeweerd, see his *A New Critique of Theoretical Thought,* 4 vols. (Amsterdam: Paris; Philadelphia: Presbyterian and Reformed, 1953–58), vol. 2, pp. 181–330; and *Roots of Western Culture: Pagan, Secular, and Christian Options* (Toronto: Wedge, 1979), chapters 3 and 4. See also L. Kalsbeek, *Contours of a Christian Philosophy: An Introduction to Herman Dooyeweerd's Thought* (Toronto: Wedge, 1975), pp. 126–141.

society's problems which have so intently occupied our attention in this book, we will have to search for it in the context of the *disclosure of society* itself.

NO READY BLUEPRINT

Having arrived at this point, however, I am in danger of being fundamentally misunderstood, especially by those who—spurred on by the brief sketch of a society in disclosure—now look forward to a manageable and concrete program of action. I will be the last to deny that disclosure can be a matter of concrete action; that will become evident in subsequent pages. But the impression that it is merely a matter of the expert design and execution of a clear blueprint for a better society must immediately be dispelled. Three weighty considerations withhold me from such a misconception.

In the first place, the design and execution of a new blueprint for society might well lead us toward, rather than away from, a closed society. Before we would realize it, such a blueprint could take the place of a new societal goal which, because of its overriding importance, could lay claim to everything and everyone. Disclosure is not to be equated with the goal of attaining a disclosed society. It is not a goal; rather, it is a process. It is the opening up and unshackling of a society which has become entangled in the toils of obedience to the autonomous forces of progress. The disclosure of a society may therefore follow paths on which not every step of the way can be foreseen. It will occur spontaneously in totally unexpected places and along avenues which have not been mapped out. It is not a prefabricated package.

Secondly, every program for an ideal society should be greeted with a healthy measure of skepticism. The great illusion of the eighteenth-century Enlightenment that liberty, equality, and fraternity would blossom forth spontaneously with a new direction in society was quickly followed by disillusionment. Gandhi once said that no structure of society can be so good that it can overcome the evil in man. Putting all your eggs in the basket of necessary change in the structure of society, while being silent about man as the permanent source of evil, is a dangerous ideology. Even a successful process of disclosure cannot bring us to an ideal society. That kind of society is not a product of our hands. A sense of relativity is therefore indispensable when we speak and think about the disclosure of society. Disclosure cannot be a question of the total and complete healing of society. We do have good grounds for expecting certain traces or elements of healing to become visible in a process of disclosure, but only to the extent that people themselves are prepared to accept responsibility for it.

The third objection is directly connected with the last point. A program of action drawn up to carry out a blueprint evokes the impression of a short-term realization of objectives. But disclosure is greater than this, in both scope and penetration. It touches society in its totality, for it involves not only a change in the entire societal perspective and idea of meaning (the religious dimension), but also in lifestyle and social values (the cultural dimension), as well as in the distribution of tasks and responsibilities in society (the structural dimension). It is nothing short of the moving of mountains.

For those who have followed the overall argument of this book so far, the last statement cannot come as a surprise. Social structures are more than methods of societal organization or management systems. They are rooted in a culture and in a belief about the meaning of human life. That is also why my sketch of the rise of capitalism has depicted a process in which not only structural but also cultural and religious barriers had to be broken through. If that is true of the rise of capitalism, then effective realization of the disclosure of society will certainly not involve fewer obstacles. Disclosure implies a genuine change in the order of society because progress may no longer function as the absolute criterion for society. But this change, in turn, has no chance of success, now or in the future, unless it is supported culturally by society as a whole, and harmonizes with what people in that society as a whole experience as the meaning of life. In material terms alone, societal disclosure may require such sacrifices that people will simply shrink back from it. The road to societal disclosure is not only difficult to find; it is also difficult to travel.

What follows below, therefore, presents no program of action. *It can perhaps best be described as a search for the necessary conditions for the disclosure of our society, coupled with a number of personal thoughts on how those conditions might be met.* I have neither the right nor the desire to make greater claims. But that need not rob the attempt of significance, for only on the basis of some knowledge of the possibilities and conditions of disclosure can we individually and collectively consider whether the price is not too high, and whether it is indeed worthwile to pursue this route.

THE BARRIERS REVISITED

To get a clearer picture of the content of these conditions, it may be useful to call to mind the three barriers encountered in Part One of this book: of church and heaven, of fate and providence, and of paradise lost. It was no accident that these barriers constituted a watershed between two totally different types of social order. If we must consider a fundamental change in our society, then the recollection of these barriers can help us discern the true nature and difficulty of our problems. On our way out of the existing tunnel society we might well encounter resistances comparable to those which arose in connection with these earlier barriers.

Perhaps we can approach the same topic in another, albeit more speculative way. The three barriers owed their significance largely to the fact that they had to be successively razed in order for the West to move from the medieval social order to capitalism. At the same time they functioned, as it were, in the opposite direction. When capitalism was established, they prevented it from returning to the earlier medieval structure of society. In other words, once barriers have been taken, they cut off escape, and leave open only the road ahead. But why should the limiting and hindering effect of the barriers, once taken, be exclusively a matter of the past? Is it not possible that these three barriers continue to surround our social order to this day, closing it off from every other fundamentally different direction but that of blind material progresssion?

These questions are sufficiently intriguing to investigate further. In any event, by renewing the relevance of these three barriers, we can perhaps come to a better understanding of the very real problems connected with a disclosure of our society. We shall, therefore, begin with the barrier which is historically closest to us: the barrier of paradise lost.

18. *Paradise Lost Revisited*

What was, in fact, going on in the West when the barrier of paradise lost was taken? In a word, the collapse of this barrier implied the decisive right of passage, throughout western society, for the powers of progress. The belief that human progress would never be able to bring about complete human happiness on earth took leave of men's hearts and minds. Advance of scientific, economic, and technical activities, often coupled with revolutionary political reforms, was henceforth seen as a kind of built-in guarantee of the unlimited improvement of humankind on all fronts. And of course no limit or restriction could be allowed to impede the newly born thrust for progress.

We have already had occasion to observe what momentous implications this had for the place and role of technology, science, and economics. Together these three managed to achieve the elimination of abject poverty, the reduction of terrible diseases and infant mortality to a fraction of their earlier incidence, the extension of educational opportunity to all classes, and the shortening of the workday to eight hours or less. In view of these results, there is every reason to be thankful for what has been achieved. Poverty, disease, and ignorance cried out for forceful and systematic reforms. Therefore, there is certainly no reason to describe the last two centuries of western society in exclusively critical terms, or as a chronicle of retrogression. But, on the other hand, the positive achievements should not blind us to the evils which the course of progress carried in its train, nor to the fact that certain developments, once set in motion, can overshoot their mark and thus lose their meaning. The phenomenon of "overshooting the mark," certainly as regards the combined effect of economics, technology, and science, is a distinct possibility in our modern western world. In the period behind us these three trailblazers of progress have, in roughly two ways, embedded themselves in the whole structure of our society.

In the first place, these trailblazers have attached themselves to our society as forward-moving forces which are *their own justification,* as sources of progress which are good in themselves, and therefore in principle need not be subjected to any critical assessment. Technical innovations are by definition considered desirable, all scientific findings are positive contributions, and in economics it is self-evident that bigger is always better. For decades the three trailblazers of progress have enjoyed a position of almost unassailable authority; it was axiomatic that the direction they pointed out was reliable and secure.

Secondly, the forces of economic growth, technical innovation, and scientific aggrandizement have established themselves securely in our society as *ultimate standards.* They need not measure up to society, but society must measure up to them. Progress does not need to adapt itself to the wishes of people and institutions; people and institutions must adapt themselves to the demands of progress.

With respect to being both its own justification as well as the ultimate standard for society, the regime of progress is, of course, in perfect harmony with faith in a coming man-made paradise. By that faith we are taught to look upon progress as something to trust implicitly at all times.

All of this may seem quite out of date. After two world wars not many people are likely to speak optimistically about the unlimited progress of the human race or about the coming of a paradise. Our faith in progress has soured on us. Many people have become conscious of the fact that ever-expanding economic prosperity, together with constantly increasing sophistication in science and technology, might well rob society of whatever happiness is left to it. Aldous Huxley prefaced his book *Brave New World* with a quotation from Nicolas Berdiaeff, in which the latter confronts our time and civilization with the troubling questions our utopias evoke: "How can we avoid their definite realisation?"[52] All of this rings true enough, but it does

---

52. The original French reads: "Comment éviter leur réalisation définitive?"

not at all justify the conclusion that consequently the barrier of paradise lost has lost all relevance for us. That kind of reasoning would even betray a fundamental misunderstanding of the true state of affairs. Religious and cultural forces, including faith in progress, can indeed wane and wither away. They can even undergo a reversal, and thus become their opposites. But that does not mean, certainly not immediately, that the power and influence they once exerted on the entire *structure* of society is thereby nullified. In its relation to a culture, a societal structure is comparable to a flywheel. A flywheel is capable of taking over momentum from an external impulse. It continues to whirl around long after the original impulse has ceased. This can also be said of our social order. We may be absolutely convinced that our culture's faith in progress has long since had its day— a debatable assumption!—while at the practical level within our social order we are daily faced with its consequences.

This rule certainly is true for our present western society, which has been profoundly changed, deformed, and reformed since the days of the industrial revolution. The transformations have been so penetrating that many consider it incorrect to describe it as a capitalist society. Indeed, if capitalism is defined in terms of a free, unhindered market economy (that is, defined in terms of one of its *stages*), such a view is perfectly understandable. Capitalism thus defined indeed no longer exists in any significant sense. But if we understand capitalism as a dynamic, progress-oriented form of societal organization, then there can be little question but that it has maintained itself in its essentials to the present day. Our society has to this day remained progress-oriented throughout; that is to say, it is internally stable only when economic growth and technological progress are constantly guaranteed. An important reason for this is that capitalism, understood as a dynamic form of social organization, is equipped (and in a sense continues to equip itself) with instruments which serve to ensure this progress as much as possible.

A telling example of this is the increasing influence of modern advertising in our society. From its original role as a perfectly acceptable means of informing consumers about available products, advertising has developed into an increasingly subtle and sophisticated means of persuasion. It is thus able to postpone the consumer's point of satiation, which would lead to a decrease in effective demand and a slowdown in economic growth. Advertising has become a tool to guarantee progress.

In modern industry a business must make provision not only for the maintenance cost of its production equipment, but also for the cost of maintaining demand. It is compelled to engage in such expenditures in order to ensure sufficient continuity in sales. In other words, when human needs turn out not to be as limitless as textbooks in economics would have us believe, they are *made* limitless for the sake of progress in our social order.

For this reason, unfortunately, the thesis that the barrier of a lost paradise is no longer relevant for us is untenable. It is true that the images of a paradise of a guaranteed happy future for everyone have lost much of their influence. Yet, in our societal structure they continue to be artificially and carefully maintained every day. They come to us in the messages prepared by modern sales techniques. These messages propagate the paradise we must seek, which is still one of bounty and affluence.

If we attempt to translate the foregoing in terms of *conditions necessary for the disclosure of our society,* two immediately claim our attention. The first condition is that we must call into question the claim of economic, technical, and scientific progress to be its own justification. It must remain possible for man to evaluate critically, and if need be to reject, certain crucial developments along the path of progress. The second one is that these forces of development have to relinquish their role as the ultimate standards of society. We must find ways and means to challenge the unquestioned autonomy which enables these forces to impose their program of modernization upon society, and thus to force people and institutions into a position of almost helpless compliance.

THE CHALLENGE TO SELF-VALIDATING PROGRESS

In the section "Traits of a closed society"[53] we compared contemporary society to a tunnel. A full-fledged tunnel society is one in which everything proceeds under the aegis and at the behest of the overriding imperative to move forward, and in which the impulse for that forward movement derives from economic expansion and the drive for ever new developments in technology and science. As a natural result of this situation

53. See pp.183ff.

a certain fixed sequence arises in which questions are asked and problems are solved. The first question concerns how we can ensure sufficient economic, scientific, and technological growth. Only thereafter is it asked to what extent we are able to counteract whatever harmful effects may result from such growth; for example, its effects on the environment, on the working conditions of laborers, on the economic status of the poor nations of the world, on the decreasing world reserves of energy and natural resources, on the freedom of consumers, and on interpersonal relationships in society. In a tunnel society such an order of priorities is self-evident. After all, its underlying premise is that the optimum solution of all these problems lies precisely along the trail blazed by our achievements for progress. The growth of affluence and technology provides the best solutions for ecology and pollution, dwindling energy supplies, and the crying needs of the third world. By this assumption, progress continues to function as its own justification.

A society with a measure of disclosure will be characterized by a conscious effort to reverse this sequence of posing questions. Its first concerns will be man's responsibility to protect and respect nature, the meaning of human labor, the human dignity of the consumer, and the opportunities for development of the poor nations; and to preserve for posterity sufficient energy and other natural resources. Only in this context can answers be found to the question of which economic, technological, and scientific developments are possible and desirable. This appears to be the right sequence of concerns for a society not obsessed with the idea of progress.

It will be immediately clear that in such a society—at least in Western Europe and North America—there will hardly be room for further economic development in terms of increased income and consumption. Consequently, it will look more like a "sustenance" or steady-state economy than a growth economy. The development of technology must occur in the light of a conscious choice on the part of society in favor of more modest, small-scale forms of production. In a later context we will return to the two implications of an overextended economy and the dislocation of large-scale technology.

At the moment it is more pertinent to ask how in our society a "reversal of questions" or a reversal of priorities can be implemented in practice. Is it not a mere pipe dream to speak of a "critical evaluation" of progress in the light of more basic criteria? It should be pointed out that at some points a modest beginning of this reversal has already been made. This is important because it shows that the possibility can be realized in principle. A clear example of this is provided by a paper, issued early in 1977 by the Dutch government, which outlined the framework for an economic policy. It starts from the important assumption that every process of economic growth must be bound to observe a number of preestablished conditions ("marginal conditions") with respect to such "facets" as the frugal use of natural resources, the quality of the environment, the position of the developing nations, and even (though stated in very cautious terms) the quality of human labor. Of course, we must not exaggerate the importance of this document. It does not reflect an entirely unified conception and it still tends to accept technological development as an absolute given. But in its main thrust, in its proposal of a so-called "facet policy," at least a toehold for a reversal of priorities in principle and practice is present. Such a document signifies a small beginning of disclosure, however hesitant and limited it may be.

Furthermore, in a number of areas national and international "codes" are being developed. Codes are essentially voluntary agreements concerning acceptable behavior in a given sector. Physicians have had a code for centuries, for the understandable reason that they apply their medical science directly to human beings. Today codes are being developed in the area of advertising and the behavior of multinational corporations. To be sure, these two codes reveal a measure of economic self-interest. In part they attempt to forestall and obviate government intervention. Despite this, or perhaps precisely because of it, the observance of codes provides an interesting possibility for the protection of human interests. They could conceivably be developed in all areas where the advance of the economy, technology, and science, whether separately or in combination, threatens to do violence to basic human needs. The use of codes would be especially appropriate in scientific research, both pure and applied. Certainly contemporary research in hereditary characteristics and their possible manipulation, as well as research in new products and technologies, calls for new codes. To the extent that external compulsion may be necessary next to internal discipline, consideration could be given to government legislation in these matters.

Moreover, the possibility of establishing separate monitoring agencies could be pursued. Existence of such agencies could be very pertinent, especially when developments or discoveries have reached the point of practical applicability. Minimum standards of health and safety, for instance, are already applied to all new products. But evaluation in terms of minimum standards and criteria could easily be extended to such matters as a consideration of the social cost of new products and technologies as they affect energy supplies and the environment. The various sectors of the economy themselves could take national as well as international initiatives along these lines. The above examples serve to show that practical options for the disclosure of our society do indeed exist. The imperialist stranglehold on autonomous progress must and can be broken.

In connection with this challenge to the autonomy and self-validation of progress, two additional areas claim our attention: modern advertising and military technology. Advertising is important because in a profound sense it guides and shapes the manner of economic growth, and thereby also engages economic potentials which could be employed in other ways. It would not be appropriate, nor necessary, to prohibit advertising. But prohibitive measures could certainly be taken against the kind of advertising which depends largely on the power of suggestion. (There even exists advertising which appeals directly to the consumer's subconscious, bypassing his conscious perception.) Moreover, the increase in advertising expenditures in society as a whole could certainly be curbed, for example, through fiscal policies.

Military technology is even more difficult to influence and control. Here, if anywhere, it is unmistakably clear that progress holds society in its grasp instead of the other way around. It is no longer possible to discover any real—normative—meaning in the design and production of sophisticated weaponry with the capacity to destroy whole regions, nations, and humankind itself. The fact that the development and production of this kind of weaponry continues apace, despite its pointlessness and potential absolute destructiveness, is an index of how powerless excessive power can make us, and how progress can produce monstrosities which directly threaten our very lives and the lives of others. Only the courage to make unilateral decisions, with all attendant risks and perils, would enable us to break through the vicious spiral of modern nuclear armament. It is my personal conviction that we must muster such courage, an example of which might be a non-first-use declaration with respect to all nuclear arms. The persistent postponement of necessary unilateral decisions inevitably puts us in a situation in which it is no longer possible to escape the forces of annihilation we ourselves have conjured up.

THE DESTRUCTION OF IMPERIALIST PROGRESS

Modern military technology is an extreme example of "imperialist" progress; that is, progress which holds society in thrall and gives it the character of a closed or tunnel society. But in an important measure this imperialist influence is also present in modern science and its impact on our society, and in our production and consumption processes. Today's imperialist tendency of progress does not, of course, rest on our wish to subordinate ourselves voluntarily to the forces of progress. Modern progress has a coercive character. This will be evident immediately if we decide to implement an across-the-board reversal of the sequence of societal questions, in line with the proposals we have discussed. It goes without saying that more stringent standards for energy and environment, elimination of various forms of meaningless labor, and a cutdown in advertising growth, would lead to the gravest difficulties for every industry in our society. A sharp increase in unemployment and inflation would make it plain that we simply cannot afford this kind of action against progress. There is something binding and ironclad about modern progress.

What is the basis for this binding power? Here we unquestionably hit upon the *autonomy* of progress in our social order, its character of being a law unto itself. It is this autonomy which we must now examine.

INTERTWINEMENT OF ECONOMICS, TECHNOLOGY, AND SCIENCE

Up to this point we have usually referred to economics, technology, and science in one breath. But at this stage of our argument it is important to ask how they are actually related to one another. What is the secret of their firm, indissoluble intertwinement?

It is one of the merits of Egbert Schuurman to have concerned himself with this question in *Techniek en toekomst*.[54] Per-

54. See Part Four, note 1.

haps his findings can best be illustrated by using the image of a funnel. Economics, technology, and science, so to speak, consist of three independent funnels, each one of which is firmly fitted into the other two. First we have the funnel of *scientific development*. At its inception western scientific development was characterized by an amazing breadth and depth. Nevertheless, at a later stage a certain narrowing can be detected, particularly because of the influence of positivism, which imposed the method of the *natural* sciences as the only correct method in every scientific discipline. As a result, a funnel-like narrowing in the horizon of scientific reflection occurred. This narrowing is the basis for the assumption on the part of most contemporary social scientists that determined processes in society are also the most desirable processes. This, too, is the reason why they regard society itself as a mechanical system which can best be administered and governed by means of natural-scientific methods.

The second funnel is that of *technological development*. This is the development of instruments and the manner in which man uses them. A similar narrowing process has taken place here. The specific meaning of technology, according to Schuurman—who is influenced by Dooyeweerd[55]—is the free shaping of given materials. But this specific meaning requires disclosure and deepening. For instance, technology should contribute to social interaction and, "ethically" speaking, it should increase rather than decrease man's love for work. However, it is precisely this particular "meaning" and disclosure which does not show to full advantage when, as is often the case, technology is developed for the sake of technology. This is how Schuurman describes the resulting situation:

> When technology is developed for the sake of technology—which may be a result of the elitist thinking of engineers or a consequence of the naive belief that technical progress automatically brings about the progress of mankind and its society—then we subject technological development to the single norm that what can be made must be made. Whether or not it has meaning is irrelevant. The consequence of such *technicism* and of this *technical one-dimensionality* is disregard for the relationship between man and technology.[56]

55. Cf. Herman Dooyeweerd, *In the Twilight of Western Thought* (Philadelphia: Presbyterian and Reformed, 1960), pp. 90–93.
56. Schuurman, *Techniek en toekomst*, p. 381.

The third funnel represents *economic development.* Its narrowing is present particularly in the dominant role of the yardstick of money for everything that can or cannot be done, so that economic considerations systematically tend to be reduced to mere commercial, monetary considerations. "Nonpriced scarcity," like the natural environment which is used at no cost, appears to suffer most in that situation.[57] A culture which regards entities without a price tag as having no economic value will continue irresponsibly to sacrifice such entities.

In short, the western scientific, technological, and economic developments have each undergone their own narrowing process. One by one they have become funnels. But funnels have the peculiar characteristic that they can be fitted into each other. And this is precisely what happened in western society.

To begin with, the funnel of *science* was fitted into the one of *technology.* Schuurman explains this by referring to the conception which regards technology as merely "applied science." "Viewing technology as applied science," he writes, "signifies the sole dominance of the technico-scientific method. Technological development then becomes the mirror of natural-scientific knowledge." In other words, in addition to its own "narrowing" process, technology is also burdened with the narrowing process of the natural sciences. Schuurman then aptly continues: "This leads to the theoreticisation of technology . . . and consequently to the elimination of human creativity . . . and of human freedom with respect to technical formation."[58] Technology becomes applied science and thus acquires its modern determinist character.

In the second place, the funnel of *technology* in turn has been fitted into the narrowed funnel of a *money economy.* Technology has been trapped in the iron law of maximizing monetary efficiency. The application of this law can systematically eradicate every degree of freedom and flexibility with respect to man's use of technology. "All emphasis is then on saving as the sole economic motive, as a result of which our eyes are closed to the specific meaning of technology as the free shaping of

57. For a more theoretical discussion of the question of economic costs, see B. Goudzwaard, *Ongeprijsde schaarste* [Nonpriced Scarcity: Social Costs and Uncompensated Effects as a Problem for Economic Theory and Policy] (The Hague: Van Stockum, 1970), with English summary, pp. 163–170.

58. Schuurman, *Techniek en toekomst,* pp. 377f.

given materials. The entrepreneur and the enterprise want to control technological development with their vast power."[59]

Thus, western progress in economics, technology, and science can be depicted by three funnels, all fitted into one another, each of which transfers its own specific narrowing focus to the others.

The necessity of competition in a market economy made it imperative for all branches of business to increase their efficiency in terms of monetary standards. This efficiency, in turn, called forth a technological development which, reinforced by natural-scientific determinism, could only permit the violence of single-track, mostly large-scale progress. Thus our technological progress, in the shape of continual increase in productivity, became "wedged" between the funnels of economics and natural science.

Increase in productivity continues even when it forces businesses to lay off personnel or to create an artificial demand for their own products. Technological development, in its turn, reinforces the necessity for the greatest possible economic growth: sales must expand in order to get a proper return on technological investment (in the form of increased productivity). It seems that at this point we have put our finger on the crux of the matter. The autonomy of progress in our social order is essentially based on the mutually reinforcing and determining forces of monetary economics, technology, and natural science. Their joint operation is comparable to a colossal three-stage rocket which propels the spaceship of our society ever higher along its single-track course toward the promised land of material abundance.

An immediate consequence of this analysis, if it is correct, is that a genuine disclosure of western society can become a reality only if the tightly knit bonds uniting economics, technology, and science are at least partially loosened. Without this the obligatory one-track course of progress continues on its way unhindered. In other words, the three funnels, which are presently jammed immovably into each other, must at least become partially *disengaged*.

We have, therefore, detected another concrete *condition for the disclosure of our western society*. We will have to achieve certain degrees of freedom within our socioeconomic order to

59. *Ibid.*, p. 378.

guarantee a position of greater flexibility on the part of economic development *vis-à-vis* the dictates of technology and, conversely, to emancipate the development of technology from the tyranny of scientific determinism and a compulsive drive for monetary efficiency. In other words, we will have to introduce a certain amount of play between the three funnels.

This is no small task. Our scientific determinism and the omnipresent demands of compulsory efficiency are not dismissed lightly. But it would be wrong to think of the task as impossible. The important question, with respect to the relationship between economics and technology, is not so much whether it is theoretically possible to disengage the two but whether it is possible to limit our wishes for income and consumption in society.

ACHIEVING DEGREES OF FREEDOM

It is not difficult to elucidate this point. There are two main compartments in our economic order: production and consumption. In the production compartment goods and services are prepared which are subsequently used by public and private consumers in the consumption compartment. In itself this is not unusual. Such a division of economic activities (production and consumption) occurs in every economic order, certainly in those of modern vintage. But there is something unusual about the way the two relate in the capitalist economic order. In the words of Adam Smith, that relation is one in which "the sole end of production is consumption." To put it somewhat more pointedly: life begins with consumption. Production, at bottom, does not have a meaning of its own. Production and labor are only means—instruments—to arrive at subsequent satisfaction of needs. The satisfaction of needs, in turn, consists of the consumption of goods and leisure time. This goes without saying in a society which assumes that happiness is possible only on the basis of material progress.

In such a society it is natural to judge production only by the criteria of productivity and efficiency. If the true goal of society is consumption, then the means (production) must be mobilized as efficiently as possible for that purpose. For the production sector this implies that in any given time the greatest possible number of consumption goods and capital goods is to be manufactured. Only when that has been achieved will the production sector have accomplished its purpose.

In such a view of life, technology and economics are an intimate part of the production sector. Technology, in this view, can have no other goal than to increase productivity in such a way as to ensure the highest possible net result of the production compartment in society. Only when that goal has been attained can technology be considered successful.

Is such a division between production-as-means and consumption-as-end, between toiling and living, necessary and inevitable? Of course not. This kind of division is necessary and inevitable only as long as it is assumed that the net result of the production sector (goods) can have no other goal but consumption. However, this one-way traffic between production and consumption is not the only choice we have. It is also possible to strive consciously *not* to use up the entire net result of the production sector. In other words, we can make the conscious decision to moderate or reduce income (and therefore consumption possibilities) which we are accustomed to extract from the production sector in order that we may gain the necessary "degrees of freedom" to return to production and labor a meaning of their own; to allow production and labor to respond to standards other than those of productivity and monetary efficiency. Why should the only goal, the only meaning, of production be consumption? It is possible to sacrifice some of our income and consumption, for instance, to utilize the resultant means for a more human technology or for an economic development attuned to broader norms than the exclusive requirement to produce as cheaply as possible for the market.

It is, therefore, not at all impossible to acquire certain degrees of freedom, even if we take the existing economic order as our point of departure. It is possible, in production, to adopt a freer attitude toward the technological requirement of unrestricted increase in productivity. In that connection it is also possible gradually to develop technologies which, although they may be considered less efficient, nevertheless make labor and production a more joyful activity than has often been the case.

Many technicians will eagerly seize the opportunity to develop technologies with precisely this orientation, and thus to contribute to what Schumacher called the "revolution in technology"—a revolution which is imperative if we are to reverse the autonomous trend toward an increasingly large-scale technology.

These remarks are not meant to promote small-scale technology as an end in itself, nor to discountenance every step in the direction of increased mechanization and automation. I do not wish to replace one kind of single-track technological development with another, but rather to open up a multiplicity of tracks in technology. For example, this would mean concretely that in labor situations where the production technique is such that work has become a mere mechanical activity, without any challenge or creativity, automation should take over altogether. In situations, however, where the scale of technology still permits a measure of creativity and variety, these positive elements must be preserved and fostered by the development of a technology especially designed for that end. One possible consequence of such a selective approach to technology might well be a significant decrease in absenteeism.

In summary, my argument does not favor a reactionary attitude to technology; rather, it points in the direction of a much more subtle and flexible approach to technological possibilities and developments. Only such an approach will promote genuine progress: a (technological) development which involves disclosure, that is, an orientation to principles with a substantial normative content.

Perhaps all of this strikes the reader as simplistic and utopian. To be sure, in the following sections we will encounter problems which will serve to add qualifications to the bold strokes of the sketch I have drawn. But these qualifications, it should be pointed out in advance, will not materially affect the basic outline of this picture. That basic outline consists in the thesis that the autonomy of technoeconomic progress in the production sector of society is, in fact, the result of our tendency to organize the processes of labor and production in such a way that the decisive criterion is always financial profit. The accusation employers and employees commonly hurl at one another is that the other claims too large a share of the *out*put of the business. Unfortunately, it is almost never asked how much joint *in*put is necessary to promote more human production techniques and more meaningful labor, or to counteract an exaggerated and artificial stimulation of demand. Yet, it is precisely this question that is crucial for the genuine disclosure of society.

19. *Fate and Providence Revisited*

What really happened when the barrier of fate and providence was broken through in western culture? The assault on this barrier amounted to a declaration of war against all "supernatural" norms and influences which still prevented western man from taking his fate in his own hands. For the sake of this unrestricted self-determination—particularly in economic life—divine Providence had to be transformed into the great Cheerleader on the sidelines. For the same reason a clean sweep had to be made of the remaining obstacles from the tradition of natural law and ethics. As we observed in Part Two, in the eighteenth century natural law was transformed into a legal theory whose first purpose was to make room for the expansion of the free market. At the same time, the barriers from the classical tradition of ethics were eroded by a utilitarian morality which required humankind not to pay any attention to motives but only to useful results.

It cannot be denied that the consequences for western society of this "instrumentalization" of the norms of justice and ethics have been enormous. We can sense this even today. It is present, for instance, in the mentality which limits questions regarding social justice and ethics merely to problems of distribution—the question of how to divide the quantities of welfare, income, and power—without a normative consideration of the meaning and possible use of income, power, and wealth. But the consequences go even deeper; they affect the very heart of western society. There, in the midst of the configuration of our social order, we are confronted once again with the barrier of fate and providence.

204

PARADOX OF UNRESTRICTED FREEDOM

Here we note a paradox. While the original motive for razing the barrier of fate and providence was the unrestricted expansion of man's self-determination, the razing resulted in the contraction of human freedom. Today this contraction is so severe that the concrete possibilities for the disclosure of society have largely disappeared. So we arrive at the strange conclusion that even if the desire for disclosure were fully present, in practice it might not be realizable because the possibility of a free human choice itself has increasingly diminished. The paradox of the modern age is this: freedom pursued as unrestricted self-determination in the end defeats itself. It appears that we are approaching that end today.

The continuous decrease of the possibilities of a free human choice was, in effect, already built into the very manner in which the barrier of fate and providence was removed—the avenue, namely, of a conscious instrumentalization of the norms of justice and ethics. What, after all, was the direct result of this instrumentalization? On the one hand it undoubtedly meant that from a moral and juridical standpoint a great deal of room was created for the "free" expansion of the market by adventurous entrepreneurs. But on the other hand it meant that the accompanying social abuses could no longer be evaluated directly and independently on the basis of universally accepted norms of justice and ethics. Application of limited corrections *as an afterthought* was, as we noted earlier,[60] the only remaining option.

This fundamental deviation from the principle of a "simultaneous realization of norms"—which presupposes the simultaneous validity of legal, ethical, and economic standards for every human decision and act[61]—has contributed to a pattern in which the opportunities for a free human choice have increasingly crumbled and weakened. When the norms of ethics and economics are not applied *simultaneously* in society, they also no longer need to be applied by the same *persons* or *agencies* in society. Thus it is not only possible but in effect very efficient and natural to let the risk-taking entrepreneurs be occupied with only technological and economic affairs, while other institutions are held responsible for matters of a moral, social, ethical, or

60. See Part Two, section "Evaluation of the industrial revolution," pp. 63ff.

61. *Ibid.*, pp. 65f.

juridical nature. Such tasks can readily be delegated to institutions such as the government, churches, or private charities.

In other words, in a society in which the "right" of unlimited autonomous self-determination in economic life is primary, norms of social justice and social ethics of necessity acquire a secondary or a "roundabout" character. They are not considered to apply simultaneously; they are at best held to be valid as an afterthought. Moreover, the primary and original decision makers do not apply them; other agencies in societies are supposed to do that. These agencies must try, in a roundabout way, to shape the final result from a juridical and ethical viewpoint to make it acceptable to everyone.

When toward the end of the nineteenth century, partly because of faith in social evolution, unlimited economic and technological growth became an unavoidable necessity in the West, forcing everyone to continual adjustment, this societal pattern of the diminution of freedom and responsibility could of course only be reinforced. It resulted inescapably in a concept of economic self-determination whose scope became ever narrower and scantier. In line with this "roundabout" ethics, business enterprises today not only do not *have to* concern themselves with matters of ethics; it is insisted that they *ought* not. After having fulfilled their formal legal obligations, their only concern *ought to be* to produce as cheaply and expand as rapidly as possible. Other institutions are expected to pay due attention to issues of social justice, general well-being, and a responsible use of the environment. The tasks delegated to them have been so well-defined that it would only lead to confusion if industrial enterprises would concern themselves directly with these matters as well. Business should stick to what is expected of it: efficient production for the free market within the limits of civil law. That is the limit of its own "free" self-determination. If industry goes substantially beyond that, society as it is structured today will make sure, via competition, that the enterprise has to pay a heavy economic penalty for its overextension: it will definitely become the loser in the commercial struggle.

We need not spend much time on the desirability of this situation. This compartmentalization of society with respect to supposedly primary and secondary norms impoverishes life. Life is meaningful only if there is a measure of simultaneous response to all the norms for human existence. Thus, socioeconomic life should not be separated from the rest of our existence.

The partial isolation of this dimension of life from the prevailing multiplicity of norms has no doubt also contributed to a top-heavy society. Insoluble problems have emerged, particularly for those institutions—such as government—whose task it is after the event nevertheless to guide the entire system to a still humanly acceptable outcome.

In the chapter "Changes Within Capitalism Since 1850"[62] we noted that the force of circumstances led to an ever closer involvement of the government in every phase of socioeconomic life, providing both correction and support as it finds itself increasingly interwoven with it. This meant that the government's task expanded enormously. In fact, in many respects the task became too much for it, and it seems as though more and more problems were left unresolved. But this is hardly the government's fault. It is no wonder that a multitude of insoluble problems arise in a society which is concerned above all with securing progress in the production sector, and only secondarily with the question of how to deal with the enormous responsibilities toward such diverse groups as the unemployed and underemployed, those afflicted by pollution, those in the international economic order who continue to be poor and are often exploited, the energy needs of our own posterity, and so forth. It is simply impossible to take care of all these duties and responsibilities as a mere secondary concern.

A DANGEROUS PSEUDOSOLUTION

Confronted with this situation, many have come to the conclusion that only one solution remains: the transfer to the government of all crucial socioeconomic and technical decisions.

In his book *Kommunismus ohne Wachstum?* (Communism without Growth?) the communist Wolfgang Harich has tried to illustrate the inevitability of this step for western democracies.[63] Harich argues that western democracies, if they continue to insist on the importance of full employment, internal stability, and an unpolluted environment, cannot escape the fact that the government, in the interest of the "collective community," will gradually take control of the entire socioeconomic arena. The

62. See Part Two, pp. 89ff.
63. Wolfgang Harich, *Kommunismus ohne Wachstum?* [Communism without Growth?] (Reinbeck bei Hamburg: Rowohlt Verlag, 1975).

limits to growth, he argues further, will simply force western democracies into collective control of all socioeconomic affairs. Thus, communism will become victorious even in the capitalist West, because "capitalism without growth" is simply inconceivable.

Harich's book is only one possible reading of a reality already acknowledged by many, namely, that the internal dynamics of our social order seem to result in a progressive erosion of decision-making power within the business world. A significant indicator of this trend is the present discussion in several western European countries—Sweden, France, Italy, and Holland—about possible direct government supervision of investments in order to secure sufficient employment. The cries of protest raised against such measures—because they would constitute an attack on the "freedom" of enterprise—sound at the very least somewhat hollow and impotent—hollow because the freedom of enterprise in these countries hitherto has often been nothing but an élitist freedom of the few; impotent because it is indeed futile to expect business to find its own solutions to the above-mentioned problems, given that business understands itself as a production sector merely producing means-for-satisfaction, and as a series of workplaces with no concern other than the efficient combination of production factors.

It is extremely doubtful that the allegedly "logical" consequence of complete government control over all crucial economic decisions will really bring any relief at all. Such a takeover of economic control is not a solution but its opposite: acquiescence in an accomplished fact. It is the recognition of man's impotence to curb a "progressive" society of giant scale and complexity in any other way than by an external governing system of giant scale and complexity. In a sense society thereby closes itself off even more, for only by shifting the burden to the allegedly democratic collectivity can "responsibilities" still said to be borne and experienced. But who will guide the system, and by what criteria? In this way political and economic power, both of which are very influential and open to abuse, will be inextricably combined with each other. The result might well be the opposite of acquiring degrees of freedom; instead, the existing degrees of freedom are being lost. The paradox of sovereign self-determination has not found its solution here; it has found only its bizarre point of culmination.

But is all of this really necessary and inevitable? On the basis of the internal trajectory of a closed tunnel society, the answer must be yes. Within that context the laws of the dialectic of progress are indeed ironclad. There can be no absolute individual freedom which does not in due time conjure up, through its consequences, the necessity of central control and domination.

In other words, classical liberalism—which advocates decentralized, autonomous freedom of progress for business—logically leads to the necessity of growing central control of society. The natural complement of autonomous and decentralized freedom in the production sector of society is the centralization of social responsibility in the state. Classical socialism—the pursuit of centralized responsibility—is therefore not only the opposite of liberalism, but also its consequence. It is precisely in their opposition that they presuppose one another.

But as soon as we begin to speak of a disclosure of society, the ground for the dialectic of progress falls away. Why should it be true that processes of production can only be blind processes of progress? Why should we remain caught in the dilemma of decentralized freedom versus centralized responsibility, when it is possible to proceed on the basis of norms and responsibilities of a unique and specific kind in each area of life, including the area of socioeconomic activity? These norms and responsibilities have to be emancipated from their tacit servitude to the laws of progress. We have seen that the root of the problem lies with the erosion and instrumentalization of the norms of justice and ethics, as well as for economics, for the sake of an advance commitment to autonomous progress in the production sector. It should be possible to make a direct connection again between these norms—translated in terms of more broadly delegated responsibility—and all socioeconomic activities in the production sector.

This brings us to a *third condition for the disclosure of society:*[64] the reintroduction of direct, full responsibility in the production sector of society, to be executed there in accordance with obligatory and unbroken norms of morality, justice, technology, and economy. Only on this basis can the degrees of freedom we have mentioned be meaningfully exercised and the communal codes of behavior be developed.

At first sight this third condition seems easier to fulfill

64. For the first two conditions see p. 193; cf. also p. 200.

than the first two. But appearances are deceptive, for the fulfillment of the last condition of disclosure requires no less than three conditions of its own: (a) knowledge and acknowledgment by business of unbroken norms of morality, justice, technology, and economy, each with its own validity;[65] (b) such organization of business that the internal realization of these norms becomes a real possibility;[66] and (c) a society which is designed to make business live up to its obligations.[67]

ACKNOWLEDGED NORMS

Every genuine process of disclosure requires the recognition and fulfillment of norms. Without norms it immediately loses impetus and effectiveness; without norms our values and standards, too, lose all material content which we might apply as criteria for progress.

But how can we come to a communal knowledge and acceptance of such norms? That raises a special problem, for norms can never be formulated outside of a committed life perspective, and there are, therefore, definite limits to their acceptability to people of different persuasions. This difficulty leads many to give up on the whole matter of acknowledgment of norms in a pluralistic society, or else to look for such broad formulations that they will be acceptable to all. Both reactions are counterproductive, however. To let the whole matter rest is like burying one's head in the sand. This only leads to the dominance of pseudonorms, such as "give everyone the freedom they need" or, "do everything in a democratic manner." The search for generally acceptable formulations, on the other hand, only makes the norms referred to more vague and devoid of content. In this way they lose their force completely.

It is much better to let everyone speak his or her own mind in these matters, in accordance with his or her own convictions. On the basis of my convictions, therefore, I openly claim that the norms of justice and morality, as well as those of economy and technology, do not find their deepest origin in man and his autonomous choices. Norms are valid in a world which was created and was designed to allow us, in everything

65. See the section "Acknowledged norms" immediately following.
66. See the section "Responsible structuration of economic life," pp. 214ff.
67. See the section "Public monitoring," pp. 219ff.

we do, think or speak, to respond to God and one another. In other words, norms are nothing more, nor less, than guidelines and avenues of response to God and neighbor. For that reason we can ignore norms only to our own detriment, for without this dimension of response our life and society in this created world run amok. Norms are not intended to rob us of our freedom; rather, they enable us to retain life and liberty, to prevent us from threatening the lives of ourselves and others.

Thus, this stance with respect to norms is clearly Judeo-Christian. Yet in certain respects it is, fortunately, also part of a *communal* cultural heritage. Our western "sense of values," nourished as it is by both Christian and nonchristian sources, is still a reality in our culture, despite threats to its existence. This creates the possibility of mutual appeal. There is a certain basis for our calling upon one another not to let the good elements in our sense of values be lost altogether.

Against this background I will present the following comments concerning the content of certain norms like economy and technology, morality and justice, especially as they apply to the production sector of our society.

1. The norm of economy

We are all acquainted with the facile identification of acting economically and efficiently, that is, acting in such a way as to acquire the greatest possible result in terms of goods or money. But it is not difficult to discern that in this way the economic norm for human life is both narrowed and distorted. It is narrowed into something which is limited to the creation of material or financial surplus, and it is distorted into something which is primarily a matter of self-interest. Such a conception of economics has been emptied of almost everything which might be reminiscent of a response to God and to one's neighbor. It has become an empty growth imperative.

In classical antiquity two distinct Greek words were used to describe human economic activity: *oikonomia* and *chrematistike*. *Oikonomia* (the origin of our word *economics*) designated the behavior of the steward whose task it was to manage the estate entrusted to him in such a way that it would continue to bear fruit and thus provide a living for everyone who lived and worked on it. Central to this concept, therefore, was the maintenance of productive possessions on behalf of everyone involved. *Chrematistike,* however, meant something quite different. This word expressed the pursuit of self-enrichment, for ever greater monetary possessions, if need be at the expense of others. It is remarkable to observe that in western civilization the meaning of the word *economics* has increasingly become synonymous with *chrematistike,* while progressively it lost the meaning of *oikonomia,* the careful maintenance as steward on behalf of others of all that is entrusted to man.[68]

A business is not run economically if it is efficient merely in a monetary sense. *It is economically responsible only if it possesses the ability to render a net economic fruit.* In terms of a normative-economic cost-benefit analysis, many financially viable businesses may be called economic fiascos, whereas the opposite might be true of a number of businesses which are losing money. As an example of the first we might cite producers of goods which can actually be marketed only by means of intensive advertising campaigns, but which pollute the environment (either during production or consumption), are energy intensive, and use up the world's dwindling supply of nonrenewable resources. Another example would be those firms which damage the health of their laborers during the process of production (health, too, is an economic good!), fail to utilize their workers' mental capacities, or even brutalize them by overdoses of mechanical and deadening drudgery. Corporations can also fail economically—despite great apparent success from a financial point of view—in their operations in developing countries; for example, when they engage in the accelerated exploitation of natural resources in a capital-intensive way (that is, with minimum employment of natives), only to disappear from the scene as soon as they have made their profits. The society which is left after such a visitation may well be left without the natural resources necessary for its own development, with no less unemployed than before, and with the dubious blessing of having come into contact with a standard of living and consumption which may be forever out of its reach. A more poignant illustration could not be given of the chasm dividing *oikonomia* from *chrematistike.*

Business enterprises, in other words, should be genuinely economic organizations, that is, institutions of stewardship. That is the key norm by which they should be judged, without neglect of market factors.

68. This was already noted by Karl Marx. See *Capital,* vol. 1, p. 152, note 1.

2. The norm of technology

The question of whether something is technologically responsible has come to mean almost the same as the question of whether it "works"—whether it successfully performs what you expect it to perform. But, once again, this is a dangerous concession to a technological development which has nothing to do with genuine human response. It fosters a technology which is judged only in terms of the arbitrary goals for which it is developed.

Technology has a meaning and norm of its own. This is found in the opening up of possibilities for creative use of typically human tools. The term *creative* links up with the deep-seated need of the human creature to be involved in creative activity to express something of himself in what he fashions. A technology which kills rather than fosters creativity is therefore antinormative. The same is true for a technology which can no longer be looked upon as *human*—either in the sense that it exceeds the measure of man in its large-scale dimension (a point expressed especially by Schumacher), or in the sense that its design is such that it isolates man from his neighbor. The last point is illustrated particularly by those forms of technology which deprive human labor, on a fundamental level, of its social and cooperative nature, thus robbing human work relations of their life's blood by the systematic removal of the element of social contact in the workplace.

Just as business firms may be held accountable for meeting the norm of economy (stewardship), so they may and should be held accountable for meeting the technological norm. Society, including its production sector, cannot ignore these norms with impunity.

3. Norms of morality and justice

Earlier we encountered morality and ethics as norms which had been bent in the direction of *a priori* service to the ideal of progress. Morality found expression in an ethics of utility or usefulness which condoned anything eventually leading to useful results in terms of progress. The norm of justice, in turn, became a rule requiring only the observance of existing formal civil rights. (This is probably the origin of the still widely accepted rejection of bringing norms of justice and ethics into play in the business world.) But it is precisely the application of the norms of morality and justice to business life that is indispensable for any kind of disclosure process in our present tunnel society.

The most obvious norm in this connection is *morality,* which requires that people should not be treated as objects but as subjects. Objectification of people can occur with reference to employees (who are accordingly plugged into the production process as mere suppliers of almost infinitely divisible units of labor), as well as with reference to consumers. Consumers are made into objects when they are manipulated by marketing techniques as just so many bundles of psychic impressions and motivations. The mark of objectification is that people are no longer treated as bearers of responsibilities. A business enterprise, for example, treats a consumer as an object when it no longer appeals to his sense of responsibility, but instead attempts to overrule or manipulate his choice. Employees, similarly, can be reduced to objects by the minimization or destruction of the possibility of making responsible choices of their own. Morality is always a matter of the recognition of other people's responsibilities. For that reason we certainly cannot exempt business from meeting its specific ethical norms.

Doing *justice* is closely related to this. The consumer has a right to a product of good quality and durability, and this right must be respected. In the case of environmental pollution, inhabitants of cities and neighborhoods have a right to protection against such pollution, which includes noise pollution. Suppliers of capital also have certain rights—not in the sense that they may demand exclusive control of an enterprise (a topic we will discuss later), but in the sense that they should receive a fair return on their investment. And last but not least, there are the rights of the laborer. These include the right to a fair wage and the right to a fair share in the final profit, but no less the right to be recognized as a member of the work community. These rights, however, may never be divorced from responsibilities, and thus should always be formulated in the context of bearing responsibility.

RESPONSIBLE STRUCTURATION OF ECONOMIC LIFE

Asking business to assume the responsibility of engaging in economic activity in the proper sense, of developing human technology, of refraining from objectification of people, and of recognizing the rights of consumers, residents of the environments, laborers and investors: all of this is no incidental matter. For such an exercise of responsibility, a business enterprise requires sufficient economic means,[69] a suitable structuration of its production plants, and a proper attitude toward its task.

With respect to attitude, we can reasonably assume that a considerable segment of the business community is quite positive about a conscious reorientation toward a more normative and more broadly conceived industrial task, provided society will furnish the economic resources required for its execution.[70] Nevertheless, a fundamental obstacle remains, namely, the implication such a reorientation would have for the decision-making process within the business enterprise. It is undeniable that the perspective of a real disclosure process in our society implies a fundamental recasting of authority and responsibility in business firms.

A business enterprise of the classical capitalist type comprises a workplace where efficient production factors are combined so as to make a profit in the market. In principle that's all that is involved, and for that reason it is easy to look upon and treat such an enterprise as an object of ownership. The owners possess the workplace, by means of which they engage in production and sales, and ultimately realize a sufficient return on their invested capital. All activities can be tested in a simple way against the goal of profit. Assurance of present and future profit is obviously of paramount significance in a capitalist conception of the enterprise as workplace.

The unadulterated capitalist enterprise has become something of a rarity in our society. Modern business is a good deal less dependent on the suppliers of capital than was its older counterpart.[71] Nevertheless, in many instances the internal functioning of an enterprise still follows the traditional pattern: it is almost exclusively geared to profitable production in a growing market; its management combines the production factors in an efficient manner and is accountable for that to the shareholders. In many respects the business enterprise has not advanced be-

69. See "Paradise lost revisited," pp. 190ff.
70. In Holland, the work of the so-called "Young Management" group of the Dutch Christian Employers' Union, for instance, is very encouraging in this regard.
71. See Part Two, "Changes within the enterprise," pp. 90ff.

yond the stage of being solely a workplace, even if increasing importance is accorded to company councils in which the workers share a measure of codetermination.

But is it proper to view a business concern in a society moving toward disclosure as nothing but an efficient workplace? Just to ask the question is to answer it. In a society which expects business to live up to the norms for authentic economy and technology, as well as to the norms of morality and justice, it is indeed impossible to regard firms as mere centers of efficient production. Moreover, the involvement of personnel must then go beyond the mere supplying of manpower. Employees must be given co-responsibility for effective decision-making. Increased responsibility of the business enterprise should be translated into increased co-responsibility on the part of the members of the concrete work community.

We can arrive at the same conclusion by considering the matter of ownership of an enterprise. As long as the enterprise is considered to be nothing but a workplace for combining production factors, it can indeed be regarded as being owned. But as soon as it is looked upon as it normatively *ought* to be—as a work community of living people—it is possible to speak of its being "owned" only in a derivative sense. One can be the owner of the capital goods of an enterprise, but not of the work community itself. For example, one can speak of a church building being owned, but one cannot speak of a church community being owned. To speak of ownership of an enterprise, therefore, may well reflect the same leveled view of society which has led people to treat businesses as no more than profitable workplaces. As soon as they are regarded as institutions bearing responsibility for their actions, and comprising workers as members, it becomes obvious that the suppliers of capital cannot lay exclusive claim to the activities of the enterprise. Once an account has been rendered of how their capital investment has been handled, the rights of investors are fully satisfied. It is neither possible nor lawful for a business enterprise as a responsible work community to act as though it were an extension of the will of investors or a mere object of ownership. This implies at the same time that the enterprise carries its own particular responsibility, precisely as a work community. Everyone in a business, whether belonging to management or labor, bears a certain communal responsibility for the overall behavior of the enterprise in society. And this in turn requires some form of effective input and codetermination on the part of all personnel for the main contours of company policy.

The best and most incisive treatment of the proper delegation of authority and responsibility in a genuinely responsible enterprise has probably been given by the English businessman George Goyder in *The Responsible Company*.[72] Goyder speaks of the necessity of restoring a *balance* between the interests of workers, consumers, and suppliers of capital. Such a balance is absent when the scales tip decisively to one side as soon as the weight of the interests of capital are added. Sometimes the required balance of the scales can be restored only by the government. Accordingly, Goyder favors legislation which would guarantee employees the right of codetermination in matters of general policy making, possibly coupled with representation of consumer interests in the governing board of an enterprise. He does not intend thereby to transfer responsibility for the weighing of interests to the government. Rather, his concern is the creation of such forms of control that the enterprise itself can come to the point of seriously weighing one interest against another. It is crucial that the enterprise live up to its own special responsibility toward its workers, consumers, financial backers, and surrounding natural environment.

However, it may be questioned whether legislative changes alone will be a sufficient remedy to restore the required balance. To obtain a genuinely balanced scale on which the enterprise weighs the various interests, we must realize that every decision within the enterprise has its own economic implications. In other words, pure balancing is not just a matter of weighing rights and justice; it is equally—probably primarily—a matter of the presence of sufficient *economic* weights. Every interest group should be able to add, as it were, its own economic pressure to the scales; it should have its own voice with respect to the liabilities and risks associated with every decision.

When we recalled the barrier of paradise lost in the discussion of the disclosure of society, one of the conclusions was that economic degrees of freedom must be regained to allow for a more responsible development of economy and technology. This conclusion is thrown into sharper relief by what we have just said. Humanization of labor, more concentrated at-

72. George Goyder, *The Responsible Company* (Oxford: Basil Blackwell, 1961).

tention to the living and working environment—in short, responsible management of a business enterprise in terms of broader norms for economics and technology, and in terms of the norms of morality and justice—requires economic elbow room which, in the business enterprise itself, can count as weight in the scales. Its weight should carry not only via the direction of management but also via the input of the employees. The latter as a group should have an opportunity of "investing" in the disclosure of the company, bringing with them an economic weight of their own, so that they can have a real voice in the charting of general company policy.

Practical avenues for the realization of this process in principle seem to be available. In this connection we can point to Sweden, where legislation requires that a small but fixed percentage of national wage increases be set aside for the humanization of labor. A more dubious approach is chosen in Belgium, where government subsidies to business are made contingent on the prior approval of the investment plans by the company's workers' council. Another interesting proposal has been made by the Christian Labour Association of Canada. This organization has suggested[73] that employees in industries chosen for this purpose be persuaded to allocate part of their wage increases for a number of years to funds under their own control. The monies made available could be used by them for a variety of purposes; for example, to provide aid to handicapped workers and their families, or to make better and more human forms of industrial technology financially possible. An opportunity could thus be provided for the introduction or continued use of those forms of technology which would have little chance of success without this kind of earmarked subsidy.

We can even go beyond this and ask whether in the long run—given the standard of living achieved by skilled labor, especially in the United States and Canada—the possibility of a more direct balancing of wages and meaningful employment opportunity exists. It would be quite in tune with a conception of growth toward responsibility in the production sector if all personnel together would opt for a wage reduction in favor of retaining or increasing the kind of meaningful employment which this might provide.

73. This suggestion was made by Gerald Vandezande when he was general secretary of the Christian Labour Association of Canada.

The legal structure which seems to lend itself best to this kind of internal arrangement, at least in a number of cases, is that of the production cooperative. In this structure the choice between wages, profit, and employment is, in principle, the common choice of management and labor. This legal structure not only reminds us of the important initiative of Robert Owen at the time of the industrial revolution, but also has promise for the future. Just as a limited liability company is the most characteristic organizational form for a closed capitalist social order, so a particular form of production cooperative might be characteristic of a society that is more open. In any event, it is a legal structure easily adaptable to broader norm orientation and greater sharing of responsibilities in business enterprises, especially if they are of a small or moderate scale.[74]

PUBLIC MONITORING

The opening up or disclosure of society means that responsibilities for one's neighbor are not just exercised via the detour

74. This is not the proper place for a detailed elaboration of the implications of this approach for the structural organization of our society. One general observation is in place, however. Allocating more immediate responsibilities to business does not have implications just for the structure of individual businesses but for that of whole branches of industry. It would be unreasonable to expect each single business enterprise to respond appropriately to all these responsibilities. They need certain guidelines, and these can best originate at the so-called middle level of society, that is, between the macro-level of the national economy as a whole and the micro-level of the individual enterprises. By consultation at the middle level—in bodies within each branch of industry, composed of parity representation of employers and employees—agreements would have to be reached on how the companies in the industry would concern themselves with such tasks as the promotion of meaningful work, reduction of excessive advertising, prevention and combat of environmental pollution, the battle against disposable utensils, and the advocacy of a better international division of labor. Such agreements would have to be sufficiently broad to allow for individual variations of emphasis among different individual businesses within a given industry but, on the other hand, they should have enough specificity and force to convince the government of the usefulness of making them legally binding for the entire industry.

Variations would be possible, of course. Coordination could be done in bodies other than those representing one industry. Government involvement from the very outset in this industry-level consultation will be advocated by some. Personally I would be wary of the latter approach, for thus the responsibilities of government and industry would be mingled in a somewhat corporate, fascist manner. Be that as it may, however, in the future structuration of our society the level of branches or sectors of production must on no account be neglected as a basis for communal consultation and decision-making.

of "society as a whole" and its "agencies," but are at least partially brought back to the sphere to which they originally belonged. With respect to our theme, it is not enough to recognize the original responsibilities of a business enterprise or to give it the appropriate internal decision-making structure. Something else is still necessary: society must have the ability and desire to make business *live up to* its responsibilities. Business firms will have to be reminded of their responsibilities. Disclosure can never be a matter for just one sector of society. It is a thoroughly cooperative matter, in which consumer organizations, the government, and the labor movement can each play an important role.

1. Consumer organizations

For many years consumer organizations have given advice to consumers on only two points: the quality and the price of products. Gradually, however, they are coming to a slightly different stance. In some instances the information they provide is being extended to include questions as to the origin of raw materials used, the nature of the enterprise making a product, and aspects of pollution and energy waste.

This shift in orientation is a positive development, especially insofar as it reflects a change in attitude among the consumers themselves. Today's consumer is more conscious of being co-responsible for the effects of his buying. Protest campaigns and boycotts organized by consumer groups against certain businesses or products are not always successful and are sometimes carried out in an awkward and arbitrary way, but as expressions of a sense of co-responsibility they deserve our respect and often merit our support.

A real disclosure of society may well call for even greater involvement on the part of consumer organizations. All instances of clear, conscious, and systematic company violation of the norms which apply to them in economic, social, technological, and moral areas[75] could be noted by consumer organizations, and the name of the company and its products could be publicized. In cases of particularly blatant and gross violation of the most basic norm of morality and other norms for economic life, consumer organizations might well go even further by

75. See "Acknowledged norms," pp. 210ff.

blacklisting the companies concerned and calling upon consumers to boycott them temporarily.

Consumer power, if responsibly used, can have enormous influence for good in our society. It not only puts pressure on a blacklisted firm to mend its ways, but also on other firms to avoid this kind of public loss of prestige. The modern business enterprise is extremely sensitive to public opinion. After all, their often gigantic advertising campaigns are aimed at directly influencing public opinion. Accordingly, negative advertising organized by responsible consumer groups against improper corporate behavior could be more effective than reams of government rules and regulations.

2. *The government*
It is impossible, of course, for the government to bring about disclosure on behalf of society. Disclosure is a responsibility for society as a whole. It is a matter of a mutually accepted willingness to shape culture in a different direction. However, a government can definitely contribute to a process of disclosure by creating the necessary political conditions. Moreover, it can itself begin to take steps toward an open society by a redefinition of its priorities. For instance, in its relationship with the industrial sector, the government can create a measure of room for individual enterprises to accept a broader conception of their task, and it can stimulate them to implement this task.

A few limited illustrations will be helpful here. In the area of environmental control the government could make differentiated stipulations for the relevant branches of industry to attain a reduced level of pollution within definite time limits. This type of government intervention is especially effective if it is accompanied by the legal threat of closing down an industry in case of total noncompliance. Such intervention is to some extent different from what we are generally used to. In environmental control it is more customary either to tax an industry or subject it to a number of prohibitions.[76] But insofar as the above proposal involving a fixed time span is followed, we are dealing with something essentially different. In that case an effort is made to place industrial life itself on a broader footing.

76. This is the general situation in Europe. Fortunately, in certain instances environmental legislation in the United States does prescribe specific tasks industries must perform to protect the biomilieu.

What I have in mind is this: a business enterprise ought to be made publicly responsible for "opening up" the economics and the technology of its operation to a proper respect for the environment. In the light of the norm of stewardship I dare say that the concern for nature is a responsibility that properly belongs to all producers and consumers. The role of the government in the future must be such that this responsibility is brought back to where it belongs, even if this requires a special type of intervention. In this way industry is given the time and the opportunity to mature, within its own sphere of responsibility, toward the assumption of a neglected task. This is only an example from the area of pollution and environmental control, but the principle which it illustrates is applicable in many cases where we are confronted with analogous problems.

A government can also move industry in a more positive manner to a beginning of disclosure. In that context we can point to a fascinating suggestion made by George Goyder in *The Responsible Company*.[77] The author proposes that certain concerns be given the privilege of carrying the legally protected predicate of "public company," which they could then use in their sales promotion. Only those companies would qualify which have given sufficient evidence of adequate concern for the environment, good internal social relations, and service to the consumer in the form of quality products. This is still a modest proposal but one with potentially interesting consequences. If certain companies could obtain the distinction to use this predicate as a result of their responsible social, economic, and ethical behavior, they would not only receive positive recognition for the benefit of society, but they would also have the right to appeal directly to the responsible consumer. In this way competition could be a more constructive force than it often is today, because it could stimulate competitors to meet the conditions for the same privilege. Furthermore, employee and consumer organizations might receive the power to propose the names of firms which in their mutual estimation meet the required conditions for the special title "public company." In this manner another small beginning could be made in the process of disclosure of economic life.

77. See Part Four, note 72.

3. *The labor movement*

What about the role of the labor movement in the recovery of an open society? The labor movement can play a very significant role in the reversal of the process of functional delegation and shifts in responsibility which caused the onesided focus of industry on economic and technological expansion. But it should not be forgotten that the conduct and goals of labor unions can be as leveled and irresponsible as those of industry itself! Today union activity often appears to be oriented almost exclusively to increases in wages and decreases in working hours. If that is the case, labor unions only contribute to the denaturing of the business enterprise, whose meaning and purpose have been reduced to the production of a pie large enough to satisfy the vested interests, including those of labor.

But labor unions can also conduct themselves differently. They can initiate efforts to reintroduce the meaning of responsibility in labor within the industrial horizon. How can this be done within the present setting of labor relations? Perhaps we should consider the possibility of a labor union negotiating a more favorable collective bargaining contract with those companies that have shown a willingness to heed social norms, to respect both worker and consumer, and have made a genuine effort to adopt a distinct style of stewardship in their daily operation. A business which has learned to conduct itself as a "public company," that is, a business which acts in a responsible way toward its suppliers, its investors, its employees, its clients, and its natural environment, is entitled to the backing of the labor movement. Such support might stimulate other companies to follow suit. In that way the labor movement can definitely contribute to the recovery of an open society.

In short, an attempt to transfer appropriate responsibilities to agencies which should have exercised them in the first place is not doomed to failure from the start. The old biblical rule that we must conquer evil with good may well appear to be a very useful guide in bringing about the necessary changes in society.

20. *Intermezzo: Possibilities and Limits of Disclosure*

So far we have dealt with two barriers to real disclosure of western society. The first hinged upon the renewed recognition that human progress as such does not open a perspective on a future paradise. For that reason the blind, single-track process of autonomous economic, technological, and scientific progress must be broken through, in order to critically examine progress itself. A necessary minimal condition for this is the creation of economic "elbow room" or degrees of freedom. The second barrier hinged on the recognition that people and institutions cannot play the role of providence in their own affairs. In their societal development they will have to reckon with obligatory norms. These norms also apply to economics and technology, and they constitute a basis for appeal by others when they are not lived up to.

Before we proceed to the third and last barrier, it may be meaningful to subject what we have asserted to a kind of acid test. Is it not true that an insuperable obstacle to any attempt toward disclosure in societies like Canada and the Netherlands is their great economic and political dependence on other countries? Besides, would not a critical approach to our kind of progress have severe negative implications for the developing world? And would not one of the first results of a deceleration in consumption be increased unemployment?

Moreover, in connection with the concrete possibilities for initiating disclosure, other questions arise. How, for instance, could it begin, and where would it end? All these questions will have to be faced squarely.

224

VULNERABILITY OF THE DISCLOSURE PROCESS

The above questions are serious and not just captious quibbling. This becomes clear immediately if we imagine what it would be like if, for instance, Canada or the Netherlands chose in favor of a general business policy oriented to broader external responsibilities and more human production technologies. It is not difficult to guess what the economic consequences would be. Every move in the direction of a more normative functioning of enterprises *vis-à-vis* society at large would lead to considerable cost increases. Moreover, more human production technologies, as a rule, will cause a reduction in the rate of increase of productivity. But, in the fierce competition of international trade, businesses with higher expenditures and lower productivity are in danger of going under immediately. They can be easily outflanked by their rivals who produce more cheaply. In an open economy, which is extremely sensitive to the fluctuations of the export market, this means a greater number of layoffs. Unemployment may well rise to uncontrollable heights, accompanied by runaway inflation.

These potentially malignant effects of an arbitrary beginning of disclosure indicate that the problem of blind progress must be perceived from the outset as being more than national in scope. Throughout this book it has been stressed that we are dealing with a problem which touches our entire western society and has its roots in the common culture of that society. We can expect no lasting benefits from disclosure which would remain only a national affair, and would not, at least in part, "spread" to other countries in the West. Our entire social order tends to be a tunnel society which imposes its demands for progress on each of its constituent national economies. These economies have profited from progress in technology and economics by way of the international market, but at the same time they have become dependent on that progress. Their production pattern has been geared to the demands of an international division of labor which is at all times being shaped by international competition. The "internalization laws" which we traced in Part Two,[78] in other words, emanate from the center of progress and apply to the individual national economies. These economies cannot

78. See the section "Internalization of science, management, and technology," pp. 92f.

withdraw with impunity from the supranational dictates of progress in western society.[79]

These circumstances might make us lose hope altogether. They seem to frustrate in advance any initiative undertaken at a national level. Nevertheless, it is possible to list a number of factors in this context which can serve as counterweights.

To begin with, we must not forget that all western countries not only have technological and economic progress in common, but they all face the same problems and difficulties that this progress has inflicted upon us. These problems cry out for a reaction. The European Common Market, for example, as well as the United States, has become involved in an enormously difficult energy situation, in acute environmental difficulties, and in a well-nigh ungovernable wave of inflation and unemployment. Accordingly, a discussion within the Common Market—laborious and surrounded with disappointments, to be sure—has emerged concerning a possible broadening of the goals of the original treaty of Rome in the direction of a European Union, that is, a federation comparable to the United States of America. This Union could then pay explicit attention to these new areas of concern. The crisis surrounding progress is an international one, and it is undeniable that even on an international level opportunities for raising the question of societal disclosure are increasing.

In the second place, as we consider possibilities for beginning disclosure at the national level, we must be mindful of the connection between the razing of the first and second barriers. If we think of societal disclosure exclusively in terms of razing the second barrier—that is, broadening the range of responsibility—then a worsening of the financial situation of business will be the immediate outcome. Matters stand quite differently,

79. The Netherlands provides a particularly striking example of this general rule. First of all, it has a very "open" economy, that is, it exports half of all its products. Moreover, it belongs to the European Common Market, which has hitherto been dedicated to an unrestrained policy of progress. The goal of this economic federation, as formulated in the treaties of Rome, is the establishment of a common market in order to assure increased economic growth for its member states (cf. article 2 of the Common Market treaty). Through the harmonization requirements of the Common Market, an important segment of Dutch economic policy instruments is bound to the achievement of the supranational policy goal that was agreed upon. Consequently, not only an economic, but also a political obligation exists on the part of the Dutch national economy to meet the demand for increased material growth.

however, if a given national economy is creating economic room for disclosure. For a particular enterprise this would mean, concretely, that on the one hand certain cost increases and productivity losses will have to be absorbed, while on the other hand the financial "claims" to the results of the enterprise's activity decrease. For example, if a decrease in wage demands on the enterprise were to be accepted, it would not necessarily imply that the wage cost per unit product would increase with a slowdown in the development of productivity. In that situation, the slowdown in the development of productivity calculated per worker is counterbalanced by a reduced wage increase per worker. And it should be remembered that the development of wage cost per *unit* is decisive in the arena of competition.

Consequently, a national beginning of disclosure does not have to be ruled out, even though in the long run cooperation from other countries will be indispensable. Moreover, it is an encouraging thought that a conscious deceleration in the rise of business productivity can entail more employment. In this way structural unemployment in society as a whole could be gradually reduced.[80]

But what about the developing countries? Will they not be the first victims of an attempt on the part of western nations to restrict consumption and moderate the development of productivity? This argument often has great effect on the debate, for to restrict demand in rich countries means a concomitant loss of a market for poor countries which, in turn, hampers their growth even more. Who would want that on his conscience? However, this argument is not as cogent as it appears to be; indeed, it even turns against itself if we take a longer-term view. It seems more cogent than it is because it is predicated on the

---

80. With the aid of the simple equation $q=(q/a)a$ we can perhaps clarify this further. q represents the total material production in society; a the total working population; and (q/a) is the production per employee, or labor productivity. If the rise in total production (and consumption) would amount to only two percent per year ($q=102$), then nonetheless an unchanged labor productivity ($\frac{q}{a}$ is constant) is already sufficient to make room for a two percent increase in the total working population (a).

This does presuppose, of course, that the incomes drawn from the production process by the working population are completely adjusted to this lower productivity of labor. That means in this case that the gross income per capita would show no increase at all.

assumption that third-world development opportunities are best aided—even if the present international division of labor is continued—by expanded foreign markets for their products. From the developing countries themselves, however, voices are increasingly heard which argue passionately for greater self-reliance, for the chance to develop themselves via their own resources, without becoming the extension of western markets and capital.[81]

The international division of labor which determines the marketing possibilities for developing countries is certainly not advantageous to poor countries. To some extent it deepens the present chasm dividing poor and rich nations. The poorest population groups are often not benefited at all, and the flow of money *from* the developing countries often exceeds the flow *toward* them. Accordingly, the International Labour Office (ILO), in the recent report entitled *Employment, Growth and Basic Needs: A One-World Problem* (1976), does not favor vigorous economic growth in western countries as a solution to problems of the poor countries. Instead, it advocates a completely different approach, centering on the provision of basic needs in both rich and poor nations.

However, the change in the international division of labor which is required for this will never be achieved on the basis of the present progress-oriented course of the western world. That has been a clear lesson of the last few decades. But this implies at the same time that the conditions for a more equitable international division of labor can be created only on the foundation of a genuine disclosure of western society. Before anything else, therefore, the production sector of the western nations themselves must be opened up toward more immediate concern for the real interests of the developing world.

The potential loss of a market for developing countries as a consequence of more moderate economic growth in western society therefore cannot be as convincingly argued as it seemed at first. In fact, in the long run this argument also turns against itself. As soon as we take into consideration such matters as the limited world resources of energy and minerals this will become

81. For further details, see the excellent book by Willem G. Zeylstra, *Aid or Development* (Leiden: Sijthoff, 1975), and the penetrating study by Bernard Zylstra, "Modernity and the American Empire," *International Reformed Bulletin,* first/second quarter 1977, no. 68/69, pp. 3ff.

obvious. It has been calculated that if every inhabitant of the earth were to use up the same quantity of energy and minerals as is now used up by the average inhabitant of the rich western nations, it would—even according to the most optimistic predictions—take less than ten years for the world's energy supplies and most vital mineral resources to be completely exhausted. By continuing to stimulate our economic growth, therefore, we progressively curtail the long-range chances of poor nations to come to a development of their own—chances which are intimately connected with their mineral and energy resources and with the possibility of increased trade among developing countries themselves. Thus it is not surprising that the 1976 RIO report of Jan Tinbergen and others explicitly notes that the gap between rich and poor nations can be narrowed only if economic growth in the industrialized countries gradually decreases. This would require the rich nations to develop new styles of consumption of a less wasteful nature, demand fewer resources, and gear themselves to social services instead of an excess in durable consumption goods. In a personal contribution to the report Tinbergen states that there is no contradiction between the simultaneous assumptions of less growth for the developed nations and more growth for the developing ones.[82]

All in all, the conclusion seems justified that, precisely for the sake of the world's poor nations, we must look upon the disclosure of our western society as an unavoidable obligation.

A SMALL BEGINNING

A process of disclosure can be started on a small scale. In fact, a small beginning can already bear fruit before society as a whole is ready for a new disclosure. Such fruit can especially be seen in the potential recovery of *shalom*—of wholeness, peace, and happiness—in the concrete setting of one's immediate life and work.

What do we mean by a *small* beginning? In this context it involves a change of direction in those social structures where one can oversee the effects of transformation. Here I am thinking notably of those relationships which can display a distinct measure of solidarity in areas like consumption or work. Fam-

82. Jan Tinbergen *et al., Naar een rechtvaardiger internationale orde* (1976) [Reshaping the International Order] (RIO report, 1976), pp. 98, 193, and 103.

ilies and local church congregations belong to this category of potential agents of social transformation. For instance, we can imagine a group of families living closely together which drastically rejects the feverish quest for an ever higher level of consumption and the resultant pursuit of a greater income. In our terminology these families have chosen a different horizon of happiness, reflected in a considerably reduced pattern of consumption. They will dispose of certain luxury items, especially if these consume time, pollute the environment, or waste energy. Other goods, particularly expensive and durable ones, may well be voluntarily shared with neighboring families. In this way certain forms of "open" private possession—once present in ancient Israel[83]—can be reintroduced in the family life style. Both the disposal of certain time-consuming articles as well as the voluntary "opening up" of one's own property toward sharing by others will strengthen a sense of community. The tendency to live in isolation from one another—the root of much loneliness—can thus also be partially reduced, and opportunities for genuine personal contacts are increased. But such a start may have much greater ramifications.

A lower level of consumption enables one to make do with a more modest income. This in turn makes possible the allocation of funds for a variety of purposes, such as the alleviation of other people's needs, the protection of our biomilieu, or the creation of a different day-to-day work environment. This could have significant effects—especially if a large number of employees of one or more enterprises were involved in the formation of common funds of this type. Such funds could then be used to finance what at first would be relatively small but eventually would become substantial structural improvements in the organization of the work situation and in the techniques of production.

Attempts in this direction could, no doubt, give rise to

83. According to Mosaic law, the farmers of Israel were not allowed to harvest the grain at the edge of their fields, but were to leave it for the poor, the widow, the orphan, and the alien. Similar regulations pertained to the harvesting of grapes. (Cf. Leviticus 19:9f.) Were these rules restrictions of what we call "private property"? Indeed not. Rather, they were signs of the disclosure of private property to the service of one's neighbor. Both private property and communal property can be either "open" or "closed." This distinction between *open* and *closed* property relations often appears to be more significant than the simple distinction between *private* and *public* property.

new problems. For instance, management as well as a segment of the work force might not support such endeavors. Moreover, the administration of funds could create certain difficulties which might require outside assistance, such as the input of labor unions. However, none of these problems would be insurmountable. When part of the employees' purchasing power is consistently set aside for the betterment or, if necessary, the drastic restructuration of work conditions, avenues could be opened up which would eventually lead to an essential improvement in the life of every worker involved in projects of this kind.

In other words, a small beginning can definitely bear certain positive fruits. But such a start will gain considerably in significance if it is expanded by the persons and groups who initiated it, that is, if it is applied to society in the broader sense of the word.

INFLUENCE AT LARGE[84]

In principle, nearly every person in a western democracy has access to two or three avenues of direct influence on the society which surrounds him or her. First of all, in the political sector citizens have the right to vote, which may or may not be combined with membership in a political party. Secondly, in the industrial sector persons can exercise an influence via employers' organizations or labor unions of their choice.[85] Finally, there is what one might describe as "the consumer's right to vote." Because everyone still has in principle a great degree of freedom in the use of one's purchasing powers, it is possible to express one's approval or disapproval not only of a particular product but also of the manner of its production and distribution.

Let us assume for a moment that a significant part of the population of the western world is prepared to choose a responsible—"response-oriented"—life style and a horizon of happiness in line with that. Let us further assume that this part of the population is willing to use the three avenues just mentioned in order to influence society in the direction of a non-

84. For a popular elaboration of the themes dealt with in this section, see B. Goudzwaard, *Aid for the Overdeveloped West* (Toronto: Wedge, 1975).

85. In the United States and Canada, labor legislation severely limits workers' freedom of association. But this has not entirely curbed the liberties under discussion.

materialistic, responsible life style. Can a positive redirection be expected of this?

1. To begin with, it would have to be made eminently clear to both *political parties* and the relevant *government agencies* that they should fight for the acceptance and implementation of a series of regulations specifically directed to make possible the disclosure of society. A few specific suggestions are in order here. The responsibilities of the industrial sector itself with respect to environmental protection would have to be pointedly delineated in governmental regulations. Advertising, especially radio and television commercials, should be radically curtailed, and noncommercial sources for the support of these media would undoubtedly have to be found. An all-out effort should be made to explore the possibilities of policy formation leading to a gradual stabilization in welfare per capita of the population. Again, the complex matter of giving a special classification to publicly responsible industries might well have to be tackled. Here we are thinking especially of industries whose products—like cars—have a phenomenal impact, for good or ill, on the economy as a whole because their use necessitates consumption of additional resources and energies. Nearly the entire packaging industry, which contributes so dearly to our "wasteland," would require close scrutiny. So one could continue. The question is whether political parties, legislatures, the courts, and other relevant governmental bodies would be willing to support—in their diverse ways—the necessary redirection suggested here. I, for one, still have enough confidence in the political processes of the western democracies to hope that this indispensable support would be forthcoming on the condition that an articulate body of the citizenry were to exert its legitimate influence. What I am suggesting here might well be one remedy for the political apathy which is so prominent today in Europe and North America.

2. The responsibility for the direction of the industrial sector of our society rests to a great extent upon *entrepreneurs, boards of directors, managers,* and the numerous organizations they have established to make their influence felt. To a great extent the responsibility for the redirection of the industrial sector also rests upon them. Simple considerations of self-protection will in the future accentuate this responsibility, since the sensitivity of the public as well as of the government for corporate conduct is noticeably increasing. There is a maturing consciousness of

the public accountability of industry. But self-protection is not the only factor here. For two hundred years the business enterprise has been one of the leading shapers of culture in the West. This alone makes it the bearer of an immense responsibility which it cannot simply shrug off. This responsibility affects the very place of the enterprise itself in our culture. Since our society has become affluent, abundant, and materially saturated, the industrial sector will have to be redirected to the needs of persons and societies that do not want to live by bread alone. An industrial sector which does not sense the need for creativity on the part of the work force, which is indifferent to the environment, which is careless with the remaining resources of this limited earth, which emphasizes quantity above quality, which produces for obsolescence, which is not oriented to alleviate the authentically material needs of the have-nots at home and abroad, is not in any way worthy of remaining in existence as a supposedly responsible shaper of our culture. Therefore business concerns, and persons responsible for decisions within them, must assume a major share in a real disclosure of western society.

3. Then there is the avenue of the *labor movement*. Here again a part of its membership could exert considerable pressure on the whole. For instance, such a part could pointedly propose that their labor union in its negotiations with management should primarily stress the importance of meaningful work conditions, the quality of the products, and the role of the workers in the decision-making process, especially with respect to concrete work situations. This would, at least partially, be an alternative to the customary demands for increased pay. Furthermore, labor unions might explore the establishment of employees' funds, perhaps based in part on profit-sharing schemes. Such funds could be used to pay for various kinds of improvements in the work situation, and would reflect the employees' willingness to share the economic sacrifices required for a change in industrial life. Finally, labor unions could be more flexible in collective bargaining agreements negotiated with firms that have acquitted themselves of their "public" responsibilities.

I don't intend to be exhaustive here. Nor do I want to create the impression that the labor movement will quickly make a reversal in the pursuit of its present goals which are also highly influenced by the materialist direction of our culture. But the point I do want to make is that the labor movement, at least in part, may be willing to accept new challenges—especially when these come from within its own ranks.

4. Finally, a few words can be said about the role of *consumers*. The future will require a more responsible pattern of consumption. Persons and families who have rejected the materialist horizon of happiness should be able to live in accordance with such a responsible pattern. Consumers' organizations can play an important role here by regularly publishing carefully researched reports containing the names of products which are harmful to health, social life, and the environment. Such negative reports should, of course, be paralleled by lists of companies and products that evidence a positive sense of stewardship. Consumers' organizations can perform other tasks as well. Truthfulness in advertising, packaging, and labeling of products are other concerns that readily come to mind.

Each one of these measures does not mean much by itself. However, in mutual combination they will definitely influence the activities and operations of business concerns. In this manner enterprises whose entire managerial policy is strictly commercially oriented will in many ways encounter obstacles. In the first place, they will experience definite losses on the market as soon as they, or their products, are entered on the blacklist. Secondly, they will be quite unprepared for the assumption of new tasks imposed by the government—such as those concerning the environment—since they have not anticipated them. Thirdly, they will have to face a confrontation with the labor movement which will attack them especially with regard to working conditions in their plants, including the range of responsibility of the average worker. On the other hand, enterprises which long desired to reorient themselves toward broader purposes with respect to their own work community, their customers, and society at large, will now at least obtain an opportunity for such a reorientation. To begin with, as "public companies" the demand for their products will increase if there are enough responsible consumers. At the same time, their wage costs will decrease if they are dealing with responsible labor unions. Finally, their concern for the environment and quality production will begin to pay off, especially if these factors will assume a larger role in government policy and consumer preference. It would be a relief to know that well-intentioned enterprises are at least partially enabled to fare better in our society than those with strictly commercial intentions.

TOWARD AN OPEN SOCIETY

The society which could ultimately develop along these or similar avenues of disclosure will be different from our society in several respects. It will be helpful to describe some of the contours of an open society which can still be shaped by concerted effort. Since such an effort is largely a presupposition of our argument, and not an object of empirical observation, what follows is not a prediction but the expression of a hope.

An open society does not call a halt to technological development. This simple statement cannot be fully elaborated here, but what I have in mind is this: an open society will direct technological development toward a deepened, much more subtle and multifaceted unfolding. It will aim technique at the making of tools and instruments fit to alleviate pain and distress, as in medicine, and structured to enhance human responsibility and creativity, as in production. Moreover, while in an earlier stage of industrial expansion technology helped save human resources, the technology of the future must help save material and energy resources. Furthermore, if there is a willingness to make the necessary economic sacrifices, the average size of a unit of industrial production can be considerably reduced in a number of branches of industry. Small-scale production cuts into profits but often enhances the meaning of work.

This might bring about other benefits as well. The present imbalance in population density and the shift from country to city are in part a result of the technological revolution with its requirement of huge work forces. Small-scale production can be relocated at least partially in towns outside of the large metropolitan centers. A reduction in the scale of production can contribute to the renewal of the local community. And this, in turn, will have a positive effect on the cost of living. Studies have indicated that living in small communities is considerably less expensive than living in large urban centers. Quite clearly, flexibility in human choice increases when we are liberated from the self-imposed burden of limitless technological expansion. An open society is marked by such flexibility.

An open society will have a different technology; it will

also have a different economy. In line with a successful process of disclosure, various business enterprises gradually will have been obliged to revise their criteria of growth so that they will direct their efforts to an enhanced quality-production for society. Competition between enterprises will be focused on the gaining of public respect because of the emergence of greater responsibility in the consumption sector. Enterprises will perhaps gradually learn to take pride in being recognized as "new style enterprises." The production process itself may become more personal and creative in character, not because the entrepreneurs have become more cordial all of a sudden, but because the employees themselves have made the necessary financial sacrifice—thus guaranteeing their own say in the matter—to enlarge the possibility of an atmosphere of creativity and initiative. New criteria for economic development can also open up new avenues in the external dimensions of the industrial sector. Less concern for rising incomes will increase flexibility in concern for such matters as the environment.

On the basis of a more modest and selective pattern of growth, the indigenous needs of the developing nations can also be more fully heeded. They will not so easily be considered merely as convenient suppliers of cheap natural resources and energy. Moreover, in a less competitive context the third world should no longer be viewed just as a convenient market for our surpluses. Instead, genuine efforts can be undertaken to build an economic infrastructure suited to the respective developing countries, in both areas of food production and industrial growth geared to local potential and need. Normative economic consciousness at home should contribute to a wider range of options abroad. Less emphasis on material growth in the West may well diminish the gap in welfare between the rich and the poor nations of the world.

Finally, an open society will be characterized by more healthy relationships between the various social structures. There should be more respect than there is now for the integrity and dignity of each societal bond and also—and this is of utmost importance—in the relationship between state and industry. Specific tasks which belong to the sphere of responsible stewardship will again be performed mainly by the industries. Similarly, the matter of employment opportunities will more fully become the concern of the industrial sector itself, because responsible persons—employees and management together—will have more of a chance to make a responsible choice between larger incomes for fewer people or expanded work opportunities for more people. Moreover, if the willingness to make the required economic sacrifices exists in society to move toward small-scale production operations, the present trend toward phenomenal power formations in the economic sector will be at least partially reversed. These power formations will then become less of a threat to the independence and integrity of the government. In the long run—but here we enter the area of almost utopian expectations—the present centers of economic power concentration might dissolve in a multitude of smaller industrial units. The basis of existence of these centers is the law of unlimited technological, industrial, and commercial expansion. That oppressive law is repudiated by an open society. Without that law, the present accumulations of economic power might gradually lose their chance to survive.

21. *Church and Heaven Revisited*

In our search for the conditions for a possible disclosure of our society we now appear definitely to have come to an end. These conditions consist of a testing or monitoring of all allegedly progressive measures, the expansion of the degrees of freedom for the redirection of technology, and the restoration of human responsibilities to their original sphere. Can anything else be meaningfully added to this substantial list of conditions?

There is indeed a problem which we have not as yet faced squarely. In our discussion of the conditions for societal disclosure we have paid insufficient attention to the human factor in history. We have, as it were, tacitly assumed that human beings are perfectly willing to act responsibly when a normative disclosure of their society requires this. But is this assumption correct? After all, people would have to be prepared to sacrifice part of their income for the required disclosure of society. They would have to be prepared to accept greater responsibilities in their working and living situations, and not let self-interest guide their actions. Politicians, businessmen, corporate managers, and labor leaders would have to be prepared to set new directions. But is there any chance at all that even a minority of our society could or would take this upon itself? Does this not require a completely different mentality, and even a completely different perspective on the meaning of life and society? At this point we meet up with a last and perhaps decisive obstacle to disclosure— an obstacle which immediately reminds us of the barrier, razed so long ago, of church and heaven.

THE RENAISSANCE VIEW OF LIFE

When the barrier of church and heaven was razed under the assault of the Renaissance—and, in another sense, the Reformation—considerably more was at stake than a challenge to the ecclesiastical lordship over natural earthly life. More significant was that thereby the way was cleared to a fundamentally different belief about the meaning of life and society. Room was created for a new perspective on society. It is important to realize that the basic contours of this new belief have remained with us in the West for nearly five hundred years.

It must readily be admitted that there was indeed a real need for a changing view of the meaning and perspective of human society. Hence this breakthrough definitely contained positive elements. Human action in the areas of politics, economics, art, and science was emancipated from subservience to the overriding societal goal of Scholasticism: the elevation of the realm of natural life to the realm of grace. Room was created for the unfolding of art, the economy, technology, and science according to their *own* nature.

Yet this was not an exclusively positive breakthrough. In the course of time one type of closed society—the medieval—was replaced by another, equally closed societal type. The difference was that it was now oriented to earth instead of to heaven, and that it was now driven forward in time instead of being forced to rise to eternity. In view of this ultimate result, we must conclude that there was also something fundamentally wrong about the razing of the barrier of church and heaven.

Precisely what was wrong is not so easy to pinpoint, however. Nevertheless, we will not be far from the mark if we assert that Renaissance man was not just confident, but *over*-confident in his own powers, especially his powers to investigate and dominate nature.

Despite the literal meaning of its name, the Renaissance is in many respects more reminiscent of a stormy process of wanting to reach adulthood than of a process of being born again. An adolescent reaching adulthood chafes at the many norms his elders prescribe. Norms and maxims are only hurdles in his path. Moreover, he hardly ever—if at all—associates happiness with a sense of security within familiar and traditional human communities. Happiness is something you must make for yourself, something you must conquer, something you must gain by putting forth the necessary effort. Of course there is a healthy side to this new attitude to life, but such an attitude also carries the seeds of excess and overconfidence, of going to extremes. In large measure this is in fact what happened in the Renaissance, the "storm and stress" period of modern western civilization. There is an overreaction to the norms which the church, in an often traditionalistic way, laid down. The desire to be completely a law unto one's self (autonomy) becomes central. Any norms coming from outside one's self are experienced as obstacles. In this context happiness is no longer considered to be a fruit which grows spontaneously in a climate of obedience and societal security, but primarily a *result* which can be achieved only by exercising one's own drive to action. Accordingly, the I-it relation contributes more to man's purpose than the I-thou relation; more and more, nature and the world are viewed as a platform for human self-realization. This also puts human labor in a new light. Labor is no longer regarded as a self-evident and inevitable necessity, bearing the curse ever since the Fall, but, instead, as the indispensable dynamic factor for either fulfilling man's vocation or for wresting human happiness from nature. In line with this changed orientation, the basic points of reference for human life and society are changed into *objectives* and *goals.* Gradually these take the place of the norms of the past. The idea of *beginnings,* of points of departure, implicit in "principles" (Latin: *principia*), is replaced by that of *ends* or objectives, as S. U. Zuidema pointed out. He argued that in our time *beginselen* (principles) have been replaced by *"eindselen"* (ends).

I have discussed this transition at some length in order to make it clear that a new and integral *vision of life* was emerging—a vision which brought about a shift in existing evaluations and insights on many levels at once. There was a shift in the appreciation of nature, but also of norms, labor, human happiness, one's fellowman, goals of life, the place of the church, God, and religion. It is important to emphasize this point, for it is this selfsame vision of life, though at present subject to so many disruptive forces, which has from the beginning given impetus to modern culture and the rise of our societal order. Its effect continues to be felt to this day in the mentality of the West. Its impact is present in our individualism and aggressiveness. Its influence is also detectable in the circumstance that economic and financial stimuli are generally more effective in our society than stimuli deriving from the need to be recognized and re-spected as human beings by each other. Its presence is felt as well in our appreciation of labor itself. Both a puritan work ethic—which elevated hard work to direct proof of piety—and a humanistic evaluation of labor—which proclaimed it to be *the* road to a happier future—have probably affected our attitudes more than we realize. The western sense of values probably lost rather than gained in depth, especially in the twentieth century. Contemporary man hardly thinks in terms of generally valid norms. He thinks almost exclusively in terms of personal and societal goals-in-the-future, and of rules necessary to achieve them. To be sure, these goals still embody certain normative elements from the past, but these normative remnants lack the original vitality and independent, directly binding validity for human decisions which real norms have.

This persistent western life perspective, with its valuation of norms, labor, and happiness, appears therefore to be a crucial obstacle to the disclosure of our society. Our society involves not only a tunnel structure; it also brings with it a tunnel vision, a tunnel mentality. There is little point in talking about breaking through these tunnel structures if the underlying tunnel vision is not fundamentally changed.

THE BREAK WITH UTILITARIANISM

The last statements are sweeping, and therefore require further substantiation. The best way to do this is to address ourselves once more—now for the last time—to the utilitarian conception of norms, labor, and happiness. This conception has been an important component of the western mentality for the last two centuries.

As we have seen before, a utilitarian lifestyle relegated labor efforts to the rubric of "disutilities," the negative factors of happiness, at the same time viewing them as the indispensable instruments to achieve "utilities" as the positive factors of happiness. These "utilities" in turn were considered to be concentrated in those results of labor which enable man to spend his leisure time in satisfying individual and collective needs. More-over, utilitarianism declared everything which contributes to happiness (thus defined) as morally good. Consequently, norms do not correct this style of life; they affirm it in advance. They have become defenseless, as it were, without a content of their own.

Here—in terms of labor, norms, and happiness—we meet the most consistent expression of the tunnel vision which fits our tunnel society and makes its continuance possible. We have seen above[86] that there is a direct connection between this tunnel vision and the law of undiminished escalation of labor productivity. Another result of this vision is the above-mentioned bisection of life into toiling and living, into production as means and consumption as goal. Finally, in this conception enterprises are not responsible social structures but goal institutions designed to produce goods and to acquire income. In the utilitarian view of life there is no other norm to answer to, to be responsible to, than the satisfaction of needs, especially as these become apparent in the market. In short, there is not a single element in the tunnel traits of our society which is not reflected and confirmed in the utilitarian view of labor, norms, and happiness.

But for that very reason the converse is also true, namely, that it is only by a fundamental disavowal of this utilitarian view of labor, norms, and happiness that a disclosure of society can be successful. This, then, is the *fourth and final condition for disclosure:* the radical break with the horizon of utilitarian happiness, including its perspective on labor and human normative responsibility.

Some of my readers will perhaps find this a fatalistic conclusion. After all, to look for a turning of the tide in our attitudes and actions regarding norms, labor, and happiness seems like a hopeless cause! This is correct, and I certainly do not want to underestimate the seriousness of the situation. Nevertheless, I would certainly not want to call our conclusion fatalistic.

AVAILABLE OPENINGS

An important factor with respect to disclosure at present consists in the hard realities of the contemporary situation, and the manner in which they are developing. It is possible that current developments will lead persons and societies to take stock of their attitude to norms, human labor, and our happiness.

Earlier we spoke of norms as rules which do not originate in man. The purpose of norms is to bring us to life in its fullness by pointing us to paths which safely lead us there. Norms are

86. See Part Three, section "The victory of utilitarianism," pp. 139ff.

not straightjackets that squeeze the life out of us. I stated as my conviction that the created world is attuned to those norms; it is designed for our willingness to respond to God and each other. If man and society ignore genuine norms, such as justice and restitution of rights, respect for life, love of neighbor, and stewardship, they are bound to experience the destructive effects of such neglect. That is not, therefore, a mysterious *fate* which strikes us; rather, it is a *judgment* which men and society bring upon themselves. This concrete, created world was designed by God for our exercise of justice, stewardship, and love of neighbor. That is why a negation of that stewardship leads to dreadful pollution in that same world, why a negation of the norm of justice leads to violence and terrorism, and why collective egoism leads to economic disruption such as unemployment and inflation. Genuine norms do not hang in the air. They are not the speculations of noble minds. They give evidence of their *validity*, of being concretely in force. To ignore given norms out of an *a priori* illusion of autonomy only seems to afford freedom, but in the long run it removes genuine freedom. Martin Buber was right when he translated the Old Testament word for "law" *(torah)* as *Weisung*, that is, "instruction," "guidance." Genuine laws or norms are pointers that guide us along safe and passable roads. Apart from norms our paths run amok.

It is crucial how we interpret the enormous problems of our time, ranging from pollution, unemployment, and inflation to alienation, loneliness, and terrorism. We can interpret them as invitations to build an even more closed type of society, in which even more strict forms of governmental centralization hold, and in which science and technology occupy an even more dominant position. Our life would then be regulated by means of "bio-engineering" and "social engineering." But there is still another possibility, namely, the way of coming to our senses, the way of reflection and reassessment. This way can lead us to reorient our cultural goals and our societal arrangements once again to vital norms and to responsibilities directed toward those norms. This is the kind of reorientation which W. A. Visser 't Hooft had in mind when he compared the West with the prodigal son in Jesus' parable.[87] That was the son who had deprived himself of all life's possibilities by "squandering his

---

87. See W. A. Visser 't Hooft, "Moet het Westen worden verdedigd?" [Must the West be defended?], *Wending*, 1956.

inheritance in reckless living," and only in that situation "came to his senses." (Cf. Luke 15).

This possibility of a turn, a fundamental change in the western outlook as a result of an accumulation of inescapable practical problems, can also occur on the level of our assessment of labor and the happiness it is supposed to bring. Many people are out of work. Even more people have jobs which give them no satisfaction whatever. The increasing incidence of absenteeism is one symptom of this. At the same time, however, more and more people are beginning to question openly the supposed connection between increased income and greater happiness. These developments could be harbingers of a new view of labor and happiness.

As to the increasing levels of income and consumption, the realization is growing that this increase may well entail hidden demands on our happiness, on our experience of genuine community, and on the time we spend with each other and with our individual selves. We are also beginning to sense how our material standard of life is making phenomenal demands on scarce natural resources, limited energy, a vulnerable environment, and the disclosure of societies in the so-called third world. In other words, many people are beginning to realize that an increasing level of income and consumption can turn into a "disutility" after reaching a certain limit; it can in fact turn into a negative factor for the happiness of themselves and others. With reference to employment or unemployment, the insight is growing that meaningless labor probably does most damage to one's happiness. Increasingly, the view is gaining ground that labor must no longer be treated as a "disutility," but must have sufficient quality to be a "utility"—to become a positive factor for happiness.

In this light we can arrive at a tentative conclusion. In our progress-dominated and progress-plagued society we can detect the first signs of a willingness to consider the *reversal of our happiness horizon.* Consumption and income might well, in the opinion of many, remain the same, or even (in the case of a more equitable distribution) decline, *if* this could be offset by the gain of more meaningful labor. A considerable number of people are now prepared to affirm that we are being misled by our distorted view of human labor and happiness, and that consequently the meaningfulness of both our labor and our consumption is being eroded.

This is undoubtedly a hopeful development. If a majority of the population would indeed see through the illusion of ever-increasing material prosperity, and would therefore agree to a stabilization of income and consumption (for example, in the context of a generally accepted income policy), then in course of time the necessary degrees of economic freedom, of which we spoke in connection with the barrier of paradise lost, would automatically appear in the economy. We could then make use of those new economic possibilities precisely in situations of dehumanized labor and in places where small-scale labor arrangements can be developed or saved from extinction. A shift in our own horizon of happiness could indeed gradually give rise to a genuine process of societal disclosure—a process which would gain in depth and breadth if it were supported by concomitant changes in the structuration of our society.

As we have said before, this does not mean the birth of an ideal society. But it could mean that certain features of "substantial healing"—to use Francis Schaeffer's term[88]—would begin to be visible within our society. And that by itself would provide immense relief.

---

88. Cf. Francis A. Schaeffer, *True Spirituality* (London: Inter-Varsity Press, 1972; Wheaton, Ill.: Tyndale House, 1972), chapter 11.

22. *Epilogue*

The brief sketch in this book of a possible process of disclosure of western society, and of the preconditions necessary for it, is undoubtedly incomplete. We have left all kinds of complications out of consideration which would certainly muddy the waters considerably. The question therefore arises whether it was meaningful to bring forward all that we did.

I personally believe it was. The purpose of this study has not for a moment been the spelling out of a precise program, or the drawing up of blueprints for a "completely disclosed society"—whatever that may be. Rather, the purpose was to make two things clear. In the first place, nearly all of our societal problems are a reflection of ourselves—of what we are in our lifestyles, our culture, our outlook, our vision of life. Societal problems are not merely "structural." They are also "cultural" in the sense that they are the fruit of western civilization and the style of life it affords. In the second place, because of this background we are not entitled to look upon our predicament as a *fate* that is overcoming us. References to fate, to an inescapable destiny of western civilization, are avenues of escaping our responsibility in history. Such escape attempts, in effect, accept the autonomy of the powers of science, technology, and economics. This book has been written on the basis of the belief that this autonomy is pretended, never real. An acceptance of fate leads to a decline in responsibility.

Over against such a decline, we have posited the theme of the disclosure of society. By this we do not mean a politically manipulable program but, first of all, an appeal to our own conscience. It is an appeal to acknowledge the real roots of our problems, an appeal to listen anew to long-neglected norms for human existence, including the norms that hold for the supposedly a-normative domains of science, technology, and industry. It is an appeal directed to all of us, Christians and nonchristians, no matter what our political party or persuasion may be. Collectively, we are all guilty of the disarray in our social order, and all of us share the responsibility for a fundamental reorientation of our social order and the lifestyle that undergirds it.

It is about this reorientation, both cultural and structural, that I have been concerned in this book, in the hope that seemingly insurmountable problems can be brought back to proportions we can cope with as human beings, small as we are. I have intended to say only "This might be a way to go"; not "This is *the* way to go." My concern is not a perfect society, for that is not the work of men's hands. But there has indeed been a burning conviction behind what I have written—the conviction that human societies can experience ever anew a liberating and healing power if men take norms seriously. For taking norms seriously is the essence of every genuine process of disclosure.

However, do we really *want* a disclosure of our society? That is the question which still begs an answer at the end of this book. In all honesty, I am not sure that the answer to that question will be positive. After all, the conditions for disclosure listed in the foregoing are anything but easy. The last condition, especially the one under "church and heaven revisited," is of such proportions that its fulfillment is hardly a matter of course. That condition of a shift in mentality, of a conversion in outlook, transcends the categories of extra effort or trying harder. The central meaning of life and society is at stake here, and that is not lightly changed in a civilization. At this point we touch upon the *religious* roots of human life.

I am keenly aware that I must tread very carefully here, because one can be so easily misunderstood. Yet I cannot refrain from pointing out, at the conclusion of this book, that the theme of progress has penetrated western society so profoundly because it was able to present itself as a *faith* in progress, as a religion of progress. That is also why the present-day crisis of the idea of progress has the depth of a crisis of *faith*. There is more at stake than a somewhat reduced confidence in "progress" on the part of western man. His whole life perspective has undergone a shock. The unfulfilled promises of progress have brought about an emptiness, a vacuum, with respect to the *mean-*

ing of life and society. Many among us even experience the demise of the idea of progress as a kind of divine betrayal. The very thing in which we had placed all our trust is turning against us to devour us. And what does one have left when one's gods betray him?

If this observation is correct, then we find ourselves at a very critical juncture in the development of western civilization. No society or civilization can continue to exist without having found an answer to the question of meaning. The emptiness created by the death of the god of progress must be filled with something else. But what will that be? It seems that we have two choices: either the vacuum will be filled by a new, awe-inspiring myth, possibly built around the leaders of a central and large-scale world authority, who are authorized by their populations to direct all available technical, economic, and scientific means to new objectives with which to assault both heaven and earth; or else there will take place a turnaround of Christians and nonchristians together, a turnaround which directs itself to the Torah or normativity which the Creator of heaven and earth has given to this world as its meaning from the beginning, and which points forward to a new earth, coming with the return of the crucified One. Without such a turnaround I can hardly imagine a real and permanent disclosure of our western civilization.

Therefore our deepest choice appears to lie between an enslaving autonomy and a liberating heteronomy, or, to put it another way, between restricting utopias and the inspiring openness of the biblical *eschaton*.

Bibliography

Adorno, Theodor W., *Negative Dialectics*. New York: Seabury Press, Inc., 1973.

Ashton, Thomas S. *The Industrial Revolution: 1760–1830*. London/New York/Toronto: Oxford University Press, 1948.

Augustine. *The City of God*. New York: Random House, 1950.

Bacon, Francis. *Essays, Civil and Moral and The New Atlantis* (with essays by John Milton and Thomas Browne). The Harvard Classics. Edited by Charles W. Eliot. New York: Collier & Son, 1909.

Baillie, John. *The Belief in Progress*. London: Oxford University Press, 1950.

Barber, Richard J. *The American Corporation*. New York: E. P. Dutton & Co., 1970.

Barrett, William. *Time of Need: Forms of Imagination in the Twentieth Century*. New York: Harper & Row, Inc., 1973.

Becker, Carl Lotus. *The Heavenly City of the Eighteenth-Century Philosophers*. New Haven: Yale University Press, 1932.

Bell, Daniel. *The Cultural Contradictions of Capitalism*. New York: Basic Books, 1976.

Bentham, Jeremy. *The Principles of Morals and Legislation*. New York: Hafner Publishing Co., 1948.

Biéler, André. *La pensée économique et sociale de Calvin*. Geneva: Librairie de l'Université, 1959.

Bouman, Pieter Jan. *Van Renaissance tot Wereldoorlog* [From Renaissance to World War]. Groningen, the Netherlands: P. Noordhoff, n.d.

Bouman, Pieter Jan. *Van tijd naar tijd* [From Time to Time]. Assen, the Netherlands: Van Gorcum, 1972.

Buber, Martin. *I and Thou*. New York: Charles Scribner's Sons, 1970.

Buchloh, P. G. "Vom 'Pilgrim's Progress' zum 'Pilgrim's Regress' " [From 'Pilgrim's Progress' to 'Pilgrim's Regress']. In *Die Idee des Fort-*

schritts [The Idea of Progress], pp. 153–178. Edited by Erich Burck. München: C. H. Beck, 1963.

Burckhardt, Jacob. *The Civilization of the Renaissance in Italy.* 2 vols. New York: Harper & Row, Inc., 1929; Harper Torchbook edition, 1958.

Burckhardt, Jakob Christoph. *The Letters of Jacob Burckhardt.* Translated by Alexander Dru. London: Routledge & Kegan Paul, 1955.

Bury, John Bagnell. *The Idea of Progress: An Inquiry into its Origin and Growth.* London: Macmillan, 1920.

Carnegie, Andrew. *The Gospel of Wealth and Other Timely Essays.* Cambridge, Mass.: Harvard University Press, 1962.

Cassirer, Ernst, *et al.,* eds. *The Renaissance Philosophy of Man.* Chicago: University of Chicago Press, 1948.

Commoner, Barry. *The Closing Circle: Nature, Man, and Technology.* New York: Alfred A. Knopf, 1971.

Commoner, Barry. *The Poverty of Power: Energy and the Economic Crisis.* New York: Alfred A. Knopf, 1976.

Condorcet, Marquis de. *Sketch for a Historical Picture of the Progress of the Human Mind.* London: Weidenfeld & Nicolson, 1955.

Cramp, A. B. *Notes towards a Christian Critique of Secular Economic Theory.* Provisional Paper. Toronto: Institute for Christian Studies, 1975.

Dalton, George. *Economic Systems and Society.* Harmondsworth, England: Penguin Education, 1974.

Dawson, Christopher. *Progress and Religion: An Historical Inquiry.* London: Sheed & Ward, 1929; Westport, Conn.: Greenwood Press reprint.

Deane, Phyllis. *The First Industrial Revolution.* Cambridge/New York: Cambridge University Press, 1965, 1966.

Dooyeweerd, Herman. *In the Twilight of Western Thought.* Philadelphia: The Presbyterian and Reformed Publishing Co., 1960.

Dooyeweerd, Herman. *A New Critique of Theoretical Thought.* 4 vols. Amsterdam: H. J. Paris; Philadelphia: The Presbyterian and Reformed Publishing Co., 1953–58.

Dooyeweerd, Herman. *Roots of Western Culture: Pagan, Secular, and Christian Options.* Toronto: Wedge Publishing Foundation, 1979.

Dorival, Bernard. "The Realist Movement." In *Larousse Encyclopedia of Modern Art from 1800 to the Present Day,* pp. 159–176. Edited by René Huyghe. New York: Prometheus Press, 1961.

Ellul, Jacques. *The Technological Society.* New York: Alfred A. Knopf, 1964.

Employment, Growth and Basic Needs: A One-World Problem. Geneva: International Labour Office, 1976.

Ernst, Eberhard. *Die Fortschrittsidee in Wirtschaftslehre und Wirtschafts-*

wirklichkeit [The Idea of Progress in Economic Theory and Economic Practice]. Ph.D. Dissertation, University of Mannheim, 1951.

Ferguson, Wallace K. *Facets of the Renaissance.* New York: Harper & Row, Inc., 1963.

Fogarty, Michael F. *Christian Democracy in Western Europe: 1820–1953.* London: Routledge & Kegan Paul, 1957; Westport, Conn.: Greenwood Press, 1974 reprint.

Frey, Dagobert. *Gotik und Renaissance als Grundlagen der modernen Weltanschauung* [Gothic and Renaissance as the Foundations of the Modern World View]. Augsburg: Filser, 1929.

Friedman, Milton. *A Program for Monetary Stability.* New York: Fordham University Press, 1961.

Gabor, Dennis. *The Mature Society.* London: Secker & Warburg, 1972.

Galbraith, John Kenneth. *The Affluent Society.* Boston: Houghton Mifflin Co., 1958; 3rd rev. ed., 1976.

Galbraith, John Kenneth. *American Capitalism: The Concept of Countervailing Power.* Boston: Houghton Mifflin Co., 1956.

Galbraith, John Kenneth. *Economics and the Public Purpose.* Boston: Houghton Mifflin Co., 1973.

Galbraith, John Kenneth. *The New Industrial State.* New York: New American Library, 1968; New York: Houghton Mifflin, 3rd rev. ed., 1978.

Gay, Peter. *The Enlightenment: An Interpretation.* 2 vols. New York: Alfred A. Knopf, 1967, 1969.

Gill, Richard T. *Economic Development: Past and Present.* Englewood Cliffs, N.J.,: Prentice-Hall, Inc., 1973.

Ginsberg, Morris. *Essays in Sociology and Social Philosophy.* 3 vols. Melbourne/London/Toronto: William Heinemann Ltd., 1956–1961.

Godwin, William. *Enquiry concerning Political Justice and its Influence on Morals and Happiness.* 3 vols. Toronto: University of Toronto Press, 1946.

Goudzwaard, Bob. *Aid for the Overdeveloped West.* Toronto: Wedge Publishing Foundation, 1975.

Goudzwaard, Bob. *Ongeprijsde schaarste* [Nonpriced Scarcity: Social Costs and Uncompensated Effects as a Problem for Economic Theory and Policy]. The Hague: Van Stockum, 1970. With English Summary.

Gouldner, Alvin Ward. *The Coming Crisis of Western Sociology.* New York: Basic Books, 1970.

Goyder, George. *The Responsible Company.* Oxford: Basil Blackwell, 1961.

Gras, N. S. B., "Capitalism: Concepts and History." *Bulletin of the Business Historical Society* 16 (1942), 21–34. Reprinted in *Enterprise and Secular Change: Readings in Economic History,* pp. 66–79. Edited by Frederic C. Lane and Jelle C. Riemersma. Homewood, Ill.: Richard D. Irwin, Inc., 1953.

Groen van Prinsterer, Guillaume. *Unbelief and Revolution: Lectures VIII and IX.* Amsterdam: The Groen van Prinsterer Fund, 1975.

Grossman, Gregory. *Economic Systems.* Englewood Cliffs, N.J.: Prentice-Hall, Inc., 1967.

Halm, George Nikolaus. *Economic Systems: A Comparative Analysis.* New York: Holt, Rinehart & Winston, Inc., 1960.

Hamilton, Earl J. "Profit, Inflation and the Industrial Revolution, 1751–1800." *Quarterly Journal of Economics* 61 (1942), 256–273.

Hammond, John L., and Hammond, Barbara. *The Rise of Modern Industry.* London: Methuen & Co., 1925.

Handlin, Oscar, and Handlin, Mary F. "Origins of the American Business Corporation." *Enterprise and Secular Change: Readings in Economic History,* pp. 102–124. Edited by Frederic C. Lane and Jelle C. Riemersma. Homewood, Ill.: Richard D. Irwin, Inc., 1953.

Harich, Wolfgang. *Kommunismus ohne Wachstum?* [Communism without Growth?]. Reinbeck bei Hamburg: Rowohlt Verlag, 1975.

Heilbroner, Robert L. *The Making of Economic Society.* Englewood Cliffs, N.J.: Prentice-Hall, Inc., 1962.

Heilbroner, Robert L. *The Worldly Philosophers.* New York: Simon & Schuster, Inc., 1953; rev. ed., 1972.

Heimann, Eduard. *History of Economic Doctrines.* London: Oxford University Press, 1945; New York: Oxford University Press, Galaxy Book, 1964.

Hicks, J. R. "Economic Foundations of Wage Policy." *Essays in World Economics,* pp. 85–104. Oxford: Clarendon Press, 1959.

Hill, Christopher. *Reformation to Industrial Revolution.* London: Weidenfeld and Nicolson, 1967.

Huizinga, Johan. *The Waning of the Middle Ages.* New York: Doubleday & Co., 1924; Anchor Books ed., 1954.

Huyghe, René. "Art Forms and Society." *Larousse Encyclopedia of Modern Art from 1800 to the Present Day,* pp. 16–27, 146–158. Edited by René Huyghe. New York: Prometheus Press, 1961.

Jantzen, Hans. *High Gothic.* London: Constable, 1962.

Jay, Martin. *The Dialectical Imagination: A History of the Frankfurt School and the Institute of Social Research, 1923–1950.* Boston/Toronto: Little, Brown & Co., 1973.

Kalsbeek, L. *Contours of a Christian Philosophy: An Introduction to Herman Dooyeweerd's Thought.* Toronto: Wedge Publishing Foundation, 1975.

Keynes, John Maynard. "Economic Possibilities for Our Grandchildren." *Essays in Persuasion,* pp. 358–374. New York: Harcourt, Brace & Co., 1932.

Keynes, John Maynard. *The End of Laissez-faire.* London: The Hogarth Press, 1926.

Keynes, John Maynard. *The General Theory of Employment, Interest and Money.* London: Macmillan & Co., 1936; New York: Harcourt Brace Jovanovich, 1965.

Kluit, M. Elisabeth. *Het Protestantse Réveil in Nederland en daarbuiten: 1815–1865* [The Protestant Revival in the Netherlands and Western Europe: 1815–1865]. Amsterdam: Paris, 1970.

Kuyper, Abraham. *Christianity and the Class Struggle.* Grand Rapids, Mich.: Piet Hein, 1950.

Landes, D. S. *The Unbound Prometheus: Technological Change and Industrial Development in Western Europe from 1750 to the Present.* Cambridge/New York: Cambridge University Press, 1969.

Lerner, Abba P. *The Economics of Control.* New York: The Macmillan Co., 1944.

Levinson, Charles. *Capital, Inflation and the Multinationals.* London: George Allen & Unwin, 1971.

Linder, S. B. *The Harried Leisure Class.* New York: Columbia University Press, 1970.

Loucks, William N. *Comparative Economic Systems.* New York: Harper & Row, Inc., 1965.

Löwith, Karl. *Nature, History, and Existentialism and Other Essays in the Philosophy of History.* Chapter 9: "Fate of Progress." Evanston, Ill.: Northwestern University Press, 1966.

Mandeville, Bernard. *The Fable of the Bees: or Private Vices, Publick Benefits.* London: 1714; Harmondsworth: Penguin, 1970.

Manuel, Frank E. *The New World of Henri Saint-Simon.* Notre Dame: University of Notre Dame Press, 1963.

Marcuse, Herbert. *One-Dimensional Man.* Boston: Beacon Press, 1964.

Marcuse, Herbert. "The Individual in the Great Society." *A Great Society?,* pp. 58–80. Edited by Bertram Myron Gross. New York: Basic Books, 1966.

Marx, Karl. *Capital.* 3 vols. New York: International Publishers, 1967.

Marx, Karl. *Grundrisse.* Harmondsworth: Penguin Books, 1973; New York: Random House, 1974.

Marx, Karl. *Wages, Price and Profit.* In Karl Marx and Frederick Engels, *Selected Works in Two Volumes,* vol. 1, pp. 398-447. Moscow: Foreign Languages Publishing House, 1958.

Marx, Karl, and Engels, Frederick. *Collected Works.* New York: International Publishers, 1975 seq.

May, Henry F. *The Enlightenment in America.* New York: Oxford University Press, 1976.

Meadows, Donella H.; Meadows, Dennis L.; Randers, Jørgen; and Behrens III, William W. *The Limits to Growth.* First report for

The Club of Rome's Project on the Predicament of Mankind. New York: New American Library, 1972.

Mesarović, Mihajlo, and Pestel, Eduard. *Mankind at the Turning Point.* Second report for The Club of Rome. New York: E. P. Dutton & Co., 1974.

Mill, John Stuart. *Principles of Political Economy.* 2 vols. Harmondsworth: Penguin Books, 1970.

Mommsen, Theodor E. "St. Augustine and the Christian Idea of Progress." *Journal of the History of Ideas,* vol. 12 no. 1 (January, 1951), pp. 346–374.

Myint, Hla. *Theories of Welfare Economics.* London: London School of Econ. and Pol. Science, 1948; New York: Augustus M. Kelley, 1965.

Myrdal, Gunnar. *The Political Element in the Development of Economic Theory.* New York: Simon & Schuster, Inc., 1954.

Niebuhr, Reinhold. *Christian Realism and Political Problems.* London: Faber and Faber, 1954.

Olthuis, James H. *I Pledge You My Troth.* New York: Harper & Row, Inc., 1975.

Perroux, F. "Les mésures des progrès économiques et l'idée d'économie progressive." *Cahiers de l'ISEA.* Paris: n.p., 1956.

Pico della Mirandola, Giovanni. "Oration on the Dignity of Man." *The Renaissance Philosophy of Man,* p. 225. Edited by Ernst Cassirer *et al.* Chicago: University of Chicago Press, 1948.

Polak, Fred L. *The Image of the Future.* 2 vols. Leyden: Sijthoff; New York: Oceana Publications, 1961.

Polanyi, Karl. *The Great Transformation.* Boston: Beacon Press, 1957.

Prybyla, Jan S. *Comparative Economic Systems.* New York: Appleton-Century-Crofts, 1969.

Reich, Charles A. *The Greening of America.* New York: Random House, 1970.

Reich, Charles A. *The Sorcerer of Bolinas Reef.* New York: Random House, 1976.

Rookmaaker, H. R. *Modern Art and the Death of a Culture.* London/Downers Grove, Ill.: Inter-Varsity Press, 1970.

Roszak, Theodore. *The Making of a Counter Culture.* New York: Doubleday & Co., 1969.

Roszak, Theodore. *Where the Wasteland Ends.* Garden City, N.Y.: Doubleday & Co., 1972.

Samuelsson, Kurt. *Religion and Economic Action.* Stockholm: Svenska Bokförlaget; London: Heinemann, 1961.

Schaeffer, Francis A. *True Spirituality.* London: Inter-Varsity Press, 1972; Wheaton, Ill.: Tyndale House, 1972.

Schiller, Kurt. "Stability and Growth as Objectives of Economic Policy." *The German Economic Review,* vol. 5, no. 3 (1967), pp. 177–188.

Schmalenbach, Eugen. *Der freien Wirtschaft zum Gedächtnis* [In Memory of the Free Market Economy]. Köln und Opladen, 1958; originally published 1949.

Schmookler, Jacob. "Technological Progress and the Modern American Corporation." *The Corporation in Modern Society,* pp. 141–165. Edited by Edward S. Mason. Cambridge, Mass.: Harvard University Press, 1959.

Schumacher, E. F. *Small is Beautiful: A Study of Economics as if People Mattered.* London: Blond & Briggs Ltd., 1973; New York: Harper & Row, Inc., 1973.

Schumpeter, Joseph Alois. *Capitalism, Socialism, and Democracy.* New York/London: Harper and Brothers, 1942.

Schumpeter, Joseph Alois. *History of Economic Analysis.* New York: Oxford University Press, 1954.

Schuurman, Egbert. *Reflections on the Technological Society.* Toronto: Wedge Publishing Foundation, 1977.

Schuurman, Egbert. *Techniek en toekomst* [Technology and the Future: A Confrontation with Philosophical Views]. With English and German summaries. Assen, the Netherlands: Van Gorcum, 1972. English edition in preparation.

Segal, Ronald. *The Americans: A Conflict of Creed and Reality.* Toronto/New York/London: Bantam Books, 1970. Published in England under the title: *America's Receding Future: The Collision of Creed and Reality.* London: Weidenfeld and Nicolson, 1968.

Sombart, Werner. "Medieval and Modern Commercial Enterprise." *Enterprise and Secular Change: Readings in Economic History,* pp. 25–40. Edited by Frederic C. Lane and Jelle C. Riemersma. Homewood, Ill.: Richard D. Irwin, Inc., 1953.

Spengler, Oswald. *The Decline of the West.* London: George Allen & Unwin, 1918, 1922; New York: Alfred A. Knopf, 2 vols., 1945.

Spiegel, Henry W. *The Growth of Economic Thought.* Englewood Cliffs, N.J.: Prentice-Hall, Inc., 1971.

Stark, Werner. *Social Theory and Christian Thought.* London: Routledge & Kegan Paul, 1958.

Steiner, George A. *Government's Role in Economic Life.* New York: McGraw-Hill, 1953.

Tawney, Richard Henry. *Religion and the Rise of Capitalism.* Harmondsworth: Penguin Books, 1938.

Thompson, William Irwin. *At the Edge of History.* New York: Harper & Row, Inc., 1971.

Tierney, Brian; Kagan, Donald; and Williams, L. Pearce; eds. *Great Issues in Western Civilization.* New York: Random House, 1967.

Tinbergen, Jan. "Do Communist and Free Economies Show a Converging Pattern?" *Soviet Studies,* vol. 12, no. 4 (April, 1961), pp. 333–341.

Tinbergen, Jan, *et al. Naar een rechtvaardiger Internationale Orde* [Reshaping the International Order]. RIO report, 1976.

Toffler, Alvin. *Future Shock.* New York: Random House, 1970.

Toynbee, Arnold J. *The Industrial Revolution.* Boston: Beacon Press, 1956. Originally published 1884.

Troeltsch, Ernst. *The Social Teaching of the Christian Churches.* 2 vols. London: George Allen & Unwin, 1931; Chicago: University of Chicago Press, 1931.

Uytenbogaardt, W. "De grondstoffenverdeling in de wereld als mogelijke oorzaak van konflikten" [The Distribution of Raw Materials in the World as a Possible Source of Conflict]. *Transactie* (February, 1973).

VandenBerg, F. *Abraham Kuyper.* St. Catharines, Ontario: Paideia Press, 1978.

Van der Kooy, T. P. "Methodologie der economie en christelijke wijsbegeerte" [The Methodology of Economics and Christian Philosophy]. *Philosophia reformata,* vol. 40 (1975), pp. 1–32. With English summary.

Van der Kooy, T. P. *Over economie en humaniteit* [On Economy and Humanness]. Wageningen, the Netherlands: Zomer en Keuning, 1954.

Visser 't Hooft, W. A. "Moet het Westen worden verdedigd?" [Must the West be Defended?]. *Wending* (1956).

Voegelin, Eric. *From Enlightenment to Revolution.* Durham: Duke University Press, 1975.

Voltaire. *Candide.* A bilingual edition. Translated and edited by Peter Gay, Columbia University. New York: St. Martin's Press, 1963.

Von Martin, Alfred Wilhelm Otto. *Sociology of the Renaissance.* New York: Harper & Row, Inc., 1963.

Weber, Max. *The Protestant Ethic and the Spirit of Capitalism.* London: George Allen & Unwin, 1930; New York: Charles Scribner's Sons, 1930.

Wells, H. G. *Men like Gods.* Toronto: Macmillan, 1923.

Wells, H. G. *The Camford Visitation.* London: Methuen, 1937.

Wells, H. G. *Mind at the End of Its Tether.* London: Heinemann, 1945.

White, Jr., Lynn. "The Expansion of Technology 500–1500." *The Fontana Economic History of Europe,* vol. 1: *The Middle Ages,* chapter 4. Edited by Carlo M. Cipolla. London: Collins, 1972.

Whitehead, Alfred North. *Science and the Modern World.* Cambridge: Cambridge University Press, 1926.

Zeylstra, Willem G. *Aid or Development.* Leiden: A. W. Sijthoff, 1975.

Zuidema, S. U. *Communication and Confrontation.* Toronto: Wedge Publishing Foundation, 1971.

Zylstra, Bernard. "Modernity and the American Empire." *International Reformed Bulletin,* first/second quarter 1977, no. 68/69, pp. 3ff.

Indexes

SUBJECTS

PERSONS